Communication Strategies in Turkey

Communication Strategies in Turkey

Erdoğan, the AKP and Political Messaging

Taner Dogan

I.B. TAURIS
LONDON • NEW YORK • OXFORD • NEW DELHI • SYDNEY

I.B. TAURIS
Bloomsbury Publishing Plc
50 Bedford Square, London, WC1B 3DP, UK
1385 Broadway, New York, NY 10018, USA
29 Earlsfort Terrace, Dublin 2, Ireland

BLOOMSBURY, I.B. TAURIS and the I.B. Tauris logo are trademarks of
Bloomsbury Publishing Plc

First published in Great Britain 2021
This paperback edition published in 2022

Copyright © Taner Dogan, 2021

Taner Dogan has asserted his right under the Copyright, Designs and Patents Act, 1988, to be identified as Author of this work.

For legal purposes the Acknowledgements on p. ix constitute an extension of this copyright page.

Cover series design: Adriana Brioso
Cover image © Leon Neal/Getty Images

All rights reserved. No part of this publication may be reproduced or transmitted in any form or by any means, electronic or mechanical, including photocopying, recording, or any information storage or retrieval system, without prior permission in writing from the publishers.

Bloomsbury Publishing Plc does not have any control over, or responsibility for, any third-party websites referred to or in this book. All internet addresses given in this book were correct at the time of going to press. The author and publisher regret any inconvenience caused if addresses have changed or sites have ceased to exist, but can accept no responsibility for any such changes.

A catalogue record for this book is available from the British Library.

A catalog record for this book is available from the Library of Congress.

ISBN: HB: 978-1-8386-0224-6
PB: 978-0-7556-3658-7
ePDF: 978-1-8386-0227-7
eBook: 978-1-8386-0225-3

Typeset by Newgen KnowledgeWorks Pvt. Ltd., Chennai, India

To find out more about our authors and books visit www.bloomsbury.com and sign up for our newsletters.

To find yourself, think for yourself.
– Socrates

Contents

List of illustrations		viii
Acknowledgements		ix
List of abbreviations		x
Short note on methods		xii
1	Introduction	1
2	The concept of political communication	9
3	Modernization in the Ottoman era, Islamism in Turkey and AKP's rise	25
4	The AKP's code of identity	49
5	Communicating religion	93
6	Politics and p(owe)r: Evolvement of political messaging	133
7	Erdoğan's communication: Populist Islamism	147
8	Post-Erdoğan Turkey	171
Notes		177
Bibliography		193
Index		231

Illustrations

Figures

1	Elements of political communication	12
2	Erdoğan's logo	105
3	Former US president Barack Obama's logo	105
4	Morocco's Justice and Development Party's (PJD) logo	106
5	Turkey's Justice and Development Party's (AKP) logo	107
6	Themes of Erdoğan's speeches from 2002 to 2009	136
7	Themes of Erdoğan's speeches from 2010 to 2019	136

Tables

1	Themes of Erdoğan's speeches	135
2	Themes, frequency and percentage of Erdoğan's speeches from 2002 to 2019	137

Acknowledgements

At the outset, I would like to express my deepest gratitude to my supervisors Dr Zahera Harb and Dr Melanie Bunce for their continuous support, guidance and encouragement throughout my research.

I have been very fortunate to have invaluable friends and colleagues whose critical feedback and wisdom have helped me in my writing. I am particularly thankful to Professor Abdulhamit Kırmızı, Nur Sevencan, Dr Yakoob Ahmed, Imran Garda and Dr Emre Kazim. I am indebted to many of my friends who supported me throughout this journey, whether with their networks, advice on the cover photo or fruitful conversations – you know who you are. I could not have asked for more gentler editors than Rory Gormley and Yasmin Garcha at Bloomsbury. Thank you for your belief in this project.

Nobody has been more important to me in the pursuit of this research than the members of my family. I would like to thank my mum and dad, whose love and devoted spiritual support sustain me in whatever endeavour I undertake. Finally, I am deeply grateful to my wife, Sare, who has been a constant source of motivation to me. Thank you for being my muse and editor.

The journey of this research started in one of my favourite cities on earth, Cairo, continued first in my hometown in Germany, and then in the inspiring libraries of London, in particular SOAS, British Library, and at 'The Pool' at City, University of London, which used to be a Victorian feature pool converted to a PhD study room, and ended in a self-quarantine during the COVID-19 in a beautiful neighbourhood in Istanbul, Yeniköy.

Abbreviations

AGD	Anatolian Youth Association
AKP	Justice and Development Party
ANAP	Motherland Party
ANAR	Ankara Social Research Centre
CHP	People's Republican Party
CUP	Ottoman Committee of Union and Progress
DEVA Partisi	The Remedy Party
Diyanet	Presidency of Religious Affairs
DYP	True Path Party
FP	Virtue Party
GP	Future Party
HDP	Peoples' Democratic Party
IHH	Humanitarian Relief Foundation
IMF	International Monetary Fund
ISIS	Islamic State of Iraq and Syria
IYI Parti	Good Party
MB	Muslim Brotherhood
MENA	Middle East and North Africa
MHP	Nationalist Movement Party
MIT	National Intelligence Organization
MNP	National Order Party
MP	Member of Parliament
MSP	National Salvation Party
MTTB	National Turkish Student Union
MUSIAD	Independent Industrialists and Businessmen's Association
PJD	Justice and Development Party (in Morocco)
PKK	Kurdistan Workers' Party
PR	Public Relations
PYD	Democratic Union Party
RP	Welfare Party
RTÜK	Radio and Television Supreme Council
SDA	Party of Democratic Action
SETA	Foundation for Political, Economic and Social Research
SP	Felicity Party
TCCB	Presidency of the Republic of Turkey

TIKA	The Turkish Cooperation and Coordination Agency
TRT	Turkish Radio and Television Corporation
TUSIAD	Turkish Industry and Business Association
UN	United Nations

Short note on methods

This research uses both qualitative and quantitative research instruments to examine the evolution of the AKP's political messages, that is, its communication strategies. Three research methods were employed: non-participant observations, in-depth and informal interviews and quantitative content analysis. The qualitative research included twelve months of fieldwork, at election rallies and events of the AKP in different cities as well as at their headquarters in Ankara; twenty-six in-depth interviews with top AKP officials, members of the Turkish presidency's Communications Directory, Erdoğan's Strategy Team, former Turkish prime ministry and AKP's Publicity and Media, Election Affairs, Social Affairs, Public Relations, and Youth Departments, sources and experts in the media, think tanks, research centers and academia; eighty-one informal interviews with AKP party members, supporters, former supporters, and volunteers. Interviews were conducted between 2014 and 2020. The quantitative portion of the study involved content analysis of Erdoğan's speeches from 2002 to 2019.

Twenty-four interviewees spoke under the condition of anonymity because of their current positions in politics, media, think tanks or academia. Indeed, this decision is closely related to Turkey's political climate. The increasing dominance of Erdoğan's one-man rule polarized the society and became a threat for millions of people, especially after the Gezi Park protests in 2013 and the attempted coup in 2016. It was further cemented with the new presidential system in 2017, which made the president automatically the head of the government, judiciary, military and police. Because of the atmosphere of fear in the country, most of my elite interviewees decided to stay anonymous to avoid facing any problems in the future. However, the anonymity has enabled interviewees to be critical and speak up openly thus resulting in a quantitatively and qualitatively rich dataset. I have separated the interviewees into four categories: Politics (PO), Journalism (JO), Academia (AC), and Research centres and Think tanks (TT) and have assigned each interviewee a code (e.g. Politician 1 is coded with PO1).

1

Introduction

Since 2010, Recep Tayyip Erdoğan has been in a *kulturkampf*. It is a challenge to transform the Kemalist *laïcité*[1] domestically, and the perception of Muslims globally – in other words, a struggle against Kemalism and Islamophobia. In fact, Erdoğan is trying to position himself as the patron of the Muslim world as he defends the rights of Palestinians by challenging Israel, welcomes millions of refugees and Muslim exiles since the Arab uprisings have started, supports rebuilding initiatives in Somalia, restores Ottoman era historic buildings in Balkans, builds new mosques and Imam Hatip schools[2] across the country, reconverts iconic Hagia Sophia and Chora Museum to a mosque and, above all, stands for religious freedom at home. Certainly, these expansions are enabled by the vast amount of political powers Erdoğan has acquired after taking possession of the judiciary, military and the police. By changing the constitution, he has made himself the strongest politician ever in the country. Yet, although these steps are strengthening Erdoğan's reputation as a populist leader, the transformation from pluralism to Islamism is isolating Turkey every passing day, and Erdoğan's communication is playing a critical role in this isolationist policies.

Erdoğan's career started within a liberal frame when he and his reformist colleagues decided to form the Justice and Development Party (Adalet ve Kalkınma Partisi, hereafter the AKP) in 2001, following unsuccessful attempts to reform Necmettin Erbakan's Milli Görüş movement.[3] Erbakan's ideological approach to politics was not approved by the younger generation of Milli Görüş. In fact, when Erbakan became the first elected Islamist prime minister in Turkey in 1996, he ruled for fewer than twelve months, because his party's anti-Kemalist agenda resulted in a postmodern coup in 1997. The postmodern coup in Turkey had an immense impact on the religious conservatives in the country, as it involved the closure of Imam Hatip schools and headscarf bans for female university students. After this critical timeframe, the AKP came into being by emphasizing its focus on the words 'justice' and 'development' in their official name in response to Turkey's economic and judicial woes in the early 2000s. They aimed to increase the diversity of their support base by focusing on Turkish people's economic and political needs rather than on pursuing a religious ideology. The founding members of the AKP studied the political landscape carefully, presenting themselves as a party willing to embrace democracy, human rights, freedom of speech and the rule of law. The discourse and political agenda of the new party differed significantly from that of Milli Görüş, as it set its objectives around the pursuit of European Union (EU) membership, pluralism, neoliberal economics and pro-Western foreign policy. More importantly, it appealed to both Turkey and the international community as the new moderate face of Islam in the Middle East. They portrayed themselves as 'conservative democrats' in order to be at the centre of the political landscape straddling both the right and the left to create an image similar to that of the Christian democratic parties in Europe.

In the first election that the AKP contested, a mere fifteen months after its establishment, the party received 34 per cent of the votes, amounting to two-thirds of the seats in parliament which enabled them to form the government on their own. Erdoğan's successful mayorship in Istanbul from 1994 to 1998, during which he delivered crucial services to the public – such as installing new water and natural gas lines, cleaning up the streets and the Golden Horn,[4] undertaking paysage projects, improving transportation for Istanbulites – had already created an image of him as a young, charismatic and capable leader in the minds of the people. Therefore, his achievements as a member of Milli Görüş played a major role in the AKP's success story.

The support for the conservative democrats grew from one election to another, as the party expanded freedom of expression and minority rights for Kurds and Alevis in particular, implemented a foreign policy based on the concept of 'zero-problem' and forged positive relationships with neighbours such as Syria, Armenia and Israel. The AKP appealed so effectively to the international community that Western capitals referred to it as a role model for other Islamist parties and movements in the Middle East and the North Africa (MENA) region For the first time in Turkey's modern history, an Islamist party developed a positive communication with the West, which was 'the other' until that date.

The positive coverage of the AKP in the international media, which continued up until 2010, was a result of this narrative. However, a turning point came around this time, resulting from a heated exchange between President Erdoğan and the Israeli prime minister at the World Economic Forum in Davos in 2009[5] followed by the Mavi Marmara aid flotilla incident in 2010.[6] This marked a shift in the image of the AKP from that of a role model to an Islamist party in the international arena. By standing up to Israel, Erdoğan repositioned himself as the guardian of the Muslim world.[7] He came to be perceived on the Arab streets as a principled and charismatic leader, and his apparent repositioning relative to Israel gave rise to questions over whether Turkey is moving away from its Western political hemisphere. As the evidence collected for this research will demonstrate, after 2010 the agenda of the AKP started focusing on the Muslim world, fighting smoothly with the Kemalist elites on an ideological level. In addition, in terms of foreign policy, Erdoğan became less willing to follow Washington and Brussels' lead by opening up Turkey's horizons to Russia and China, moreover, introducing the *Blue Homeland* doctrine for maritime claims in the eastern Mediterranean. This repositioning became increasingly apparent in the rhetoric employed domestically by the AKP and Erdoğan himself after the Gezi Park protests in 2013, which were partially provoked by the enforcement of new conservative policies and a harking back to the country's Ottoman heritage. This new rhetoric continued into Erdoğan's speeches in the post-2010 period, and in policy changes following the coup attempt of July 2016. The role of Islam after this period started changing in the public sphere. From reconverting Hagia Sophia to a mosque, to naming new bridges and highways after Ottoman sultans and building Ottoman-Seljuki mélange mosques, schools and palaces, banning pride marches and queer-friendly events, and polarizing the society along cultural and religious lines, a new approach to politics emerged within the AKP – one which is related to what this book terms as Erdoğan's 'populist Islamist' ideology. Yet Erdoğan's aim with all these steps is to leave an imprint behind. Furthermore, he wants to have a pious generation that, later, will take over his legacy and 'be leaders of the society'.[8]

However, the latter remains unfulfilled after two decades of governance when considering the fact that generation Z (born between 1995 and 2010), who have not had the opportunity to witness the rule of any other party, shows less support for Erdoğan's AKP. Similarly, compared to ten years ago, young people in Turkey describe themselves as less 'religious' and 'pious', embracing a modern lifestyle and respect for diversity.[9] It is the same generation that consumes more social media than traditional mainstream media which is 85 per cent under Erdoğan control.[10] The fear of losing generation Z leads Erdoğan to control digital communication by introducing new social media laws and confronting platforms such as Netflix to regulate the content regarding LGBTQ+ characters – further step of limiting freedom of speech.

In an attempt to understand the above-mentioned transformation that has taken place within the AKP and Turkey, this book will examine the AKP's political communication strategies to unpick the development of and changes in its political message, discourse and language. The discussion divides the period of AKP rule into two eras: 2002 to 2009, which was characterized by a liberal political ideology and pluralism, and post-2010, which witnessed a shift towards a populist Islamist discourse, questioning the objectives of the democratization and liberalization process. In reference to the first period, the AKP is described as the first post-Islamist party in Turkey willing to embrace democracy and moderate Islam.[11] However, the changes in both discourse and policy after 2010 suggest that the new strategy of Erdoğan's AKP is to change the dominant secularization policies of Atatürk and 'rescue the Islamic world from Western colonization to once again achieve a dominant position in world politics'.[12] Thus, the development of the AKP's political communication can be characterized by the transition from post-Islamism to populist Islamism.

The global rise of the 'populist zeitgeist', as Mudde[13] describes, has put Erdoğan into the same category as that of populist leaders, such as Donald Trump, Boris Johnson, Vladimir Putin, Xi Jinping and Narendra Modi. This global development and AKP's polarizing discourse – of differentiating between 'us' as the majority of religious conservatives who seek national independence, a strong economy and religious freedom, on the one hand, and 'them' who favour old Kemalist policies that make Turkey dependent on the West, on the other – have strengthened Erdoğan's leadership. Yet when German historian Winkler speaks about Putinism in the context of Russia vis-à-vis the West, he underlines that it is not an intellectual challenge to the West as Leninism or Marxism once were.[14] Because for him, homophobia, anti-feminism, anti-liberalism and anti-rationalism are crucial aspects that need to change course in Russia. The same applies to the communist regime in China according to the historian. In this regard, Erdoğan's political approach, or 'Erdoğanism' in the context of Winkler, is not an intellectual contribution to Turkey's political sphere. Erbakan's suggestion of formulating an alternative economic model of 'Just order' (*Adil Düzen*), or his vision of creating the D-8[15] (an EU-like political union among Muslim nations) and having a common currency – in other words, standing for an alternative political agenda – were what made his approach fundamentally different from Erdoğan's when it comes to intellectual discussion about religious conservatism in Turkish politics. Despite Erbakan being more moderate when he came to power, as compared to the early 1970s when he started his political career, and leading a coalition government, he has not tarried to strengthen his base and gain credibility like his student Erdoğan. In fact Erdoğan's conviction in challenging the West, its institutions and his anti-Israel discourse is a result of the confidence he gained after transforming the country economically from 2002 to

2010, winning one election after another, securing the presidency by appointing Abdullah Gül in 2007 as well as making changes to the judiciary and military with the support of the Gülenists.[16] But in spite of the power he gained – especially after changing the constitution in his favour, abolishing the prime ministry and being the most powerful president of all times in Turkish history – his leadership was not able to forge unique models in politics, economics and education, which are the three fundamental areas vital for the future of any country. As a result, despite Erdoğan's seemingly more power-emanating discourse after 2010, as will be examined in this research by concentrating on communication strategies and on the incorporation of more images and symbols based on his populist Islamist approach, he has not been able to present an alternative model that will back up what his discourse proposes.

This research contends that effective communication of a party's message and charismatic leadership are fundamental to its political success. Of particular interest will be how changes in policy have been reinforced by Erdoğan's charismatic leadership style. He has effectively used a variety of political communication strategies, including images and symbols, to create a collective identity among the AKP's supporters, which has kept the social movement alive for a long period. However, starting with the Gezi Park process, this collectiveness among the AKP's leading figures has drifted apart. The 2019 local elections were a clear sign of this dissolution as Erdoğan lost in major cities such as Istanbul and Ankara for the first time after a quarter century.[17] The departure of two prominent political figures, namely the former prime minister Ahmet Davutoğlu and the former economy minister Ali Babacan, from the AKP was another crucial indicator of Erdoğan's assertive leadership style which does not leave any room for criticism and dissent, as he recognizes diversity not as a fundamental principle of democracy but as a threat to his authority. As a result, Erdoğan's authoritarian leadership polarized the society in Turkey and recently gave birth to two new parties within the AKP. While Davutoğlu formed his Gelecek Partisi (Future Party, or GP) in late 2019, Babacan established the DEVA Partisi (The Remedy Party), which stands for democracy and progress, in 2020. More importantly, the rise of Ekrem Imamoğlu, an unknown politician from the ranks of the opposition People's Republican Party (CHP) as Istanbul's new mayor, elected with an 800,000 vote difference to AKP's most popular and empathetic candidate, former prime minister Binali Yıldırım, and CHP's Mansur Yavaş, mayor of Ankara, are seen as a threat to Erdoğan's authority. Although it is still early to foresee if new dynamics and political figures can prevent Erdoğan's rise in the near future, seven million[18] digital natives who will vote for the first time in the next elections will add a whole new dimension to the political dynamics in Turkey. But certainly, the majority of this young generation is less interested in polarization, division and confrontation. Rather it favours diversity, investment in future job opportunities, development of AI technologies, a better education system and more collaboration with Western institutions. Also, political identity is less relevant for this generation. In fact, it is digitalized communication that increases the role of popular culture globally and creates a common identity. As a result, the Weltanschauung and political demands of young university students in Europe are not much different from those of students in Turkey.

Erdoğan continues to expand his populist discourse and politics day by day, intervenes in Syria to prevent the birth of a new territory for Kurdish Democratic Union Party (PYD) in post-Syria civil war, becomes involved in the Eastern Mediterranean, and builds drones and warships. Meanwhile he constantly underlines the importance of remaining strong and acting in unison in order to be among the strongest ten economies in the world as part of his 2023 vision of the Turkish Republic's 100th anniversary. Moreover after the COVID-19 outbreak in Turkey, Erdoğan criticized some European countries for standing for liberalism and human rights but not being capable of handling the pandemic crisis in their countries and collaborating internationally. Erdoğan emphasizes that Turkey will be the country of the twenty-first century by overcoming the economic damage in the post-pandemic period, mentioning not only Vision 2023 in his speech, but Vision 2053, the 600th anniversary of Istanbul's conquest, and Vision 2071, the 1000th anniversary of the Battle of Manzikert, which was the beginning of the end of Byzantine Empire in Anatolia and the start of the Turkification era.[19] Yet, despite economic failures, at every possible opportunity he makes references to the Ottoman past in his speeches, which the religious conservative majority in Turkey associates with the glorious rule of Islam across the world for 600 years.

Structure of the book

This book aims to bolster the literature concerning the AKP and Turkey; however, it will also be relevant in the context of other Islamist parties and movements in the MENA region as it attempts to explicate the role of political communication in the political sphere. Another focus of the book is the exploration of the Americanization of political communication in a non-Western context, which manifests itself in the form of increasing professionalism, the use of symbolism, candidate-centred electioneering and the portrayal of the leader's family in the election campaign. In addition, the concept of charisma and its role in campaigning and designing of the political discourse is given significant attention.

Chapter 2 details the analytical framework for the research and also reviews relevant literature. It concentrates on political communication and political public relations (PR), and it explains the Americanization of political communication, which is associated with personalization, image-making and charisma.

Chapter 3 covers the historical development of modern Turkey from the ashes of the Ottoman era to the birth of Islamism. It begins by defining the concept of Islamism as it is used in reference to the AKP in the study. It then discusses the modernization of the Ottoman Empire, which began in the eighteenth century, and also explains the politics and individual lifestyles of some of its rulers. Furthermore, the chapter discusses the role of Sultan Abdulhamid II, known to have been a role model for Erdoğan, and his Islamist policies. The chapter then introduces the issues Abdulhamid II faced during his reign as bearing relevance to the internal challenges encountered by Erdoğan, particularly during the Gezi Park protests and the 2016 coup attempt. It also details Islamism in modern Turkey in the twentieth century in connection with the Islamist poets Erdoğan mentions during his speeches where he uses poetry as a symbol of communication.

Chapter 4 tackles the AKP's code of identity by highlighting the relevance of Erdoğan's personality as the main asset of AKP's brand. This leads to a discussion of the details surrounding the emergence of the AKP and the influences on its politics, including consideration of different events and turning points that created new symbols and images. By reflecting on the Erdoğan's polarizing discourse, the chapter goes on to explain how his leadership plays a key role in AKP's identity crisis.

Chapter 5 examines religion as a critical component of AKP's political communication. While some leaders prefer using Twitter for communicating with their citizens, as well as with the public and media, Erdoğan follows the traditional way of 'one-to-one communication', addressing hundreds of thousands of supporters at outdoor rallies. The reflections on some of the rallies I have personally attended across Turkey are summarized in this chapter. The chapter further examines the roots of the AKP's election victories, depicting the party's remarkable historic successes in the past two decades, which will be still relevant and continue to be discussed in next couple of decades when analysing populist politics, political communication and charismatic leadership in Turkey.

By exploring the opinions of the interviewees, it formulates an understanding of the shifts that occurred since 2010.

Chapter 6 presents Erdoğan's speeches over a period of eighteen years. The analysis evaluates a sample of speeches given each year from 2002 up to and including 2019. It discusses the evolution of political messaging in different fields such as human rights, freedom of speech, anti-establishment and cultural dialogue.

Chapter 7 provides a unique perspective of Erdoğan's communication. By evaluating all interviews, ethnographic observations in 2014, 2018 and 2019 as well as Erdoğan's speeches, the chapter provides a critical insight into the communication mechanisms of the party and presidency. Every domestic and international challenge and threat to Erdoğan has contributed to his political discourse and introduced new communication strategies. Hence the chapter concentrates on how Erdoğan's discourse embraced liberalism until having reached a certain level of economic prosperity that allowed his self-confidence to turn into a populist Islamist political attitude after 2010. Since 2015, a nationalist discourse was added to this rhetoric when the Peoples' Democratic Party (HDP) got stronger politically after the Kurdistan Workers' Party (PKK) had orchestrated attacks across Turkey in 2015. The nationalist dimension of Erdoğan's rhetoric grew stronger with the coup attempt in 2016, and it advanced with the refugee crisis in particular, an issue that has played a key role in the AKP losing Istanbul in the 2019 local elections. Erdoğan turned these events to a 'national survival' matter by strategically portraying himself as the only leader in Turkey and the Sunni Muslim world seeking to create a strong, independent Turkey that is free from dependence on the West and that represents freedom for religious conservative people.

The final chapter depicts post-Erdoğan Turkey by summarizing opportunities and challenges for the ruling AKP and other political parties. It explores how Erdoğan uses political communication in favour of his populist Islamist ideology to build a legacy that is the foundation of the 'New Turkey' to replace Atatürk. By doing this, the chapter presents the differences between silencing opposition voices after the Gezi Park protests and quelling religious conservatives after 2016, which will help understand how the AKP's political attitude that constituted polyphonic voices in the early days morphed into homogeneous mindset thereby creating deep societal polarization.

2

The concept of political communication

Our society is constructed around flows: Flows of capital, flows of information, flows of technology, flows organizational interaction, flows of images, sounds, and symbols. Flows are not just one element of the social organization: they are the expression of processes dominating our economic, political, and symbolic life.
— Castells[1]

The three main elements of public relations are practically as old as society: informing people, persuading people, or integrating people with people.
— Bernays[2]

This chapter evaluates the existing definitions of political communication, seeking to understand the formal role the media plays, while also providing an entry point to further our understanding of the dynamics of the AKP's political communications. Although the concept of political communication is the main analytical framework of this research, an examination of political public relations is necessary to develop a deeper understanding of political communication. Public relations is a management function responsible for connecting an organization with its target audience:

> Public relations ... helps establish and maintain mutual lines of communication, understanding, acceptance and cooperation between an organization and its publics; involves the management of problems or issues; helps management to keep informed on and responsive to public opinion; defines and emphasizes the responsibility of management to serve the public interest; ... and uses research and sound and ethical communication as its principal tools.[3]

The definition above is applied principally in relation to political parties, highlighting the importance of influencing public opinion and public interest. Greater precision is provided by the definition given by the World Assembly of Public Relations Associations, published in 1978, which emphasizes the relationship between organizations and public interest:

> Public relations is the art and social science of analyzing trends, predicting their consequences, counselling organization leaders and implementing planned programmes of action which will serve both the organization's and the public interest.[4]

The use of the word 'serve' is indicative of the aim of public relations in general. Furthermore, as the phrase 'public interest' indicates, building awareness is an important aspect of public relations, while the reference to the 'public' evokes the critical political dimension of public relations.

When political actors – including Erdoğan and Abdullah Gül who held leading positions within former prime minister Erbakan's (1926–2011) Milli Görüş movement – decided to form a new party in 2001, they distanced themselves from the Turkish Islamist stance, with its 'anti-Western and anti-secular'[5] approach, focusing primarily on meeting the public's chief economic demands. At this time there was a need for the government to promote economic development, as it was when a financial crisis was underway in Turkey.[6] Thus, the AKP chose the slogan 'Everything is for Turkey' (*Herşey Türkiye için*) for its 2002 election campaign, concentrating not only on a specific audience composed of a single group or ideology of their own supporters, but on the whole of society.[7]

Political public relations are currently characterized by news management, agenda building, public relations and election campaigns, political marketing and public diplomacy strategies.[8] According to Strömbäck and Kiousis,[9] there is a lack of theory and research bridging the spheres of public relations, political communications and political science theory. Here, the following definition of political public relations is proposed:

> Political public relations is the management process by which an organization or individual actor for political purposes, through purposeful communication and action, seeks to influence and establish, build, and maintain beneficial relationships and reputations with its key publics to help support its mission and achieve its goals.[10]

This definition of political public relations emphasizes coherence, granting each party political agency as it seeks to influence the public by communicating its objectives. Public relations performs the role of a management function, that is, the 'management of communication between an organization and its public'.[11] This idea of a management function in public relations is a common element present in the definitions given in the literature. Thus, it is significant that public relations mediates dialogue between institutions and the public, thereby establishing a relationship between an organization and its audience while underlining the mutual benefits arising from the interaction.

In contemporary political parties, the management of communications between individual organizations and the public is the responsibility of parties' public relations departments.[12] Hence, throughout, this research will examine how the AKP professionally utilizes public relations opportunities when campaigning in order to influence their target audience. The data collected will also reveal whether the AKP has institutionalized its communication strategies, or whether it has a different structure. By looking at the coverage of the Gezi Park protests that took place in 2013, this research examines how public relations campaigns can damage political parties and their leaders by reducing their credibility internationally.

The protest occurred when what began as a plan by Istanbul municipality to destroy Istanbul's green Taksim Square and build an Ottoman barrack that would include a shopping mall sparked a series of nationwide protests. Initially, the protestors alluded to an environmental agenda, but the demonstration became the catalyst for an 'anti-government protest' that received extensive international media coverage. In truth, the main intention of the protesters was not only to draw attention to Taksim Square's destruction, but, more importantly, to highlight other 'urban development projects' in Istanbul. As highlighted in the introduction, these included, among other policies, the creation of Turkey's largest mosque, Çamlıca Mosque, which according to Ismail Kahraman, the former speaker of the parliament, should be named after Erdoğan,[13] and the naming of the third bridge linking the European and Asian parts of Istanbul after Yavuz Sultan Selim, who is claimed to have led the massacre of Alevis, and other religious motivated developments, which was alleged to have been executed top-down in an undemocratic way. Considering the role of election and crisis periods like the Gezi Park protests, this study will investigate how different incidents changed the AKP's political message and Erdoğan's discourse.

The main function of political public relations is that it can be used by political actors to 'influence the media, their agenda, and how they frame events, issues, and processes'.[14] Influencing and persuading the public, or the audience of a particular viewpoint, is another dimension of political public relations.

What is political communication?

Political communication plays a central role in the analysis undertaken in this research. Yet this study centralizes political communication as the main concept because of its relevance to the research. The topics most frequently studied by researchers interested in political communications are election campaigns. Political communications involve different actors, ranging from the non-political (e.g. journalists) to influential decision makers responsible for moulding public opinion. It is a direct method of communication with the public in which the message conveyed plays a crucial role in strengthening the impact of a campaign. The focus of political communications is on the quality of the message, in particular its capacity to prompt the receiver to develop a certain ideological viewpoint regarding specific events. As a result, this research will centralize political communication when conceptualizing communication.

The scope of political communication has been illustrated as encompassing three different groups: political organizations, media and citizens.[15] Political parties, lobby groups, pressure groups and consumer groups can all be categorized under the umbrella of political organizations. McNair[16] explains political communication as 'purposeful communication about politics, which

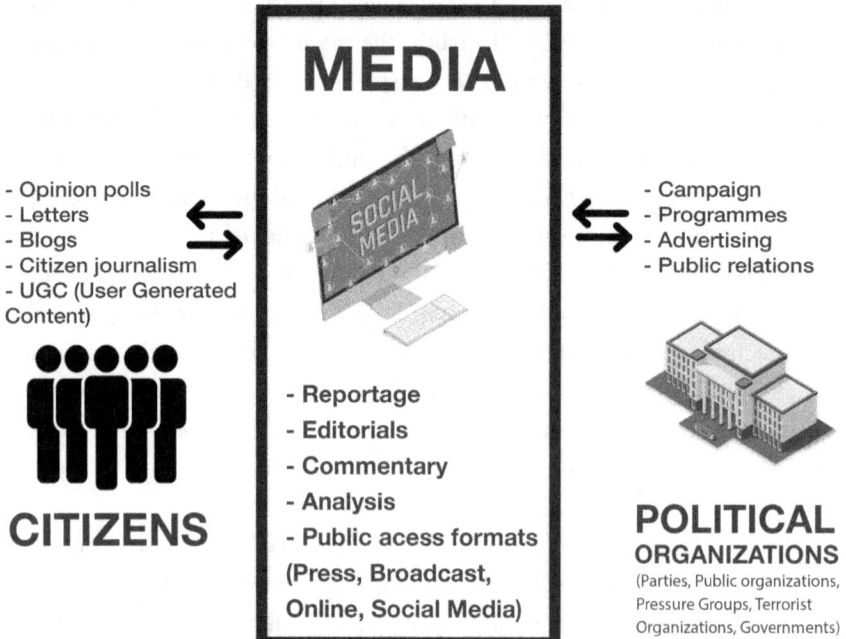

Figure 1 Elements of political communication (Source: McNair 2018: 5).

incorporates all forms of communication undertaken by politicians and other political actors'. One of the goals of political actors is 'receiving maximum favourable publicity and the minimum of negativity', as illustrated in the Figure 1.

The reactions in Figure 1 are two-way, meaning that political organizations operate symbiotically with the media, since advertising and public relations need to be transferred to media outlet, who in turn conduct analysis and report to the citizens. Conversely, political communication also rises from the bottom-up, beginning with citizens who respond in the form of digital media engagement or opinion polls which are subsequently reported and analysed by political organizations. Thus, the media serves as a bridge between politicians and citizens. Both the politicians and their audience members are key constituents of the political communication process. Although both sides are influenced via the media, audiences are the principal target of politicians, as they pursue particular objectives and take key decisions to gain public support.

Although this model appears complicated, it broadly summarizes the process of political communication. Figure 1 will be referenced in this research when analysing the AKP's political communication activities. In addition, the AKP's media advertisements during the election period and the impact of these on citizens, in other words their supporters and potential electorates, were also a key focus when conducting the ethnographic interviews as part of the fieldwork in Turkey. Similarly, the importance of opinion polls, conducted through research and development companies, will be evaluated to ascertain whether the AKP is reconsidering its policies according to the outcome of polls, and if so, what kind of impact this has on its message. Indeed, the role of digital media is an important part of this process in the twenty-first century.

Symbols play a crucial role in political communication. They are an additional communication tool, conveying shared ideas and concepts and disseminating political beliefs in a manner that is culturally meaningful. Political communication recognizes cultural norms and values, as well as laws and constitutions, as forming the basis of a healthy relationship between political actors and the public. Cultural, social, political, institutional and systemic contexts provided the basis for the AKP to communicate with the public. As an 'Islam-sensitive' political party [17] their shared background enabled them to communicate readily with the 'authentic, humble, and uncorrupted Turkish-Muslim people who were dominated and oppressed by secular and modernist elites'.[18]

When analysing the role of the AKP's political communication in Turkey, it is impossible to overlook the incidents that occurred between the AKP and the Fethullah Gülen movement from 2012 onwards. This movement has no official name but its members refer to themselves as *hizmet* (the service), and are widely known as *cemaat* (the community), the 'Gülen Movement' or the 'Gülenists'[19] in Turkey.[20] When investigating the role of communication based on religious values, it is important to recollect the struggle between the two groups in terms of symbols and messages. A new public relations era began in December 2013, following a corruption scandal that revealed a deep power struggle between the two parties. However the climax of the struggle took place on 15 July 2016 when a coup was attempted by the same group.[21] By evaluating a combination of cultural, social, political and institutional factors, this research will consider how different events throughout last two decades of AKP governance has shaped political communication of Erdoğan.

Americanization of political communication

> [The] Western model of modernization exhibits certain components and sequences whose relevance is global. Everywhere for example increasing urbanisation has tended to raise literacy; rising literacy has tended to increase media exposure; increasing media exposure has 'gone with' wider economic participation (per capita income) and political participation.
>
> – Lerner[22]

This section of the discussion explains how the American style of political communication has become the modern and professional method of campaigning in democratic countries.[23] It is a personalized and candidate-centred mode of electioneering that centralizes the politician's image and portrays their approachability at a personal level by actively including their family members in the campaign process.[24]

During the First World War, US President Woodrow Wilson established a Committee on Public Information to manage public opinion about the war. This marked the beginning of political public relations and was followed by the establishment of public relations offices to manage party political issues, first by the Democratic Party in 1928, and then in 1932 by the Republicans. Once reputed as an effective tool, the number of political public relations consultants increased rapidly, especially during the second half of the twentieth century. Thus, the field of public relations and communications, including infotainment, is considered intrinsically American; the United States has been described as the so-called Mecca of political campaigning.[25] The rapid expansion of this field is attributed to America's dominance after the Cold War and the increasing reliance on soft power.[26] Simultaneous with the greater cultural and ideological appeal of America, the significance of a popular culture in general was also strengthened.

Jean Baudrillard[27] states, 'America is the original version of modernity', with other countries being merely imitators. In particular, after the Second World War, America's domination was manipulated to amplify the 'homogeneity and interdependence of cultures'.[28] The homogenization process was either termed 'modernization or Americanization',[29] and was recognized as a means to 'transform traditional societies'.[30] In fact, Americanization can be considered the 'younger brother of globalisation', as it was the initial force responsible for creating a global economy and global culture, leading to the 'globalisation of everything',[31] and in the case of this research, also political communication.

Furthermore, it is interesting to consider the suggestion that Americanization is itself dependent on modernization, as it is the latter that underpins expectations of long-term societal change.[32] Indeed, it was modernization that first weakened political parties and facilitated the rise of modern campaign practices. Undoubtedly, typically the modernization of a society leads to greater individualization, thereby reducing the impact of the collective identity of a political party or movement.

In *The Passing of Traditional Society: Modernizing the Middle East*, Lerner[33] identifies the role of modernization relative to industrialization, secularization, democratization, education and media participation. In addition, he underlines that the West is the driving force of modernization in the Middle East, generating organic societal change.[34] According Niyazi Berkes[35] 'secularization and laicization mean the transformation of persons, offices, properties, institutions, or matters of an ecclesiastical or spiritual character to a lay, or worldly, position'. Change begins at the level of the individual and continues with exposure to media, finally reaching into the domains of 'economic as well as political participation'.[36]

Due to its economic growth and development, and the resultant rise in socio-economic conditions, the United States became a leading actor in designing political communication strategies for use during election campaigns. Therefore, not only did the Americanization of political communication effect 'changes in communication practices'[37] and the social structure generally, it also triggered widespread changes to electioneering practices.[38] The Americanization of political communication demanded technical expertise and 'professional advisers, growing detachment of political parties from citizens, development of autonomous structures of communication' and the personalization of politics.[39] Some critics suggest that it is inaccurate to refer to these changes as Americanization, because other modernized countries, such as Germany, France and the UK, also export campaign experts and international advisers.[40] However, as the election techniques originated from the United States, and as Swanson and Mancini[41] favour the use of the word 'Americanization', it is adopted herein.

As a pioneer of modernization, the United States founded a political public relations model comprising 'public and private opinion polls, telephone canvassing, computers, direct mail, fax machine, campaign consultants, market research, television saturation', among other techniques.[42] Obviously, despite some of them being still relevant today, these tools are from the second half of twentieth century. Particularly in today's world, digital communication needs to be added to this list as it plays a key role because American presidential candidates, particularly with the Obama campaign, have started to use digitalized political advertising.[43] In fact the rise of the 'fake news' has started increasing in the media literacy with the presidential campaign of Donald Trump in 2016, who, on Twitter, blamed the mainstream media for spreading fake news about himself.[44]

Many democratic countries imitated the US model in their communication. However, evidence suggests that 'what works in one country may not work in another' and that 'what works in one election may not work in the next'; this also needs to be considered when discussing multiple examples of election campaigns.[45] Yet, election campaigns are becoming more Americanized in the Western world, as reflected in the strategies and actions of 'candidates, political parties and news media'.[46] Although other nations have borrowed press and media models from the United States, this does not necessarily mean they also have American-style media machines. The fact that Bill Clinton relied on advisers from the British Labour Party demonstrates that in some cases US politicians benefit from adopting practices from abroad, and that progress is not just achieved a 'one-way flow of influence'.[47]

By conducting in-depth interviews in Turkey, I establish what type of communication the AKP applied. Comments by personalities close to Erdoğan, such as Erol Olçok, who was in charge of Erdoğan's public relations for twenty-five years and was Erdoğan's spin doctor, and sources from the Communications Directory, party, presidency and former prime ministry provide an important source of information for evaluation. The role of independent, professional consultants is also relevant to the AKP's political communication model. Since Olçok[48] had forged no direct ties with the party, he was empowered to act independently. The in-depth interview I conducted with him provides a valuable contribution to this research as it helps clarify the functioning of the AKP's campaigning model until 2018. After 2018 when Turkey entered a new presidential system, when power relations were redesigned, a new department responsible for communication affairs was founded under the name of

'Communications Directory', which will be also part of the discussion to reflect on post-2018 period communication.

Personalization of political communication

The personalization of political communication is an additional aspect of Americanization – one that is closely related to candidate-centred politics. With the increasing dominance of populism, this is a phenomenon that is on the rise globally, and appears to have emerged alongside notions of globalization and the free market. Arguably, personalization has led to a diminishment of the 'traditional affective ties between voters and parties'.[49]

Two different forms of personalization can be identified from the literature. The first form is 'individualization', which concentrates on central actors, highlighting their ideals, capacities and political policies.[50] The second is 'privatization', which relates to the 'public role of the politician as a private individual'.[51] The latter arises from interest in and 'media focus on the personal characteristics and personal life of individual candidates'.[52] Both forms are becoming increasingly important aspects of political communication, as the personal influence of political candidates on voters is growing, and the personalities of 'individual politicians are becoming more central in media coverage'.[53] This process is described as the 'politicisation of the private persona'.[54] Consequently, in an era when parties and government institutions are losing their appeal, elements such as 'family, personal appearance, lifestyle, upbringing and religion' are intruding into the political arena, through the depiction of the personal lives of politicians.[55] As election campaigns become progressively personalized through the use of social media, politicians' private lives, philosophies and beliefs are increasingly becoming topics of interest among voters. This growth in personalization has impacted the efficacy of traditional election campaigning, consisting of party programmes and promises. Hence, the shift from 'political to personal characteristics, and from the politician's public life in office to their private life' is discussed herein in reference to the personalization of politics.[56]

Personalization plays a key role within the context of this study, in particular in reference to the 2014 Turkish presidential elections. This election was the first time a president could be directly elected by the Turkish people. In addition, Erdoğan's chief election promise was the introduction of a new presidential system with the ambition of remaining in power until 2028. The mechanism for ensuring this was implemented in 2017 referendum which enabled a constitutional change.

The professionalization of political communication is another aspect of Americanization that also links to personalization. The use of spin doctors, technical experts and professional advisors characterizes the modern model of campaigning. This professionalization process can be summarized in three steps: 'Changing organizational structures of political parties, the changing nature of technologies of communication, and the place of spin in modern politics'.[57]

Public image in political communication

The objectives of personalization and the Americanization of political communication are to manage a party's or a politician's public image and control the dissemination of information. Two categories of public image are relevant here: the personal identity of the political actor and the corporate image of the party. Factors ranging from personal appearance to logo design, and even the use of teleprompters to enable politicians to address their audiences naturally, are among the many components of image building, designed to construct a positive identity for a political leader. Indeed, Erdoğan's popularity as a member of the Milli Görüş rose notably after the election period for the mayoralty of Istanbul in 1994. Therefore, the significance and creation of Erdoğan's personal image is stressed when presenting the fieldwork conducted at the AKP's headquarters. To gain a clear understanding, the role of 'political consultants, image-managers, spin doctors and gurus'[58] in reference to the image created of the AKP's leader is examined.

Charisma as a pillar of political communication

When focusing on the Americanization of political communication and personalization, it is essential to consider charisma as an essential aspect of leadership. Max Weber's *On Charisma and Institution Building*,[59] the leading study on charisma, characterizes the quality from a sociological perspective. Weber explains that the rise of charismatic leaders was not from among former bureaucrats or officeholders, so-called experts, but from the heart of the people, the crowd. Weber emphasizes the appeal of those who are marginalized and living in the social context they wish to ascend from. Having innate charismatic leadership skills is another significant factor that contributes to the perception of charisma in leaders. A charismatic leader arises not from 'appointment or dismissal'; that is, there is no 'regulated career' or 'salary' that will satisfy the most charismatic of individuals.[60] Rather, charisma arises from 'inner determination', according to the German sociologist. If a charismatic person is recognized by the community he leads, then 'he is their master' and can continue to be so while attaining 'recognition through proving himself'.[61] Fulfilling the expectations of one's supporters and followers is a critical factor in maintaining an aura of leadership. The expectations here depend on the specific role taken up by the charismatic leader:

> If he wants to be a prophet, he must perform miracles; if he wants to be a war lord, he must perform heroic deeds. Above all, however, his divine mission must 'prove' itself.[62]

In accordance with this view, the expectations of a political leader, such as Erdoğan, are necessarily part of the analysis to be engaged in when assessing the qualitative research data. The question 'What are the demands of the "faithfully surrendered" people, and Erdoğan's approach to meeting them?' will deliver important answers. However, more significant for this research is Erdoğan's journey from a member of the 'crowd' to charismatic leader. His successes as a leader began in 1994 and peaked in 2018, when he introduced a new system by changing the constitution and becoming the most powerful president in modern Turkey – a system which he has changed in favour of himself with a referendum in 2017. The dynamics that inform his charismatic leadership style will be investigated to assess its significance to the political communications produced by the AKP.

Social Movement Theory

> Power…is no longer concentrated in institutions (the state), organizations (capitalist firms), or symbolic controllers (corporate media, churches). It is diffused in global networks of wealth, power, information, and images, which circulate and transmute in a system of variable geometry and dematerialized geography…Power still rules society; it still shapes, and dominates, us.
> – Castells[63]

The role of political communication, which has been explained at length, is discussed in this research in relation to social movement theory. By linking both political communication and social movement theory, the study frames the AKP's communication model. It examines different frameworks pertaining to social movements when analysing the AKP, and when addressing how far and in what ways religion influences the party's political communication.

Social movements seek to 'correct, supplement, overthrow, or in some fashion influence the social order'.[64] Put another way, it is 'the expression of the collective will', lying at the 'heart of social life'.[65] Social movements can be divided into four categories: 'transformative, reformative, redemptive and alternative'.[66] Whereas the aim of transformative movements, including many leftist movements, is to alter the entire social structure, the aim of reformative movements is simply 'partial change'.[67] Nuclear armament and the position of women in society are examples of focal issues for this second group. Given that the AKP originated from an Islamist movement, Milli Görüş, an interesting question to consider here is whether it can be said to have changed itself from a transformative social movement to a reformative one. Redemptive movements, meanwhile, perceive 'the total change of an individual whose problems are divorced from their social context'.[68] Alternative movements, the final category, are founded on the 'rejection of materialism and the development of unconventional lifestyle characteristic of some Western youth'.[69] Environmental social movements fall into this category, as they seek to 'develop viable, sustainable alternative lifestyles such as conserving of energy'.[70] Zirakzadeh[71] takes an approach to defining social movements that is different from the one proposed by Wilson.[72] He highlights three elements as crucial to understanding contemporary social movements:

> (1) Comprise a group of people who consciously attempt to build a radically new social order. (2) Involve people of a broad range of social backgrounds and provide an outlet for political expressions by the non-powerful, non-wealthy and non-famous. (3) Deploy confrontational and socially disruptive tactics involving a style of politics that supplements or replaces conventional political activities like lobbying or working for a political party.[73]

Zirakzadeh's first point aligns with Cameron's definition, stating that 'a social movement occurs when a fairly large number of people band together in order to alter or supplant some portion of the existing culture or social order'.[74] Cameron continues as follows:

> To understand a movement, it is often desirable to classify its purposes relative to those of the rest of society. Such a classification also provides an initial thumbnail description of the purposes. For this classification four familiar concepts are suggested: reactionary, conservative, revisionary, and revolutionary.[75]

Similarly, American sociologist Herbert Blumer[76] states that the main objective of social movements is to 'establish a new order of life'. In contrast, Moghadam[77] distinguishes between three kinds of social movement: those after 'capitalism and neoliberal globalisation: the women's movement, political Islam, and the global justice movement'. Social movements are frequently associated with the rise of capitalism and modernity, whereas the emergence of Islamist movements dates to early twentieth century, after the fall of the Ottoman Empire. Islamist movements can be divided into two categories: moderate and extremist. While moderate movements engage in non-violence, such as politics and civil society, extremist groups prefer to use violence and illegal means when they consider the political system 'anti-Islamic, westernized and dictatorial'.[78] The Muslim Brotherhood (MB) of Egypt, AKP in Turkey, Islah Party of Yemen and Morocco's Justice and Development Party (PJD) are among some of the movements and parties that fall within the moderate category.[79] When considering the mobilization of a moderate social movement, as in the case of this study, the 1979 Iranian revolution is deemed an important paradigmatic example. During the revolution, mosques were perceived as a crucial conduit for distributing messages and organizing people. Bayat[80] supports this view, arguing that 'Islamist movements have utilized mosques to assemble and communicate, cassettes to get messages across and agitate, and Islamic symbols to frame their ideas'. A similar case applied to the MB, in particular during and after the Egyptian revolution in 2011. It would certainly not be possible to categorize the AKP by mentioning their former affiliation with the Milli Görüş, as the separation of state and religion is constitutionally forbidden in Turkey and mosques are not empowered to politicize people directly. Yet, since the July 2016 coup attempt, and more importantly after Eroğan appointed a loyalist as the head of Diyanet, the AKP is systematically using Friday sermons to deliver unity messages during critical turning points. During the COVID-19 pandemic, in order to distract the attention from economic recession of the country, the head of Diyanet targeted LGBT individuals at a Friday sermon by claiming that '[h]omosexuality brings with it illnesses',[81] sparking a new polarization between both camps in Turkey.

Notwithstanding, I consider Bayat's 'Islamic symbol' when referring to Erdoğan's personal religiosity and his ideological motivation by investigating whether in this sense Erdoğan's charisma played a key role in mobilizing potential voters to support him during the elections. This makes it possible to determine whether Erdoğan's role in voter mobilization is more significant than the AKP's political programme. However, the use of Islamic symbols is also relevant when evaluating AKP's political communication campaigning; this is in order to discover if the AKP is using religious motifs to mobilize support.

Pakulski[82] defines social movements as 'recurrent patterns of collective activities which are partially institutionalized, value oriented and anti-systemic in their form and symbolism'. In another definition, social movements are described as 'value-oriented, power-oriented, and participation-oriented'.[83] Although 'anti-systemic' and 'power-oriented' appear to be at opposite poles, one can be an extension of the other, meaning that being anti-systemic first can inform one's power-orientation after challenging and succeeding the former system. In this sense, Ernest Gellner[84] refers to Islamist movements as 'irrational responses to the breakdown of traditional society'; in other words, they are 'revivalist' or 'anti-colonial'.[85] Initially this definition sounds insignificant when considering Turkey as a Muslim nation, but the notion of an 'irrational response' and 'anti-colonial' sentiment can be interpreted in the case of the AKP as a challenge to the 'Kemalist elite'.[86] Kemalism is another name for nationalism, secularism or modernizing.[87] However it is a uniquely Turkish term as it refers to the founder of the Turkish Republic, Mustafa 'Kemal', which emerged after the 'overthrow of the Ottoman regime'.[88] The Kemalist elites were the founders of modern Turkey in 1923. Mustafa Kemal, who initiated the 'modernization programme' in Turkey, created the CHP – modern Turkey's first political party, which remains the main opposition party today.

Collective identity

> Collective identity is an interactive and shared definition produced by several individuals and concerned with the orientations of action and the field of opportunities and constraints in which the action takes place.
> – Johnston and Klandermans[89]

The fundamental concept in social movement theory is collective identity. This is a process of 'constructing an action system' which emerges through 'exchanges, negotiations, decisions, and conflicts'.[90] Melucci observes that 'collective identity is a product of conscious action and the outcome of self-reflection more than a set of given or "structural" characteristics'.[91] It is the first step taken by social movements in the formation and maintenance of collective action. With regard to collective action, there are five vital components to note: 'interest, organization, mobilization, opportunity, and collective action itself'.[92] It is important to understand the collective identity of the AKP according to these five principles.

The parties that arose out of Erbakan's movement were challenged by the secularist elites, from the formation of the first one in 1970. Thus, Erbakan had to form new parties successively. When it became clear that the Welfare Party (RP) would soon be banned, Erbakan ordered the creation of a fourth party, the Virtue Party (Fazilet Partisi, or FP), in December 1997. Subsequently, two groups emerged within the FP: traditionalists and reformists. The de facto leader of the latter was Erdoğan, while the traditionalists were overseen by Erbakan. With regard to Tilly's[93] approach, 'interest' was deemed the first step in the collective action of reformists; they challenged the traditionalists, who were responsible for controlling the party, to introduce reform and increase the variety of supporters. However, Erbakan was not enthusiastic about changing the ideological approach of the movement. This led Erdoğan to 'organize' the younger generation within the FP to mobilize against the traditionalists in 2000 at the FP congress.

At that time, Abdullah Gül was the candidate for the reformists, because Erdoğan had been banned from political activities for five years and spent four months in prison for reciting a religious charged poem during a speech in the city of Siirt. Gül received 521 votes compared to Recai Kutan, the candidate for the traditionalists, also known as the 'Politburo', who received 633 votes. Although the reformists failed to gain control of the party, this represented an opportunity and led them towards 'collective action' – the final point that Tilly[94] notes – ultimately to leave the FP and form the AKP in 2001.[95] The courage of the reformists rested on successful political communication and campaigning during the 1994 municipal elections, which revealed the RP could succeed in major cities such as Istanbul and Ankara. The softer language of Erdoğan and the involvement of women for the first time in election campaigns in the 1994 election made it clear that there was potential for the conservative[96] majority in Turkey to prevail.

Collective identity can function as a means of unifying 'social, political, and economic conditions and action orientations'.[97] It answers the question of who key actors are as a social movement. Social movements, which have become a major area of sociological analysis, are the basis for creating 'ideas, identities and ideals' for society.[98] These fundamental aspects come together as 'collectiveness'. In this manner, 'common interest' turns to 'common identity'.[99] The literature raises questions concerning whether the role of social movements is to 'change or defend society'.[100] Lindberg and Sverrisson[101] also highlight the role of organization in social movements as follows:

> Social movements can be defined as collective action with some stability over time and some degree of organization, oriented towards change or conservation of society ... The idea of social movements tends to move between two poles in social theory. One is the vision of social movements as collective action responding to specific tensions or a contradiction in society ... The other is social movement as bearers of the meaning of history ... and the main agent of global social change.[102]

On the basis of Lindberg and Sverrisson's approach, it seems fair to surmise that the AKP sought 'collective change' in society by placing key issues such as 'development, democracy, human rights, pluralism, freedom and the rule of law' at the epicentre of its party programme in 2002. The main incentive was to deliver change by creating a conservative yet modern society. By exploring two different periods of the AKP's development, 2002–9 and 2010–19, this study will analyse how the party altered its understanding of societal change. In particular, the concepts of human rights, pluralism and freedom are critical issues when looking at both periods, as Erdoğan increased the concentration of power in the executive enhancing one-man rule and developed a populist Islamist discourse over time.

3

Modernization in the Ottoman era, Islamism in Turkey and AKP's rise

Islamism is an activist and modernist movement which in the nineteenth and twentieth centuries methodologically and cleverly rescued the Islamic world from Western colonization, tyrannical administrators, slavery, mimicry and superstitions by causing Islam as a whole (faith, worship, morality, philosophy, politics, education etc.) to 'once again' civilise and dominate life.

– Kara[1]

The leader of the Ennahda (Renaissance) movement in Tunisia, Rached Ghannouchi, stated at the Ennahda's congress in May 2016 that, following the 2011 revolution, '[p]olitical Islam has lost its justification in Tunisia'.[2] In an interview with *Le Monde*, Ghannouchi described the Ennahda as a political, democratic and civil party capable of embracing the values of modern civilized nations. When Erdoğan created the AKP in 2001, he claimed he got rid of his Milli Görüş ideology, emphasizing that the party had renounced 'the traditional aims and discourses of political Islamism and embraced secular democracy'.[3] In an interview for the *New York Times* in 2003, he explained the shift in his political ideology as follows:

> A political party cannot have a religion. Only individuals can. Otherwise, you would be exploiting religion, and religion is so supreme that it cannot be exploited or taken advantage of.[4]

The above views consider the role of Islam within political frameworks, and choose to emphasize change and reform as guiding the party's political governance. Whereas the former statement was taken from a discussion in 2016, the second example dates to the early days of the AKP. Nevertheless, both were uttered as the parties in question sought to open up internally to win over a non-conservative audience and globally to align more with the West, with the aim of becoming mainstream Islamist. Although the statements distance the parties from a sense of embodied religious ideology, Islamism is the principal source of their popular support. Certainly this reality affects not only the AKP and Ennahda but also other parties and movements in the region, such as the MB in Egypt and Jordan, and the PJD in Morocco.

The aim of this research is to evaluate the changes in the AKP's Islamist ideology over time by carefully observing shifts resulting from relevant milestones. Consequently, this section will examine Islamism and its impact first in the Ottoman era and then in the modern Turkish Republic. That the focus of the study is on a party that was established from the ashes of an Islamist movement increases the importance of conceptualizing Islamism and framing the party's position relative to critical turning points. This will assist our understanding of the political identity of today's AKP and its leader, and elaborate on the role of religion in the political communication of the party.

The next section continues by offering a definition of Islamism in order to explain how it will be framed in this research. The period of modernization of the Ottoman Empire during the eighteenth and nineteenth centuries will be examined in a later section; this will help understand the emergence of Islamism and shed a light on Erdoğan's previous affiliation to the Milli Görüş, leading to a greater appreciation of what the AKP represents today.

What really is Islamism?

The political aspect of Islam, variously known as 'Islamism', 'Political Islam' or 'Post-Islamism', describes the instrumentalization of Islam by an institution, group, organization or political party. Bobby Sayyid,[5] professor of social theory at the University of Leeds, notes that the aim of Islamism is to establish 'a political order centred on the name of Islam', locating religion centrally in the political sphere. Denoeux[6] sees this as a 'political response to today's societal challenges by imagining a future'. This is, on the one hand, a reaction to specific policies and, on the other, a response to 'secular modernity'.[7] As highlighted in the beginning of the chapter, Professor Ismail Kara, a prominent scholar of Islamism in Turkey who was also one of the interviewees in this research, offers a broader description of Islamism. For Kara, the function of Islamism is to counter Western colonization. In his comprehensive description, he analyses this from a wider vantage point than previously mentioned scholars. Similarly, in his *Making Islam Democratic*, Bayat[8] argues that Islamism emerged to mobilize the middle class to resist established economy, politics and culture. Whereas both scholars centralize 'the other' as the main aim, there is a significant difference between them. Bayat[9] asserts that Islamists' principal aim is to form 'an Islamic state', as in the case of Iran. The failures in Iran and Turkey in the late 1990s led Bayat to advance a new term, post-Islamism, to define the process of embracing democracy and combining faith and freedom, and the objectives of a 'secular democratic state with a religious society'. While Erbakan's RP represented Islamism for Bayat, the AKP stands for a post-Islamist party in Turkey.[10] In contrast, Kara[11] never discusses the idea of an Islamic state; instead, he talks about framing an Islamist struggle within the laicist Kemalist order. He argues that there is no marked difference between the RP and AKP,[12] as both Milli Görüş and the AKP are modernist movements. A closer examination of Bayat, Kara and Sayyid lend support to the claim that Kara's and Sayyid's description is more adequate than Bayat's considering the different political dynamics in Turkey, relative to those in Iran. In this regard, I prefer to use the frame of 'Islamism' for the AKP, in the way Kara and Sayyid do, but add the word 'populism'; in other words, 'populist Islamism', because compared to Erbakan, Erdoğan uses Islam in a discursive and rhetorical way after 2010 to gain credibility on the ground.

Modernization in the Ottoman era

Eric Jan Zürcher[13] noted, 'Turkey cannot be understood without reference to its Ottoman past.' To effectively assess the impact of Islamism in Turkey and the birth of the AKP, I turn now to Turkey's Ottoman past. Turkey has often been presented as the successor state to the Ottoman State, and so, to understand modern Turkey, it is useful to review the process of modernization that characterized the Ottoman Empire of the eighteenth century because it had a considerable impact on politics and society.

The signing of the Treaty of Karlowitz in 1699 was a significant event for the Ottoman Empire as it ended the empire's uninterrupted expansion and led to its first significant loss of territory. This turning point caused considerable introspection and marked the beginning of an inter-regnum period, which saw the start of a steady decline during the reign of Abdulhamid I (reigned from 1774 to 1789), which was followed by the rule of Sultan Selim III (reigned from 1789 to 1807). Following a number of defeats, Selim III modernized the Ottoman army, opening new military schools inspired by European models. Hanioğlu[14] noted that the 'adoption of western technology' proved a further means of attaining superiority over the West.

The steps taken also included some political modernization as apparent in the form of a number of social reforms. A significant step towards modernization, which had a lasting impact on Ottoman society, was the introduction of a new education system. Throughout the Ottoman era, the schools had always been *madrasas* (i.e. religious schools), in which children were primarily taught an Islamic curriculum. However, alongside these *madrasas*, Sultan Selim III introduced a new type of educational system based on European schooling that included subjects such as medicine and engineering. The primary influence behind this new Western-oriented education system and political renewal were the European-educated bureaucrats. Captivated by Europe's development, these intellectuals who returned home to Turkey were convinced that the only way to halt the decline of the empire would be to imitate the strategies of Western countries, particularly of France. During this period, the palace, in consultation with high-ranking bureaucrats, agreed that only through modernization would the empire's fortunes be resurrected.

Sultan Selim III: Symbol of modernization

The modernization of the Ottoman Empire was first embodied in the private lives of its sultans. Selim III, following the example of Louis XVI, who reigned between 1774 and 1792, even ensured his children were taught French from an early age. He established embassies in London (1793), Vienna (1794), Berlin (1795) and Paris (1796), which then became further significant means for Ottoman bureaucrats to acquire knowledge of Western diplomacy, allowing the sultan to build strong relationships with European countries and politicians. This process was continued by Sultan Mahmud II (reigned from 1808 to 1839), Selim's successor, whose reforms affected all aspects of the empire, from politics to education and even social life. Although the changes undertaken were portrayed as actions proceeding from new progressive policies by the caliphate, and characterized as part of a process of renewal and development, they ultimately heralded a long period of decline.[15]

After Mahmud II, Sultan Abdulmecid I (reigned from 1839 to 1861) came to power; he was responsible for introducing a crucial reform process in 1839 called the *Tanzimat*. Under this reform, the education system became more coherent and was institutionalized through the establishment of a new Ministry of Education, which became an important arm of the state.[16] Moreover, changes were made to the mechanisms of bureaucracy, including provincial administration, taxation and communication. Another significant example was the adoption of printing, which was recognized as a useful European invention and introduced to the Ottoman era in 1727, attracting a *fatwa* (religious opinion) from the *ulama* (religious scholars), the strongest religious and most respected authority in the Ottoman rule.[17] Thus, the *ulama* were instrumental in the process of modernization. The reforms made by Selim III and Mahmud II were characterized at the time as undertaken 'for the sake of religion and State'.[18] Although the *Tanzimat* period witnessed the institution of reforms throughout the empire, they were arguably too late, as it was already faltering and approaching an accentuated decline. The empire's difficulties proved to be an important opportunity for the British Empire, from whom it sought both economic and political concessions.

Abdulhamid II and Islamism

> If we want to rejuvenate, find our previous force, and reach our old greatness, we ought to remember the fountainhead of our strength. What is beneficial to us is not to imitate the so-called European civilization, but to the Sharia, the source of our strength ... Mighty God, I can be your slave only and ask only your help. Lead us on the right path.
>
> – Abdulhamid[19]

The reform and modernization process continued until Abdulhamid II's reign (1876 to 1909). Reflecting upon Abdulhamid II's reign is important here, as there has been some discussion in Turkey in recent years that Erdoğan is following in the footsteps of Abdulhamid II.

Abdulhamid II received a traditional education 'from private religious scholars who were known for their erudition and knowledge of state affairs',[20] which resulted in him adopting an Islamist stance throughout his life. In fact, 'the Hamidian period', named after Abdulhamid II, included opposition to some facets of Western civilization as he sought to establish a political means of uniting Muslims around the world under his caliphate,[21] leading to criticisms of his reign from both orientalists and Turkish secularists alike. However, it is interesting to note that Karpat[22] characterizes Abdulhamid II as the most Europeanized sultan, describing him as listening to European music, having a passion for theatre, speaking French, drinking wine occasionally and demonstrating a preference for European amenities. Furthermore, it was Abdulhamid II who authorized brothels to fight against the syphilis infection.[23] Although Western countries and their leaders regarded him as a religious caliph,[24] and as an enemy of civilization and enlightenment, his admiration for Western developments led him to continue with reforms to both the government and education, thereby transforming the Ottoman society during his reign. There were clearly disparities between Abdulhamid II's political stance and his personal lifestyle.

The empire had entered a period of ideological and physical fragmentation as a result of the previous sultan's modernization policies and a series of battlefield defeats, and it was continuing to decline relatively on the international stage. Against this backdrop, Abdulhamid II set about forging a new policy of Islamism to counteract European encroachment on his lands. His Islamist policy was based on *ümmet*, according to Mandaville,[25] derived from the Arabic word *ummah*,[26] and aimed to create a universal religious community among Muslims. However, Aydın[27] calls it the 'Muslim world' rather than 'ummah' because he analyses the period after 1870s as one of 'Muslim religious community' being under to influence of European powers owing to the modernization policies introduced in the Ottoman era. This political reinvention of the empire's position established a new political foundation to bind Muslims together.

Abdulhamid II's policy came to be known as 'Pan-Islamic' in the Western world and was widely regarded as modern Islam.[28] French journalist Gabriel Charmes was one of the first to use the term 'Pan Islam' in his article 'La Situation de la Turquie' (Turkey's Situation), published in the *Revue des Deux Mondes* in Paris during the 1880s.[29] According to Aydın,[30] Pan-Islamism was a secular spiritual caliphate perception. Based on this description, even Westernists in the Ottoman Empire could have been a Pan-Islamist. The term Pan-Islam became rapidly popularized in mainstream discourse, and was discussed in the British media as well as in the domains of academia and politics, subsequently reaching the international arena. Landau[31] argued that Pan-Slavism, Pan-Germanism and Pan-Hellenism shared similarities with the political steps taken during the reign of Abdulhamid II. During the same era, the writings and meetings held by Young Ottomans, a group of Ottoman Turkish intellectuals, employed the term *Ittihad-ı Islam* (Union of Islam). In the Arab world, the *al-Urwa al-wuthqa* journal, published by Jamal al-Din al-Afghani and Muhammad Abduh, the founder of Islamism in Egypt, used the term *Ittihad-ı Islam* for the first time in 1884.[32] These examples indicate that, by the end of the nineteenth century, Muslim intellectuals and politicians were making frequent use of the terms *Pan-Islam* and *Ittihad-ı Islam*, especially to describe their political project to unite all Muslims. The term *Ittihad-ı Islam*[33] was used within the Ottoman Empire, and *Pan-Islam* was the interpretation of it as understood in Europe.

Intellectuals under Abdulhamid II's rule followed three steps to support the policy of *Ittihad-ı Islam*. First, they had the common aim of returning to the Quran and the Prophetic Sunnah (i.e. the sayings and traditions of the Prophet), freeing religion from those aspects they viewed as arising from superstition and which had infiltrated the religion by contributing novel ideas. Second, they believed the door to *ijtihad* (i.e. independent reasoning) should be open to establish solutions to current social, political, economic and religious issues. Finally, they considered the 'soul of Jihad' should be awoken in order to battle in unity against the enemy, leading to a popular social awakening. These steps established because the Ottoman Empire was seeking to combat its disintegration in parallel with modernization. It is therefore impossible to compare these policies with those of Erdoğan because the Islamism process referred to here took place under a Muslim caliphate when the Ottoman Empire was still intact. In this manner, theologian Taftazani defines the fundamental responsibilities of a caliph as follows:

> The Caliph is the representative of the Prophet, on the one hand, and of the nation, on the other… [He] is the representative and leader of the Islamic nation in administering the affairs to the state and observing the interests of the nation. The power and authority that he possesses are directly derived from the nation.[34]

Despite the differences in legal framework, as one leader is a caliph and considered holder of the Islamic law and the other governs a modern secularist state, Abdulhamid II's political philosophy can be contrasted with Erdoğan's pursuit of Islamization of the country as evidenced in his messages and discourse. More importantly, Erdoğan's Islamist approach elicits memories of that of Abdulhamid II, one of the most highly reputed sultans revered by the conservative majority in Turkey. Historian Yasamee[35] who is the author of the *Ottoman Diplomacy: Abdulhamid II and the Great Powers 1878–1888* underlines in his book that 'Abdulhamid held that the first condition of any government was religion and in order to protect that religion, a little fanaticism.' Furthermore, he saw religion as a social and political force to support his reign.[36]

> He also strove to identify the State with Islam in the eyes of his subjects, through official participation in religious festivals, patronage of influential religious *şeyhs*, financial grants for the repair of mosques, and constant press propaganda… Abdulhamid gave practical priority to the interests of his Moslem subjects. He was above all anxious to raise the Moslems' educational and economic status.

> He recognized that they were backward in comparison with their non-Moslem compatriots, and that this relative backwardness posed a serious threat to the Empire's future... He was able to expand the state school network, and thereby to increase educational opportunities for Moslems. In the short term, the schools were intended to strengthen the state, by producing better-educated officials and army officers; but in the longer term, they also contributed to the formation of a Moslem middle class, composed of state employees and members of the free professions, though not, as yet, of businessmen. Paradoxically, it was this new middle class which was to overthrow Abdulhamid's regime in 1908.[37]

These sentences about Abdulhamid show clearly how Erdoğan's aim is very similar to that of the Ottoman sultan regarding the Islamist ideology. Similarly Erdoğan supports the restoration of mosques and places importance on education by opening new Imam Hatip schools (or modernizing existing ones) and private schools by proposing a new education model which combines religion with Western education systems such as Montessori Method. His family mainly manages the private schools, of which there are at least three different types. Erdoğan's aim is to have a new pious generation that continues his legacy by increasing the value of Islam first within the borders of Turkey and then globally in the long term. However the last few elections have shown that this generation in particular, the generation Z, neither approves the AKP's policies nor recognizes Erdoğan as a leader. AC5, philosophy professor at a foundation university in Istanbul, underlines that 'especially students who study at pro-government schools and universities are opposing the ruling AKP which reflects how Erdoğan failed in founding a unique solution for the education system'. Moreover, AC5 says that this new generation will be the main rival of the AKP when they become active members of the society after the graduation.

Modernist movements challenging Islamist policies

During the reign of Abdulhamid II, a number of forces, foreign as well as domestic, attempted to prevent the spread of Islamist policies. In 1889, four students[38] from a military medical college in Istanbul founded the Ottoman Unity Society (Ittihad-ı Osmani Cemiyeti), which seven years later was renamed Ittihat ve Terakki (i.e. the Committee of Union and Progress; or CUP).[39] During the Armenian crisis (1894–6), when Abdulhamid II was experiencing considerable difficulties and the influence of the CUP was increasing in the empire, Abdulhamid II's Islamist policies, in particular his unification project, were criticized by CUP members who represented the modernist wing of the Ottoman intelligentsia and bureaucracy. However, the CUP's ideology of modernization along Western lines garnered no influence within the Ottoman Empire until 1908. By 1908, however, they had begun to exert greater influence, resulting in the birth of the Turkish Republic. In 1908, when the Second Constitutional Period was announced, new reforms transformed the caliphate into a more secular institution.

A further significant opposition movement that emerged in addition to the CUP during the final days of the Ottoman period was an organization known as the 'Young Turks' (Jön Türkler, originally from French: Les Jeunes Turcs), which had a branch in Paris promoting modernization of 'Ottoman intelligentsia and bureaucracy'.[40] The Young Turks were sent from the Ottoman Empire to France to study scientific advances and experience Western progress with the aim of implementing developments in the Ottoman Empire, so as to help the empire regain its place in history.

Islamism in modern Turkey

The period from the end of the Ottoman era to the years following the First World War witnessed the nascence of various Islamist movements and parties. The birth of the Turkish Republic created new political paradigms, with the traditional autocratic governance model adhered to under the Ottoman Empire replaced by a modern, Western-style approach, focused on secularism. Samuel Huntington[41] described Turkey as a 'torn society', divided between a political elite, which considered itself a part of the West, and a larger, more religious grouping, which viewed itself as part of the Muslim Middle East.

The new social circumstances and the emergent one-party state[42] produced a number of difficulties in terms of institutionalizing Islam in politics, as was apparent by the end of the 1960s. Previously, the role of Islam had been highlighted in publications by poets and Islamist activists such as Mehmet Akif Ersoy (1873–1936), Necip Fazıl Kısakürek (1904–1983) and Sezai Karakoç (1933–). However, immediately following the establishment of the Republic, Islamic activities were banned in Turkey. At this time, the *Nakşibendi*[43] Sufi orders organized themselves into an underground movement with the intention of spreading the word of Islam to all Turkish households. Although they were not wholly successful in implementing an Islamic identity, they provided a strong foundation for the intellectual classes, who used poetry, plays and novels to focus on ideological Islam. These groups included scholars like Necip

Fazıl Kısakürek, Nurettin Topçu (1909–1975) and Sezai Karakoç, all of whom published literary journals after the 1930s. This was also the first use of the print media in modern Turkish history.

The following section focuses on these three intellectuals and their ideologies, as they proved highly influential at creating a new Islamist narrative. It was these thinkers who inspired Erdoğan in his youth. Indeed, it is well known that Erdoğan enjoys reading poems. The poems he most prefers are those by Kısakürek and Karakoç. Hence in order to understand Erdoğan's Islamist stance and historic imagery, it is necessary to comprehend the ideological messages conveyed by these individuals.

Necip Fazıl Kısakürek

Necip Fazıl Kısakürek was a prominent Turkish poet who attempted to Islamize the Turkish people using the medium of literature. His ideology can be summarized by reflecting on the following three beliefs:

> (1) Turkish-Muslim society had lost its ties with the past by losing its ties with the language, morality and historical memory as a result of Westernisation policies. (2) The Kemalist reforms deliberately sought to 'destroy' the inner spiritual power of the Turkish nation. (3) This project of de-Islamization could be reversed with the rise of new 'ruling elite' who shared a Turkish Islamic cognitive map of revival. In other words, by giving the youth a mission to restore memory and an Islamo-Turkish identity, Kısakürek mixed nationalism with Islam and offered an emotional attachment to political activity.[44]

Kısakürek's approach directly relates to Kemalism and references Mustafa Kemal, because loss of the Ottoman language was one aspect of the top-down imposed modernization programme introduced by Mustafa Kemal Atatürk. The process of modernization under Mustafa Kemal created many enduring problems according to the Islamist ideologue, who characterizes his leadership as overseeing a process of deliberate de-Islamization. In order to redress the damage done, Kısakürek emphasized the value of poems and ideological publications. In 1943, Kısakürek published the *Büyük Doğu* (The Great East) journal, which focused on Islamic ideology, while criticizing the modernization of Turkey. The primary aim of his books, poems and journal was to encourage the Turkish population to regenerate an Islamic consciousness for itself and practice a religion based on the Quran and Sunnah. Moreover, *Büyük Doğu* did not simply focus on Turkey; it also underlined the importance of eradicating the borders between Muslim nations to facilitate the building of an *ummah* thus fostering Islamic unity. In addition to *Büyük Doğu*, Kısakürek founded the Büyük Doğu Cemiyeti in 1949 (The Great East Community), the purpose of which was to organize conferences in Anatolia to spread his ideology mainly through poetry.

In 2014, in one of his speeches, Erdoğan explained that Kısakürek had made a valuable contribution to the self-confidence of the people.[45] He even attributed the expanding Turkish film industry to Kısakürek. Kısakürek's activism was highly significant for Erdoğan, and it is referenced occasionally in his speeches, especially while addressing young audiences.

Sezai Karakoç

Another influential person in Turkish history was Sezai Karakoç. He was arguably the most important figure when considering the *Medeniyet* (civilization) project, which was established after 1960s. This project relates to physical, metaphysical, moral and cultural norms. Karakoç published the *Diriliş* (resurrection) journal to circulate his ideas regarding Islamic thought, culture and art; it proved to be an important platform for bringing young people together. Prior to publishing this journal, he contributed to Kısakürek's *Büyük Doğu* between 1950 and 1955, revealing that both poets have a common ideological background. *Diriliş* journal served to foster a Muslim renaissance in literature, art, culture and Islamic thought in general.

> We need to reconsider ourselves in terms of civilization and ideals. We need to start our own renaissance to view the world from our own spirit. In short, we need to revive!
>
> – Sezai Karakoç[46]

Karakoç summarized the three responsibilities of Muslims as follows: (1) to know oneself, (2) to know the East and (3) to have a deep knowledge of Western philosophy and literature. By emphasizing the 'East', he was referring to the oriental world. He further classified the three different political forms of the nation and state: (1) great nations and states (i.e. planning for over 100 years), (2) those aiming to maintain the status quo in the international arena and (3) small nations and states, which lack vision and message. He was convinced that it was vital for Turkey to become a great nation and a great power, being able to influence world politics. For this reason, EU membership was an important opportunity for Turkey to position itself against Russia. However, he viewed an

Islamic Union as the ideal guarantee for 'liberation', as without this no safety could be guaranteed, neither for Turkey nor for any other Muslim country. For Karakoç, the Middle East was not only a geographical region, but also a representation of both civilization and culture, and the ideal region in which to implement Islamic unity and the concept of *Medeniyet*.

Following the failed coup in 2016, Erdoğan explained that there was no longer a need for the EU membership.[47] By contrast, he has emphasized on many occasions that Turkey could rise to become one of the world's ten best performing economies. This reflects Karakoç's political views, specifically those concerning the dream of creating a *Medeniyet*, a civilization to challenge the West.

Necmettin Erbakan's Milli Görüş Movement

> Zionists are seeking to assimilate Turkey and pull us from our historical Islamic roots through integrating Turkey with the European Economic Community. Since the European Community is a single state, Turkey's membership means being a single state with Israel. The goal is to create a Greater Israel by integrating Turkey into the community.
>
> – Erbakan[48]

After the demise of the Ottoman Empire, more than institutions, individual thinkers and activists attempted to raise awareness of Islamic ideology among the younger generation in the years leading up to 1969. This year marked a critical turning point, in terms of institutionalization of Islamic views, with the entrance of Necmettin Erbakan into the political arena. An engineering professor who had been educated in Turkey and Germany, Erbakan, who led the Milli Görüş, swiftly rose to become the most important figure representing political Islam in Turkey.

In terms of the origins of the AKP, Erbakan's movement played a significant part, as the founders of the AKP were members of his movement from a young age. In order to provide the backdrop against which Erdoğan's views were shaped in his youth and during his early political career, the role of Erbakan, the history of the parties he founded and his political approach will be outlined in the following sections.

Erbakan's ideology describes the movement he founded; *Milli Görüş* literally translates as 'National Outlook'. However, although the name 'Milli' literally means 'national', in this context it is better understood in terms of Islamic perspective. Erbakan summarizes the ideal behind Milli Görüş in the following sentences:

> Milli Görüş is the outlook of our people. Milli Görüş is identical with Sultan Fatih's ideology when he conquered Istanbul in 1453. Today the only solution for the problems is Milli Görüş.[49]

Sultan Fatih is also known as 'Mehmed the Conqueror', as he conquered Constantinople in 1453, wresting it from the Byzantine Empire. In the quotation, Erbakan not only makes a reference to the Ottoman era, he also ratifies its policies, drawing parallels between his movement and the objectives of the empire. Yet, every year, Erbakan's youth organization Anadolu Gençlik Derneği (Anatolian Youth Association, AGD) organizes yearly anniversary programmes to remember the conquest of Constantinople. Until Erbakan's death, these celebrations, which were held in huge stadiums in Istanbul, were attended by Erbakan. He was known for his animated speeches at these celebrations that had a motivational impact on his social movement. During such speeches, the importance of Hagia Sophia was always highlighted by Erbakan who underlined that the museum needs to be reconverted to a mosque. In fact, after 2015, Erdoğan first started arranging rallies with huge crowds to celebrate the conquest of Constantinople in Istanbul's Yenikapı district, and reconverted Hagia Sophia to a mosque in 2020, fulfilling the dreams of his former mentor. Erdoğan's loyalty to Erbakan could be recognized when considering the fact that he named his second son after his guide.

Whether in Turkey, or in Egypt, Islamists were always impressed by socialist discourse. The policy of Milli Görüş was referred to as *Adil Düzen* (just order), and presented as a third way, an alternative to capitalism and socialism. *Adil Düzen* describes the global system as a 'slave system', which was supported by the International Monetary Fund (IMF), the World Bank and other organizations, whose sole aim was developing a 'true private enterprise regime'.[50]

In contrast, Erbakan's policy drew on *Othering*, approaching politics from an ideological vantage point thus describing a 'fundamental conflict between the Western and Islamic civilization'.[51] This led to foreign policies based on an anti-Western paradigm; he opposed the EU, calling it a Christian Club, and predicted that Turkey's membership would adversely impact its cultural identity and sovereignty. He was convinced that if it joined the EU, Turkey would be paving the way for Israel to do the same. This was crucial, as at the crux of his anti-Western policy was anti-Zionism,[52] characterizing Israel as an 'illegitimate and expansionist state whose ultimate aim is to create a greater Israel by occupying Syria, Egypt and Turkey'.[53] His beliefs were strongly expressed, and also incorporated the conviction that the United Nations (UN) had been established only to create an Israeli state.

History of the Milli Görüş

Erbakan was first encouraged to engage in politics by Mehmet Zahit Kotku (1897–1980), a cleric and sheikh of the *Iskender Paşa* community of the *Nakşibendi* order. Lütfi Doğan, head of the Directorate of Religious Affairs between 1968 and 1971 and Erdoğan's companion for an extended period of time, explains the relationship as follows:

> Mehmet Zahid Kotku was the brainchild of the party. He wanted to have a party where Muslims could feel at home. We were, in fact, tired of being used by other centre-right parties. I became involved in this party because of Zahid Efendi. I remember that evening when Zahid Efendi invited five people and told us that 'you are all men dedicated to the cause of protecting and advancing this nation. The core identity and character of this wounded nation is Islam. Your main heritage is Islam and Muslims. You can heal this wound by listening to what our Turkish Muslim people want. What they want is an Islamic sense of justice and the restoration of their Ottoman-Islamic identity.'[54]

According to Kotku, the Kemalist regime's modernization policies were responsible for creating a wound that affected the identity of Muslims in Turkey. Kotku's anti-modernization and anti-Kemalist approach distinguished him from other politicians in Turkey. In conjunction with the writings of Kısakürek and Karakoç, Kotku's ideology has a significant impact on Erdoğan's political stance.

Erbakan originally aimed to be elected as part of Süleyman Demirel's Democrat Party, but following opposition from Demirel, he ran in 1969 as an independent candidate from Konya. Following this election, on the 26 January 1970 he founded the Milli Nizam Partisi (National Order Party, MNP), along with eighteen colleagues. The MNP sympathizers were typically (1) religious recipients of a modern republican education; (2) religious middle-class tradesmen and (3) Sunni Muslims living in Turkey's metropolitan and provincial regions. However, the MNP survived for only sixteen months before being disbanded on 20 May 1971 by the Constitutional Court 'on account of its alleged anti-secular activities'.[55] This was the first example in what became a long history in Turkey of the banning and closing down of religiously inspired parties.

However, the successor to the MNP was founded seventeen months later, under the name Milli Selamet Partisi (National Salvation Party, MSP). The MSP participated in the 1973 elections, receiving 11.8 per cent of the votes and forty-eight assembly seats. This election marked the party's first entry into parliament, and led to the participation of the MSP in two coalitions. In 1981, the MSP was closed down for similar reasons to those given when banning the MNP, that is, alleged anti-secular activities.

Erbakan subsequently founded a new party called the Refah Partisi (Welfare Party, RP) in 1983. The closure of each party was followed by Erbakan and the members of their main governing bodies being banned from politics for several months or years. Of Erbakan's parties, the RP was the only one that rapidly grew in strength, polling 4.4 per cent in the 1984 elections. Erbakan was permitted to engage in politics during the 1987 elections, when the party's share of the vote increased to 7.2 per cent. However, due to the national threshold of 10 per cent, the party was unable to send a representative to parliament. The party's share of the vote increased to 9.8 per cent in the local elections held in 1989, followed by 16.9 per cent in parliamentary elections in 1991. This rapid rise of the party continued in the local elections in 1994, with the RP receiving 19.1 per cent of the votes and capturing the mayoralties of twenty-nine provincial centres, including the two most important ones of Istanbul and Ankara. Following this election, Erdoğan was elected mayor of Istanbul, after challenging a number of important candidates and utilizing effective political communication strategies during his campaign. He drew on universal values to attract the necessary additional liberal and secular-minded voters. Erdoğan's campaign included visits to pubs to reassure voters that, should his party prove successful, they would continue to be permitted to drink alcohol, and the government will not interfere in private lives.

Members of the Milli Görüş invited the population to follow Islamic principles in the guises of the MNP and MSP. However, the new RP omitted references to religion, that is, branding competitors as 'bad politicians' rather than 'bad Muslims'. This change in rhetoric created a vital shift during the local elections, which in turn had a considerable influence on the 1995 parliamentary elections during which the party gained every fifth vote (i.e. 21.4 per cent) to emerge as the strongest party by winning 158 of the 550 parliamentary seats. They were also able to attract a far greater diversity of supporters than any Islam-inspired party in the Middle East had done previously, with Erbakan reportedly receiving support from 'conservative townspeople, poor urban migrants, professionals, intellectuals, and wealthy industrialists'.[56] Furthermore, it was the first time that working-class conservative women became active in an election campaign, representing a distinct advantage for conservatives.

However, the RP was unable to rule alone, which forced it to be pragmatic and form a coalition with the centre-right Doğru Yol Partisi (True Path Party, DYP). The electoral success of political Islam resulted from four factors:

> First, there has been the state policy of a Turkish-Islamic synthesis introduced by the leaders of the 1980 military coup. Secondly, there has been the political and economic liberalisation accompanied by the emergence of the new conservative Anatolian bourgeoisie, represented by such organisations as MÜSIAD. The third factor has been the prominence of a new class of Islamist intellectuals based in print and electronic media. The final factor has been the internal organisational flexibility of the RP and its ideological presentation of the Just Order (*Adil Düzen*) platform.[57]

Notwithstanding, secular-minded individuals and institutions opposed the formation of a RP-DYP government, with the result that the coalition lasted twelve months. In 1997, Erbakan was forced to resign in response to pressure from the military and the National Security Council, in conjunction with the media and other leading civil society organizations. This was termed 'the 28th February process', as this was the date that the National Security Council met. It has been presented as a postmodern coup by the coalition, working alongside the secular-minded military, the media and state institution. The overthrow and subsequent banning of the RP was (as in previous cases) attributed to its 'anti-secular activities'. Erbakan and six other leading party members were banned from entering politics for a period of five years.

Following this ban, Fazilet Partisi (Virtue Party, FP), the fourth party to emerge out of the Milli Görüş, was formed. The coup marked the beginning of a long decline for Erbakan and his movement; one from which they were unable to recover. The party lost voters at every election despite nearly thirty years of effort – a reality that triggered a process of self-criticism and reflection among its younger cadre of activist members. This introspection negated the previously 'unconditional obedience' that had been practiced towards its senior members, as in the days of the Ottoman Empire. Thus, a new group known as the *Yenilikçiler* (reformists) arose in contrast to the *Gelenekçiler* (traditionalists).

The reformists were led by Erdoğan, former president Abdullah Gül and the twenty-second Speaker of the Grand National Assembly of Turkey Bülent Arınç; all three were convinced that the RP needed to reform its policies and communicate through a more moderate and universal discourse. Both wings were challenged during the FP's Congress in 2000, and Gül was the reformist candidate because Erdoğan was banned from political activities for five years and spent four months in prison for reciting a religious charged poem during a speech in the city of Siirt.[58] Gül lost the vote by a small margin to Recai Kutan from the traditional wing (521 votes to 633). However, this was a success for the reformists, leading to subsequent opportunities when the Constitutional Court chose to ban the FP when its actions were judged incompatible with the secular character of the state. The party closure led the Islamists to split into two parties in 2001, with the traditional wing being established as the Saadet Partisi (Felicity Party, SP), and the reformists forming the AKP under the leadership of Erdoğan.

It is significant that in July 2000, one year prior to the foundation of the AKP, ANAR (Ankara Social Research Centre) conducted a poll which found 'that if a general election were held on the day, 30.8 per cent of the people surveyed would vote for the party to be founded by Erdoğan and his associates'.[59] This poll reveals that even before it was founded it was apparent that the AKP would become a popular party in Turkey. When Erdoğan read a poem in 1997 and was jailed for four months for 'publicly provoking people to animosity and enmity based on religion and race', he also 'lost his political right to stand for office'.[60] This demonstrates the desire on the part of the Kemalist elites to ban him from politics. However, this made him more popular among the conservatives, who perceived his treatment as unreasonable and his punishment 'unfair'. The potential popularity of Erdoğan and the AKP was also apparent from another poll conducted in June 2001, two months before the foundation of the AKP. On this occasion, respondents were asked who should be selected as chairman if Erbakan's fourth party, FP, were banned. Of the respondents, 40.8 per cent answered Erdoğan. Erdoğan appears to have experienced a surge in popularity because he was seen as having been victimized by the courts. This experience also endowed him with an image of courage and heroism. It is also important to consider Erdoğan's image within the party for this study as this helps explain the success of his one-man leadership approach.

Erdoğan as an aspiring student of Erbakan

In 1969, at just 15, Erdoğan joined the National Turkish Student Union (MTTB). During that time, this movement played a significant role in educating young people in accordance with an Islamic agenda; this had great influence on young Erdoğan's political views. Necip Fazıl Kısakürek and Nurettin Topçu were pioneers of the school, referred to as anti-communist, anti-Zionist, anti-Kemalist and anti-elite. The MTTB proved to be an opportunity for Erdoğan to create a network that has sustained him throughout his political career, first as mayor of Istanbul and later as founder of the AKP. Erdoğan's relationships with the MTTB enabled him to join Milli Görüş's Youth Branch, where he became directly involved in politics.

Erdoğan's popularity resulted from his political success as mayor of Istanbul. However, during the early years of the AKP, his personal success story advanced rapidly alongside economic and political achievements realized over a short period of time. Thus, he became a symbol to other marginalized and middle-class conservatives, while 'Turkey became a model of democratic governance in the Middle East'.[61] Clearly, the story of a man who played semi-professional football and sold lemonade as a boy to support his family resonated; he was thought of as an average conservative Anatolian Turk. Meanwhile, Erdoğan's personal characteristics as a leader, [and his] lifestyle and position towards daily issues have had a crucial impact on party ideology and the decisions made by the electorate.

The role of Erdoğan as party leader is one of the main areas of consideration in this research. It focuses on his charisma in particular to more fully appreciate his role in the political communication strategies of the AKP. Furthermore, Erdoğan's approach to politics has been largely perceived as pragmatist – emphasizing the available opportunities to improve living conditions for the population rather than imposing a specific lifestyle or ideology. However, Erdoğan's accumulation of power has isolated him somewhat, eroding his identity as part of a collective, a role once promoted as one of the fundamental aspects of the party. It is perhaps more crucial, in view of the research questions, to investigate how Erdoğan's growing authoritarianism resulted in the AKP's populist Islamist policies, with consequences for human rights as well as for freedom of speech in Turkey.[62]

AKP: Rising from shadows of Erbakan

> My reference is to Islam; democracy is not an aim, but a means; the system we want to introduce cannot be contrary to God's commands; human beings cannot be secular; I banned alcohol, because I believe I am the doctor of this community; in view of the future of our nation, I am against birth control.
>
> – Erdoğan[63]

Erbakan's creative strategizing played a key role in Erdoğan's new party. The AKP attached considerable importance to the reinterpretation of Islam under the umbrella of democracy, while simultaneously embracing assorted political and social groups. Diverse identity, lifestyle and ideology convened under a pluralist banner; one that was designed not to take Islamist transformation forward, but rather to focus on 'participation, inclusion, tolerance, emancipation, and human rights and liberties blended with Islamic morality, brotherhood and solidarity'.[64] Erbakan's bitter experience during the postmodern coup that took place in 1997 encouraged Erdoğan to move forward by allowing political expediency to win over religious objectives.

The principal difference between the new party and Milli Görüş was apparent from their discourse. As Erdoğan veered away from the Islamist discourse and policy that had coloured his time in RP, he emphasized global values, namely, democracy, human rights, freedom of speech and the rule of law. Moreover, Erdoğan and Gül positioned the AKP as a 'moderate, reformist, business-oriented party of the centre-right' that supported 'secularism, democracy and Turkey's traditional pro-Western foreign policy, particularly the goal of EU membership'.[65] Consequently, the 2002 elections were an opportune time for the party to redesign the political landscape in Turkey thus expanding its public sphere. The AKP's support of the Anglo-American definition of secularism included an equal approach towards all faiths and religions, as emphasized by Ibrahim Kalın,[66] presidential spokesperson and ambassador:

> AKP founders have sought to create a political identity wide enough to embrace different segments of Turkish society from the religious and conservative to the urban and the liberal.

This approach contributed to meteoric rise and successes of the party in 2002. However, arguably more important was the economic situation in Turkey. In 2001, Turkey was facing an economic crisis, which increased the need for perceived social and political 'justice' as well as 'development' of the national economy to raise standards of living overall. Both these needs are recognized and articulated in the official name given to the party: the 'Justice and Development' party. Furthermore Kalın[67] outlined the aims of the AKP as follows:

> On the one hand, they have dealt with issues of 'high politics', such as democratization, minority rights, secularism, and civilian-military relations and broken many taboos in the country's recent history. On the other hand, they have implemented effective policies to fix the economy, establish a sound financial system, increase trade and foreign direct investment, and inject a new energy into foreign policy-areas in which they have been extremely successful.

During the 2002 parliamentary elections, the AKP's slogan 'Everything is for Turkey' exemplified the universality of the new party's role in Turkish politics. This slogan caused voters to contemplate issues such as the 'universality of human rights, the Copenhagen criteria, freedom of thought and expression and freedom to economic enterprise'.[68] Alongside its pragmatic policies, the AKP can be characterized as having a national and spiritual agenda culturally, a pluralist democrat attitude regarding politics and a liberal approach to economics until 2010. Kalın[69] emphasized that the party acted as 'a voice for the silent majority and bringing the periphery to the centre'.

AKP's association with the MB

Despite the fact that the AKP embraced inclusivity and moderate position, this did not prevent the Western media from portraying it as an Islamist party, even though the AKP's spokespersons branded themselves as 'conservative democrats' rejecting any affiliation with Islamism. The AKP's understanding of secularism was predicated on the 'separation of religion and politics'; it did however emphasize the government's role in the 'protection of religious beliefs', stressing the importance of 'giving more freedom and visibility to religious identities in the public sphere'.[70] This position was witnessed during Erdoğan's visit to Egypt in September 2011, following the fall of Hosni Mubarak, when he sought to persuade the MB to recognize secularism thus leading to a 'lively debate' among Egyptian Islamists. Here, it is important to briefly elaborate on the relationship between the AKP and MB. Kalın[71] asserts that AKP sympathizers identify themselves with Islamist movements, such as the 'Muslim Brotherhood and Jamaat-i Islami, the Palestinian struggle against the Israeli occupation, the Afghan war against the Soviets, or the Chechen wars of independence in the 1990s'.

AKP's silent revolution: Reforms

The most significant reforms inside the AKP occurred between 2002 and 2009, when a number of issues impacted Turkey's progress towards membership of the EU, including the 'demilitarisation of civilian public institutions, progress on the rule of law, minority rights, decentralisation'.[72] Furthermore, the improving economic status of Turkey and the AKP's fundamental policy solutions increased the party's popularity within the region. Membership to the EU was held to be a priority for the AKP. Erdoğan even described the process of democratization in Turkey as akin to 'a silent revolution' as 'a result of the EU reform packages'.[73] Between 2002 and 2004, the AKP focused on the 'demilitarisation of civilian public institutions, progress on the rule of law, minority rights and decentralisation' in order to haste the application for EU membership.[74] The AKP's democratization process led the United States, in particular, to pronounce the AKP 'a model for the Muslim world'.[75] In addition, a further aim of the AKP was to support the Greater Middle East Initiative, set out by the Bush administration in 2004, which supported 'democracy and open market economics in the Muslim world'.[76] This proved a further factor in effecting US opinion of Turkey as a role model, with the US approach to the AKP in relation to the Greater Middle East Initiative being interpreted as White House support for moderate Islamism.

In domestic terms of politics, AKP committed itself to ending 'corruption, unemployment, the unequal distribution of wealth, and decay in moral values' and invested in infrastructure, particularly health and transportation, while sharing the benefits of their success at the local level.[77] However, the AKP's accomplishments attracted the attention of a new Islamic bourgeoisie with roots in Anatolia; they became the driving force behind the AKP's silent revolution. At this time, two crucial orientalist themes were challenged by the AKP: (1) Islam and democracy and (2) Islam and capitalism.[78] This highlighted the fact that the AKP's economic policies in particular were capitalist-oriented. Consequently, the policies of the AKP were assessed as being pragmatic rather than ideological.

AKP's foreign policy: 'Zero-problem' with neighbours

When Ahmet Davutoğlu, former chief advisor to Erdoğan, became foreign minister in 2009, the AKP began implementing his political theory as foreign policy. Turkey began forging good relations with its neighbours based on Davutoğlu's initiation of a 'zero problems' policy, which was part of his 'strategic depth' doctrine. The priority was to extend Turkey's hinterland 'from the Balkans to the Middle East'.[79] However, external actors characterized this development as the beginning of an Islamist style government, pursuing 'neo-Ottomanism'. Conversely, the Davos debate in 2009 and Mavi Marmara aid ship crisis in 2010 resulted in the worsening of diplomatic relations between Turkey and Israel, lending weight to the arguments of those with 'pro-Islamic' foreign policy tendencies within the AKP. Further challenges to the AKP resulted from the Arab uprisings in the MENA. In particular, the Syrian conflict was viewed as partly resulting from a miscalculation by Erdoğan's administration, and the 'zero problems' strategy pursued by the AKP up to that point. A further policy challenge that brought an end to the party's geo-strategic approach was the Egyptian military coup d'état against the elected president of the MB, Mohamed Morsi (1951–2019). While the AKP struggled with its foreign policy, a new challenge arose for Erdoğan in the form of the Gezi Park protests in 2013. This was followed by the corruption scandal of 17/25 December 2013 – at a time when Erdoğan was preparing for the local elections of March 2014 and the forthcoming presidential elections in August 2014. These are critical turning points for Erdoğan when he started using the term 'national survival' more often in his speeches to build a collective identity which supports Erdoğan's vision of an ideal social movement.

AKP's political message in foreign affairs

When studying the post-2010 literature, it emerges that two important events proved to be critical turning points in terms of the development of the party's principal message. The first took place at the 2009 World Economic Forum. The panel discussion in Switzerland led to a diplomatic crisis between former Israeli president Shimon Peres (1923–2016) and Erdoğan when Turkey's then prime minister 'harshly criticised the Israeli President over the fighting in Gaza' with the following words:

> Mr Peres, you are older than me. Your voice comes out in a very loud tone. And the loudness of your voice has to do with a guilty conscience. My voice, however, will not come out in the same tone… You know very well how to kill. I remember the children who died in beaches. Two former Prime Ministers in your country who said they felt very happy when they were able to enter Palestine on tanks… I find it very sad that people applaud what you said. There have been many people killed. And I think that it is very wrong and it is not humanitarian to applaud any actions which have had that kind of a result[80].

After uttering these words, 'Erdoğan walked off the stage, vowing never to return' to the World Economic Forum.[81] The Davos debate in 2009 was the first time Erdoğan raised his voice against Israel; until that time he had always shown respect and had successfully developed good political and economic relations with Israel. The volume of trade between both countries had increased after the AKP came to power in Turkey, and Erdoğan himself, as well as some other ministers and officials, had visited Israel. In particular after 2005, Erdoğan intervened in the Arab-Israel conflict. He prioritized solving problems in the region and promoted cooperation with Israel up to 2008. However after

'Operation Cast Lead', also known as the 'Gaza War' (27 December 2008 to 18 January 2009), Erdoğan felt Israel had 'ruined Turkey's peace efforts'.[82]

The second event is that of the Mavi Marmara flotilla. The Gaza flotilla raid happened in 2010, sixteen months after the Davos spat, and also affected the outlook of the AKP. The Mavi Marmara flotilla was on its way to deliver aid to the Palestinian people in Gaza on 30 May 2010 when it was attacked by Israeli soldiers. Nine activists, including one US citizen, were killed during this offensive. Following the event, the Western media's coverage of Turkey, and in particular Erdoğan, began to change. The then Turkish prime minister Davutoğlu, speaking in 2015, summarizes this change:

> There is an international media network in the world. We are doing our best, but this network made a decision to finish off Turkey's success story and demonize President Erdoğan. That's their objective. They have moved against Turkey as if a button was pressed after 2010, that is, after the 'one-minute' incident in Davos.[83]

Davutoğlu's remarks encapsulate the AKP's evaluation of the Western media's biased coverage of the president after 2010. the 'demonising of Erdoğan' is a key concern that appears to relate closely to the evolution of the party's message, and as such it will be part of the subsequent discussion.

4

The AKP's code of identity

'Natural' leaders – in times of psychic, physical, economic, ethical, religious, political distress – have been neither officeholders nor incumbents of an 'occupation' in the present sense of the word, that is, men who have acquired expert knowledge and who serve for remuneration. The natural leaders in distress have been holders of specific gifts of the body and spirit; and these gifts have been believed to be supernatural, not accessible to everybody.

– Weber[1]

The AKP's political communication has changed over time. Specifically, religious and nationalist populism have replaced the emphasis on liberal political ideology, namely democratization and expansion of freedom of speech. I will begin this chapter by analysing the roots of the victory achieved by the 'conservative democrats', depicting the party's historical successes from 2002 to 2019. A vitally important aspect to note in this study of the AKP is that the party has sustained its capacity to achieve victory from one election to another consecutively. This is an accomplishment that is unique in modern Turkey's history. I will start exploring the historical and sociological background of the ruling party by concentrating on its identity and ideology in order to delineate and interpret its development.

In addition to presenting definitions of the AKP provided by scholars, it is essential to view the party through the eyes of current and former AKP officials. Frequently, academic texts convey views that are biased or partial, depending on their authors, and similarly the opinions of politicians affiliated with the AKP could be coloured by their loyalty or dependence on the party. Thus, by considering two kinds of sources – that is, literature and interviews with party faithful as well as with former affiliated personalities – a breadth of perspective will be delivered to clarify this research's portrayal of the AKP.

In this section, details about the AKP's background are provided to contextualize the role of religion and explain how it is intertwined with communication - the principal focus of the study. This depiction of the AKP's history will form the basis for a later discussion, which will review many different facets. Furthermore, before developing an understanding of the communication strategies employed by the party, it is important to understand how the party sees itself to clarify the role played by religion.

In the interview data, Aydın Ünal, speechwriter of Erdoğan from 2007 to 2015 and linguistic expert, explains the establishment of the AKP, by recollecting the situation in Turkish politics at the end of the 1990s when three parties governed Turkey together; a situation which seriously impeded national development. As Ünal underlines, '[C]orruption, unemployment, the unequal distribution of wealth, and decay in moral values' were the main obstacles faced by Turkey at this time. Ünal further notes that the postmodern coup of 1997, which targeted former Prime Minister Necmettin Erbakan and his RP, created a psychological wound in the hearts of the people of Turkey. For him, the birth of the AKP, which he describes as a 'conservative' and 'traditionalist', was in large part a reaction to this postmodern coup.

Nonetheless, JO1, a pro-government journalist in his early 40s who is also part of Erdoğan's Strategy Team, refutes this suggestion, separating out the identity and wishes of Turkish society from the ambitions of the AKP. JO1 characterizes the AKP as 'conservative, proud of the nation's history, having nationalist reactions, but also open to developments in the modern world' when describing the stance of the AKP and its supporters. By contrast, Professor Kara focuses on criticizing the party's adoption of 'conservative democracy', taking the characteristics of European conservative parties into consideration. He underlines that while the AKP might have been inspired to draw some 'conservative' elements from contemporary political parties in Europe, there is no single centre-right democratic party in Europe that classifies itself in this way. Professor Kara notes that the adoption of the term 'conservative' was intended by the AKP as part of an image-making strategy, with the objective of receiving recognition from the Western world. However, he clarifies that this does not change the fact that the notion 'conservative' is akin to religious in the context of culture in Turkey. Meanwhile Kalın[2] argues that the AKP united 'different segments of Turkish society from the religious and conservative to the urban and the liberal'.

Party of the periphery

Here it is useful to analyse the pre-AKP landscape to more fully appreciate the relationship between Islamism, Erbakan's Milli Görüş movement and the foundation of the AKP. Erbakan's stance during the postmodern coup in 1997, which received no popular backing, caused the RP to split. The fact that it was in a position to draw on the political and historical heritage of the RP was a significant advantage for the AKP. Conversely, the past failures of centre-right parties suggested it was unlikely that the AKP would benefit from its connection with such political circumstances.

According to Ünal, the modernization process in the Ottoman Empire, which enabled the emergence of the AKP, dates back hundreds of years. He argues that as a result of the Turkey's 200-year-old Westernization process, the AKP drew on 'nativism, conservatism and Muslimness'. In this case 'Muslimness' is used to reflect indications of Islamic activism. The Westernization process in the Ottoman Empire was triggered by the recognition of the empire's decline. The development of education, the military and diplomacy were three important areas imitated from the West.

An interview with former minister of interior, PO1, revealed that the emphasis is instead on the AKP as a local party, reflecting on local social values. Similarly, TT1, who leads a think tank that conducts research for the AKP among other clients, states that the party embodies the energy present in the local environment, a fact that enabled it to move from the periphery to become the hub of the political landscape. The AKP broke down perceptions about what constitutes the centre, eroding social class differentiation to become a governing party characterized by 'the energy of the periphery'. TT1's description highlights the significance of the party's appeal to lower- and middle-class Turkish people. TT1's final definition coincides with the objective set by Erdoğan at the AKP's inception: it is 'the party of the people who are dreaming a new Turkey'.[3] Finally, he views the AKP as a party of transformation and innovation. Reflecting the assertions made by TT1, JO2, who is a well-known and respected journalist who has also been a chief political advisor to Davutoğlu when he was prime minister, also uses the word 'periphery' when describing the party. However, he continues by noting that after a specific point the AKP transformed itself into a postmodern movement with a place in the global community. TT2, chairman of a pro-AKP research center and professor of international relations, indicates that the AKP was established with the aim of serving as a melting pot, open to communications with the world; simultaneously pragmatist and realist, able to motivate people from different ethnic and ideological backgrounds to support them. As an Armenian minority, JO2 describes his support for the AKP with the following words:

> I am an AKP supporter since Erbakan's Refah Party. I am supporting these guys because religious conservatives have to become democratic in order to be

able to speak about democracy in Turkey. I cannot imagine an AKP without Erdoğan. He has experience. But the case is that AKP had a collective mind, which disappeared after 2010.

This research found that people, according to their interpretations of the party's stance, drew on a rich variety of definitions to understand the AKP. Whereas the party uses the term 'conservative democrat' to position itself at the centre of the political landscape in Turkey, the interviewees' classification of the party range from traditionalist to innovative, from Muslimness to postmodern, suggesting that it is a party that embraces contradictions. Evidently, the changing politics of the AKP contributed to this diversity of perceptions resulting in interpretations of the party to change over time. Another explanation is provided by JO2 who emphasizes that the party has not yet defined itself, suggesting that it is in fact lost from a sociological perspective, with no vision of where Turkey will be in the next 100 years. He argues that the AKP's followers to some extent determine its direction, but the party itself needs to be responsible for its repositioning. Moreover, JO2 , whom I met at a cafe at the historic Taksim square which played a key role during the Gezi Park protests, implies the AKP's primary policy is to survive, as it is a pragmatic and realistic party, just as its leader Erdoğan is. This results in the lack of a strong political identity that is able to endure and advance the governing process. Furthermore Erdoğan's pragmatism changes his policies in current affairs too: Syria is an important example of this. Erdoğan and Syria's leader Bashar al-Assad were very close friends before the conflict in Syria started in 2011; they even organized a family trip to Bodrum, in the southern part of Turkey, in addition to a joint cabinet meeting in which ten ministers from both countries participated. But when the civil war started, rather than using his close relationship to convince Assad with soft power, Erdoğan miscalculated and compared the developments in Syria with Egypt and Tunisia, and he believed that Assad will leave the office in a very short period of time like Ben Ali of Tunisia or Mubarak of Egypt. This preventable situation has turned to chaos since 2011. Syria policy has cost Erdoğan millions of Euros, and a burden of more than four million refugees in camps across the country, with only half million living in Istanbul. People close to Erdoğan mobilized journalists and members of the Foundation for Political, Economic and Social Research (SETA), according to JO4, to blame Davutoğlu for Syria policy in articles they wrote or talk shows they attended, when both leaders started having disagreements after Davutoğlu became prime minister in 2014. 'Despite Erdoğan having the final word on everything, he follows this strategy of blaming and systematic humiliating regularly to protect his image. The impact that mainstream media has on the less-educated people is such that it helps sell these stories,' says pro-government columnist JO4 who appeared to our interview in Istanbul's conservative Üsküdar district with a kitsch suit and Ottoman style ring that had a calligraphy on it.

It is traditionally expected that a social movement will embrace the notion of collective identity to inspire change in society. However, in the case of the AKP, as JO2 argues, the party's identity crisis renders this impossible. It is important to note, however, that in social movements common interest turns to common identity, which is arguably the case with the AKP. For its part, as JO3 underlines, the AKP has pragmatically identified itself as the party of 'conservative democracy' because there are more conservatives in Turkey than Islamists. Consequently, the government's definition of the party indicates that it has an identity, even though, as JO2's point implies, the leadership does not adhere to it. Moreover, their name 'Justice and Development' is another indicator that Turkey's turmoil, created by the postmodern coup in 1997 and the economic crisis of 2001, increased the need for political justice, the rule of law as well as the improvement of infrastructure and living standards. In this manner, while considering the different approaches defining the AKP, it is essential to investigate how AKP officials explain political Islam or Islamism.

Islamism and the AKP

PO1 indicates that 'political Islam' is a term used to define a political position. For him, the word 'Muslim' is a more neutral term, and hence 'obviously the identity of those who created the AKP can be explained better with the word Muslim'. He continues by underlining that the founders of the party did not aim to establish a political party with a religious foundation. Indeed, this was one of the ways in which the AKP sought to differentiate itself from Erbakan's movement. Due to their bitter experiences as members of Erbakan's parties, the AKP party elite adopted a strategy of political expediency, avoiding religious discourse. The attitude of the AKP after separating from Erbakan's party can be likened to the emergence of the Ennahda Party in Tunisia. Tunisia's most influential Sunni Islamist movement Ennahda is a unique example that reflects the relationship between the Milli Görüş and the AKP. Ennahda's leader Rashed Ghannouchi, who was in exile in the UK for twenty-two years before the Arab uprising began in 2011, announced in May 2016 that he distinguished between the party and the movement from which it developed by using the term 'Muslim democratic party' for Ennahda instead of an 'Islamist label'. This was interpreted as a reimagining process for the Ennahda, targeting first their credibility in the West and then evoking more widespread support from the Tunisian society. In other words, it marked the transition from a social movement (*haraka* in Arabic) to a political party (*hizb* in Arabic). Unlike Erdoğan, Ghannouchi achieved reforms within the original party. Erdoğan's AKP instead adopted a new politics, distancing itself from the older generation of the Milli Görüş.

The postmodern coup in 1997 led to suppression of Islam and practicing Muslims in Turkey, but taking racism, nationalism and regionalism as a red line, the founding members of the AKP chose, in 2001, to define the party as 'conservative democrat'. By conservative, the political cognoscente understood it to be upholding local social values – in other words attaching importance to religion, tradition and history. PO1 admits that 'Westerners define the AKP as an Islamist party, or a party which comes from an Islamist background', but underlines that this was never mentioned in the party's programme or statements. Rather they preferred the term 'conservatism', which encompasses social and religious values.

The references to 'Westerners' when describing the stance of the international media clearly reveal how 'we and others' – in other words, 'othering' – is perceived within the mindset of AKP officials, thus recalling Erbakan's othering policies that were based on the conflict between the Western and Islamic civilization. Noting the compelling nature of this evidence, JO3, whom I met in one of Ankara's skyscrapers where his 40 square meter office was based, observes that it is not reasonable to label a party that received more than twenty million votes, as 'Islamist' or designate it 'political Islam'. Indeed, the Ankara representative of a pro-AKP newspaper, JO3, emphasizes that Islamism in Morocco differs from Islamism in Egypt or Turkey. For him, the AKP is a 'class-rooted' party rather than an ideological one. Moreover, he underlines that the same people who support the AKP today supported the Motherland Party (ANAP) during the 1980s. The ANAP, whose leader was Turgut Özal (1927–1993), received 45.1 per cent support, amounting to 7.8 million votes, in the 1983 elections. When compared with the results of the AKP in the November 2015 elections, this equates to 15.8 million fewer votes, a fact which strengthens the interpretation of journalists. However, the diversity of voters and, more importantly, the ideology of the party aligned more with ANAP than any other party in Turkey, particularly during the AKP's first term (2002–9). This is illustrated by the fact that during that time many key people from different parties and backgrounds joined the AKP. It is for this reason that Erdoğan mentions Turgut Özal occasionally in his speeches and why he positioned himself closer to Özal than to Erbakan between 2002 and 2009. As commented by TT2 regarding this issue:

> The AKP never defined themselves as part of political Islam. On the contrary, it generated more support when it distanced itself from Islamism and political Islam. This is the reason why they underlined in the early years that they had changed. The AKP identified itself so that the West could understand it. Consequently, they used the term 'conservative democrats' referring to the 'Christian democrats' in the West. But personally, they did not deny that they were respecting Islamic references. This was an appropriate idea in terms of taking liberal steps. On the other hand, Erdoğan and his team knew that it was not possible to go any further, if they were following in the steps of Erbakan's. They changed their discourse, but they changed themselves too.

Later paragraphs will discuss how after 2013 in particular, Erdogan started playing the Islamism card with the aim of transforming his party to a social movement and building a collective identity among his electorates. The discourse used by the party is crucial as it accentuates the AKP's ideological transformation and Erdoğan's intention to position the AKP as a moderate and reformist party. Furthermore, the stated objective of the AKP was 'to embrace different segments of Turkish society from the religious and conservative to the urban and the liberal'.[4] An equally significant point to make here is that, as Professor Kara claims, it does not matter if the AKP viewed itself as the party of Islamism or not; rather it is important how it was perceived both abroad and within the country. For him, the AKP genuinely positioned itself to appear positive in terms of the political tableau, and this marked a dramatic decline in Islamism relative to Erbakan's movement. The use of the term 'decline' by Professor Kara is intended to denote the lack of a political culture reflecting Turkey's intellectual geography. Certainly, the aims of the party were best served by bringing together a deliberate set of beliefs, symbols and values.

When asked about the use of the term 'Islamism', Ünal explained that it means merging Islam with nativism, conservatism and 'anatolianism'.[5] Interestingly this leads him to describe the audience of the RP, which he claimed was generally composed of 'people who pray, attach importance to headscarf, distance themselves from alcohol, and criticize the West and Westernization'. According to him, the 'AKP has adopted this heritage from the RP. Despite offering examples to explain how the AKP was a continuation of the Milli Görüş tradition, Ünal's views are more pertinent when linked to the politics of today's AKP, rather than those it espoused in its early years. In the first election period, the AKP's political conduct was one of 'transformation that has seen it jettison its Islamist roots and thus it can no longer be considered part of Islamism'.[6] However, Erdoğan's political discourse today recalls Erbakan's position, which was once harshly criticized by Erdoğan and his followers, particularly during the separation process that led to the establishment of the AKP.

When evaluating the in-depth interview material regarding relations between political Islam and the AKP, it emerges that while political officials frequently seek to apply an authoritative definition, non-affiliated individuals take a more flexible approach. In fact, characterizing a party's identity can benefit non-affiliated people, but understanding reality is more beneficial. This is because populist Islamism is at the epicentre of the debate concerning the AKP; especially since 2010, more extensively after 2013.

The next section will look at how the evolution of the party message changed over the course of the period under review, especially in terms of how the AKP positioned itself relative to Islamism. Here it is vital to identify the events and timing of any shift in position, and to explain how the party's views developed. Specifically, it will discuss the emergence of anti-Western discourse after 2010.

Evolution of the political message

The evolution of the AKP's political message from 2002 to 2019 provides the conceptual framework for this research. The changes to the AKP's political communications suggest an apparent process of transformation over time within the party. However, it is important to first establish whether party members acknowledge that a change has occurred to determine if it is reasonable to differentiate between the two eras or whether the notion of a shift is merely a myth proceeding from a biased approach to the party and its leader.

The interviewees were asked if changes to the AKP's political message date to the post-2010 era, and are connected with the Davos crisis at the World Economic Forum and the Mavi Marmara aid flotilla, as portrayals in the literature and Western media coverage would suggest. JO2 observes the process of the development of the AKP's point of view more broadly by first analysing the Weltanschauung of AKP members:

> We need to look at the Middle East, before explaining the reality. It would be too easy to explain this reality by saying that AKP was passive and there was a turning point for Erdoğan, which changed his career and made him Islamist.

JO2 identifies an 'Ottoman-style communication' that intensifies the relationship between political parties and the society. The result of this is that Erdoğan holds himself responsible as a Turkish Muslim and is willing to serve as the voice of the oppressed. This is part of the AKP's vision, according to the former Erdoğan loyalist journalist:

> When Israel attacks the people of Gaza, it is not possible to be silent. If you do not react, and observe only, people will ask where all the vision has gone. Because Erdoğan convinced people after the Davos debate with Israeli President Peres in 2009 that he is the 'patron' of the Muslim world.

JO2 adds that mainstream Western media explains Erdoğan's responsibility to society by likening him to a 'new sultan' or even a 'dictator'. These comments call to mind Abdulhamid II's *Ittihad-ı Islam* (Union of Islam), or *pan-Islamism*, as it was referred to by scholars such as Landau[7] and Piscatori.[8] Abdulhamid II was enthusiastic about creating a universal religious community of Muslims, in which all Muslims would be bound together. Thus, JO2 argues that it is changes elsewhere in the Middle East that altered Erdoğan's political outlook.

Erdoğan's chief advisor, academic, member of the parliament and former party spokesperson PO4 questions the significance of the Davos crisis and Mavi Marmara incident for the AKP's identity. He underlines that Mavi Marmara was not an AKP-sponsored initiative or a project associated with the Turkish government or state:

> It was organized by international and Turkish civil society. Obviously, Turkish people joined Mavi Marmara because some saw themselves ideologically close to IHH. Although, we did not create the organization, as soon as we heard about it, it became our responsibility to take up the burden.

Although Erdoğan's long-term chief advisor PO4 clearly states that there was no relationship between the AKP and IHH, in reality both institutions were very closely aligned. The IHH was an offshoot of Milli Görüş, and its board included 'AKP members of parliament and people affiliated with the party'.[9] Furthermore, after the Mavi Marmara crisis, the AKP started supporting the IHH publicly. The IHH's relationship with Erbakan connects it with the AKP's stance towards Israel and Zionism.

To establish whether the party's involvement in the incident represented a shift in position, I asked PO4, who believes in the idea of Islamism in politics, whether he felt Erdoğan would have supported such an initiative had it taken place in 2002 or 2003. He immediately and unequivocally responded with a clear 'yes'. However, it should be remembered that Erdoğan publicly criticized the organizers of the Mavi Marmara flotilla in 2016 for their 'objection to an agreement[10] between Turkey and Israel'.[11] This criticism was covered by pro-AKP media outlets close to the AKP, but it was interpreted elsewhere that despite

Erdoğan's criticisms of the IHH he had benefitted from the Mavi Marmara event during the elections of 2011 because it had enabled him to 'play the victim and gain more votes'.[12] PO4 adds that Mavi Marmara's timing coincided with that of the expansion of economic relations with Israel. However PO5, a member of parliament (MP) for the AKP, argued that 'the conflict with Israel is, on the one hand, a result of Erdoğan's "the world is bigger than five"[13] slogan, which he raised for the first time in 2014 at the UN General Assembly, whereas, on the other, it is pure populism'.

In contrast with PO4 and PO5, PO1 explains how commentators, in particular politicians and think tanks in the West, believed that the AKP was democratizing Turkey whenever possible. However, he cited a turning point in the party's approach following Mavi Marmara and the Gezi Park protests[14] in 2013. Rather than accusing the 'pro-Israeli lobby' for the shift in perception as Davutoğlu did, claiming that it had 'made a decision to finish off Turkey's success story and demonise President Erdoğan after the Davos incident',[15] PO1 alleges that the self-exiled Fethullah Gülen and his movement, the Gülenists, were responsible. PO1 further suggests the Gülenists used their immense network in diaspora to influence the Western media to attack the AKP and, in particular, Erdoğan. In addition to the cases of Mavi Marmara and the Gezi Park protests, PO1 suggests that Turkey's policies towards Egypt and Palestinian territory have created an image of the AKP as an Islamist party, which, according to him, is another way of demonizing Muslims:

> We are the same. We have not changed. Our politics are the same. If you look at our official documents like government programmes, you will see this. Our discourse is the same. Moreover, now we are looking at our election programme from 2002 to 2011, a plan to work on issues we promised but could not execute before today. The AKP is a broad umbrella at the centre, which means it is a party that is organized in every township and receives support from all over Turkey.

PO1, in his early seventies and one of the most experienced politicians within the ranks of the AKP, refutes the suggestion that the AKP has changed its communications, discourse or politics. Although he holds similar views regarding Erdoğan, he admits that Erdoğan's religious references increased after 2013. That the AKP lost major cities like Istanbul and Ankara in 2019 local elections points to fact that there was a lack of trust of electorates, which was closely related to the shift of political messaging according to JO5, journalist who used to work for a pro-government media at the time of this research, and who is now working for a foreign news outlet. Ünal also affirms the suggestion that the

AKP changed its message after 2009, 'replacing conservativism with Islamism', referencing Erdoğan's post-2009 speeches:

> If you look at the speeches between 2002 and 2009, you will consider that some notions are used less frequently. After 2009, these notions have increased. However, it has peaked in 2014 when he became president.

Although Ünal was reluctant to go into more detail, he recommends that academics should study this change in the party and the direction in which it is evolving. He notes that the change in rhetoric started with the defeat of threats formerly faced by the AKP which was a result of the changes in military and bureaucratic instruction and the reduced impact of Western finance. Regional instability also affected Turkey's development, and Ünal opines that the economic growth and development in Turkey increased the AKP's self-confidence, resulting in the party becoming less cautious and controlled, and willing to more freely express a liberated discourse. According to Erdoğan's former speechwriter, 'liberated discourse' means expressing a position independent from 'Western expectations'. He notes that Erdoğan was the leader who announced this new objectivity. Similar to PO1, Ünal recognizes Davos as a turning point. However, he identifies the so-called 7 February MIT crisis[16] as the beginning of the AKP's conflict with the Gülenists:

> The message of this operation was clear: 'if you do not follow our steps, we will remove you [Erdoğan]'.

This crisis between the Gülenists and the AKP dates back to 2012, when Gülen's network were infiltrating to state apparatus. In fact the aim of this move was to control the Interior Ministry and National Intelligence Organization (MIT), which would strengthen the power of the Gülenists and enable them to have further control of other institutions, according to Ünal. In fact, Erdoğan has taken serious measures against Gülenists after the coup attempt in 2016. Until the Gezi Park protests in 2013, the organization was hand-in-hand with the AKP, which was a huge advantage for Erdoğan as he could control the judiciary, military and police with the help of Gülen supporters within these institutions. But after the MIT crisis, Erdoğan realized that the movement will be a threat to his own political future..

Discrepancy of collective identity between Erdoğan and Gül

Another important point made by Ünal was that after the overthrow of Muhammad Morsi's MB in Egypt, the next target of 'Western countries', who supported the coup in Egypt, was Turkey and the AKP government. Erdoğan clearly announced that his government would not accept the presidency of Abdel Fattah al-Sisi when the Egyptian military ousted Erdoğan's close ally Morsi in 2013. However, the then Turkish president Abdullah Gül congratulated al-Sisi on attaining the presidency.[17] Erdoğan criticized this statement, emphasizing that congratulations could not be extended as he would not tolerate a difference of opinion of this nature being publicly expressed.[18] Ünal argues that Erdoğan automatically responded harshly to these events, viewing them as a personal threat. Yet, it is also important to note that this action reduces the significance of the sense of a collective identity created within the AKP, which is the basis of any social movement. Although both Erdoğan and Gül were founding members of the AKP in 2001, and acted collectively to move on from Milli Görüş, over time differences emerged and the sense of an agreed collective identity diminished. In fact, Gül had congratulated al-Sisi two months prior to the 2014 presidential elections.

It illustrates how Erdoğan personalized the party's communications and differentiated himself from the former president, othering him as part of his strategy to achieve victory in the election. Thus, the case of Gül is an interesting one when scrutinizing the AKP's leadership. Differences in political actions between the former close friends and allies brought discussions to the fore that resulted in Erdoğan instructing AKP's lawyers not to allow Gül to run for presidency again in 2014. Gül did not address this issue publicly, but TT1 highlighted that, as a consequence of political disagreements, Erdoğan did not favour Gül running either for president or for prime minister or chairman of the AKP. This move was clearly a sign that Erdoğan was solidifying his power base by eliminating potential challengers. On these grounds, it can be argued that Erdoğan's support of Morsi was merely a product of his policy stressing collective identity. Kalın[19] emphasized that some AKP sympathizers identify themselves with Islamist movements, such as the MB. Sympathy for the MB means that supporters of the AKP, at least those known to be religiously motivated, have a 'common interest' which then becomes a 'common identity' with Islamist groups. In fact, from an Islamist perspective there are a number of similarities between the MB and the AKP. This collectiveness could also be witnessed when Morsi died during trial in June 2019.[20] Erdoğan claimed that it was not a 'natural death' but that 'he was killed', and he 'vowed to pursue justice for this sudden and unexplained death'.[21] Later Morsi's son thanked Erdoğan and Qatari Emir Tamim bin Hamad al-Thani for their stance and support.[22] Yet both leaders are the leading figures in supporting moderate Islamist movements in the region.

Kurdish peace process

According to AC2, an academic in Istanbul and a political advisor to Erdoğan, it is important to not only consider the crisis in Davos, but also the Kurdish issue as a turning point for the AKP. In fact, he describes how the AKP started a peace process in 2009 by enabling minority rights for Kurds in eastern part of Turkey. Mother tongue-based schooling and the introduction of Turkish Radio and Television Corporation (TRT) Kurdi within the rights of freedom of speech were only some of the steps taken by the government. However, this ended when the HDP was able to pass the threshold of 10 per cent and enter the parliament in 2015. The HDP's relationship with the PKK and the AKP's increasing nationalist discourse as a result of increasing dominance of the HDP across the country are two main issues that require further discussion in order to help explain why the peace process ended in 2015. AC2 conceives of the change as a 'power struggle' – more precisely the question of 'who will reign Turkey and establish the New Turkey'. The term 'New Turkey' was used by the AKP repeatedly during the 2014 Turkish presidential election campaign. It was intended to indicate a new constitution and presidential system. The phrase was also included in the election manifesto of the AKP in the 2017 referendum, which aimed to increase the executive power of the president. AC2 underlines that due to the power struggle in which he was engaged, Erdoğan's 'national reflexes' were sensitized. He did not mention with whom the power struggle was taking place. However, Erdoğan's aim was made clear: to become an actor, first in the region and then globally. AC2 pays attention to the struggle for independence by noting thus:

> The international arena did not welcome Turkey reaching for independence. The reactions to Erdoğan's politics cannot be assessed from the perspective of human rights or freedom. It is wholly an issue of power struggle and benefit. The discourse of authoritarianism is only rhetoric … If Erdoğan were to follow the same discourse as the West, he would have to be the most easy-going politician in the world.

In this regard, another source, a psychology professor who supports Erdoğan because of a 'lack of alternative for conservative people', classifies Erdoğan's politics as 'authoritarian'. This signifies that even in academic circles close to the AKP there are criticisms of Erdoğan's discourse which has increased in particular in 2016 when more than 2,200 academics signed a petition criticizing AKP's policies against Kurds in eastern part of Turkey. This petition was harshly condemned by Erdoğan.[23] However, when, after three years, ten academics, who signed this petition, applied individually claiming against 'disseminating propaganda for a terrorist organization' charges, constitutional court issued a rights violation in July 2019.[24] This time, 1,071 academics, who criticized the decision of the constitutional court, signed a petition as a response to the previous one.[25] Pro-government sources used the symbolic number '1071' for their petition. Although two academics later said that their names were used without their knowledge, the aim of '1071' was to have a reference to the Battle of Manzikert in the year of 1071 between the Byzantines and Seljuk Turks where Turks conquered a significant part of Anatolia.[26]

Generation Z and Erdoğan's social media censorship

TT1 notes that the AKP is devising new responses to internal and external developments, with the aim of strengthening its links with 'Islamic civilization' by exploring its quintessential roots. Consequently, social, cultural and political discourse is being used by the AKP and its leader to realize this 'dream'. Clearly, although TT1 contends that the AKP and Erdoğan are pursuing the same goals they held at the party's inception, he admits that a new approach to achieving them is increasingly dominant. In contrast, another pro-AKP research centre chairman whom I interviewed in his huge office with Islamic calligraphy on its walls in Ankara, TT2, commented on a policy shift by remarking the relations between the AKP government and the IMF. Until 2008, the AKP steered the national economy congruent with IMF politics, but since this time a more independent set of policies has emerged. When the Turkish currency and debt crisis happened in 2018, fresh discussions started regarding entering a new programme with the IMF; however, Erdoğan denied these rumours.[27] In fact, AC3, a 42-year-old history professor at a foundation university in Istanbul, argues that the economic developments in 2018 had an important impact on the electorate's decision in the 2019 local elections as AKP lost trust and caused an increase in inflation. AC4 also highlights this issue by giving an example from the Kartal Imam Hatip school – a well-known Imam Hatip with its close relationship to Erdoğan where also his son Necmettin Bilal studied – of which half the students did not vote in the 2019 local elections, which he found out during a research he conducted.

In June 2020, when Erdoğan addressed young students online via YouTube, hundreds of thousands of young people disliked the livestream and commented in the chat section to emphasize that he will not get their vote.[28] The hashtag #OyMoyYok ('no votes for you') later became a trending topic on Twitter in

Turkey. Immediately, Erdoğan's communications office disabled the video's comments section. A couple of days later, when Erdoğan's daughter, who is married to the Minister of Treasury and Finance, Berat Albayrak, gave birth to her forth child, she was insulted on social media. Subsequently, after both events, Erdoğan announced plans to regulate and control digital media platforms:

> Do you understand why we're against social media platforms such as YouTube, Twitter and Netflix? So that we can wipe out such immoralities.[29]

Government's plan include obligation for social media companies to open a representative office in Turkey and deal with complaints from authorities within forty-eight hours.[30] Turkey is among the ten countries with the highest number of Facebook users, and the increasing number of social media users in the country is a threat for the ruling government indeed.[31] In the same context, Erdoğan's communications office released a 'Guidebook for Social Media Use' in 2020, in other words, an instrument of censorship on social media. These steps lead to the conclusion that Erdoğan has finally realized that controlling 85 per cent of mainstream media is not enough to survive, and therefore, he concentrated on new regulations, which limits freedom of speech among youth in particular and enforces more 'morality'. Within the same political ideology, Netflix had to cancel a Turkish series after pressure from Culture and Tourism Ministry and Radia and Television Supreme Council (RTÜK) to remove a gay character.

Erdoğan's consolidation of his power

Based on the information provided by TT2, the AKP's struggle for independence was first economic, before it became political, as mentioned by AC2. Another term to describe this process would be 'real politics', which has been a hindrance for more than six years (2002–8) to the 'conservative democrats', as AC2 underlines:

> I can remember in 2006, when members of the MUSIAD[32] exerted pressure on Erdoğan to reopen Imam Hatip schools, he emphasized that the world and himself are not ready yet, and so he did not take the risk over. Today, the landscape looks different. He could not convince Turkey before making progress... I think that 2007 was a turning point. Up to 2007 the AKP followed a liberal discourse. Despite their liberal steps, the AKP faced a party closure trial in 2008.

Here the interviewee is disclosing the content of an internal meeting with Erdoğan which clearly demonstrates Erdoğan's views at such a critical turning point. The opening of Imam Hatip schools in Turkey was a highly controversial issue, in particular from 1983 until 1997, in part due to the rise of Erbakan's Milli Görüş movement. As highlighted in the introduction, Kemalists believed that these schools will Islamize the society. In conjunction with the postmodern coup in 1997, compulsory eight-year education was introduced to limit the expansion of religious schools. The AKP's conservative supporters had expected the reopening of these schools when Erdoğan came to power. However, TT2's comments above explain the situation very clearly. Although Erdoğan had graduated from an Imam Hatip school himself, he knew very well what a negative perception these schools had. Thus, he was reluctant to reopen them in 2006. In fact, it took ten years of AKP rule before, in 2012–13, a fully functioning Imam Hatip school was opened. Erdoğan explained the importance of Imam Hatip schools with the following words:

> The interest in Imam Hatip schools is high because it meets the demands and values of the students, their parents and the whole of society ... We have never intervened in others' lives. We never force people how to dress and behave ... An Imam Hatip student is someone who protects his/her own country, flag, azan,[33] and leads the struggle for independence and futurity. An Imam Hatip student can never come side by side with terror organizations injustice, violence and illegal things.[34]

Erdoğan's comments reiterate the role played by Imam Hatip schools that inculcate Islamic consciousness and pious life among the younger generation. But when I was conducting in-depth interviews with Imam Hatip students at Tevfik Ileri Imam Hatip School in Ankara in summer 2018 for a conference at CUNY in New York, I recognized that 45 per cent of the final-year students had not voted in the June 2018 elections and were criticizing the AKP for using religion as a propaganda tool. In this regard, AC4 does believe that the relationship between the ruling party and generation Z cannot be repaired 'because younger generations are always opposing the dominant political discourse; it is their nature'. This is, according to AC4, similar to young people in the United States supporting Bernie Sanders rather than other pro-establishment candidates within the Democratic Party 'because Sanders challenges the status quo, and stands for defending the oppressed across the world'.

The information presented suggests that the first period (2002–9) under the AKP was one that emphasized transition and gaining trust in order to rightly earn credibility and power. When TT2 states that 'today, the landscape looks different', he means the AKP has now transformed and developed the country and received the support of the people, which has enabled it to implement more sensitive and critical policies that might conflict with the aims of Kemalists.³⁵ However, here one should recall Erdoğan's stance towards religious issues when he and his reformist crew were challenging Erbakan; he acknowledged the need to adopt a different tone and party line after the postmodern coup of 1997. As observed by TT1, Erdoğan has always held the same ideological aims, but he consistently chooses to act pragmatically.

Effect of the West's anti-Turkey sentiment on Erdoğan's discourse

TT2 notes that Mavi Marmara incident marked a turning point in terms of the AKP's negative portrayal in the West. However, he underlines that it is not entirely apparent if this was due to the AKP itself, or to other external factors. He sees the shift as possibly part of the discussion concerning democracy and Islam in the West, claiming that Western countries' orientalist perspective resulted in its anti-AKP sentiment: 'For them [West] the only thing was that Turkey is ruled with democracy and free market economy'. In support of this interpretation, AC2 argues that Erdoğan was expected to be an easy-going leader adhering to the same discourse as that used in the Western world. Should he deviate from this, TT2 expressed confidently, the 'West' would then seek to remove the AKP by manipulating the Turkish military from within. TT2's comments might appear absurd at first glance; however, on 15 July 2016 a faction of the Turkish military attempted a coup.³⁶ Turkish Historian Halil Berktay³⁷ is clear when answering the question: 'what would a possible win have meant were the July 15 coup to have succeeded':

> What kind of military regime might have taken over – something like Myanmar, perhaps? What sort of Kemalist-Gülenist coalition would it have entailed? After a time, would the Gülenists have started moving just as insidiously as ever to eliminate their partners? Meanwhile, how many tens of thousands would have been arrested, jailed, perhaps tortured, perhaps killed by their martial law authorities? ... What if the country had lapsed into a state of civil war?

Berktay's questions are timely as regards democratic concerns, but the post-coup crackdown should not be forgotten, as Erdoğan used the opportunity to arrest hundreds of thousands of innocent people accusing them of posing a danger to the Turkish Republic. This leads us to consider the opinion of JO4, a journalist and former candidate for nomination to the AKP who was not selected by the governing board. He questions the events by recalling the time of Sultan Abdulhamid II, observing that the sultan was as reactive then as Erdoğan is today. According to the journalist, Erdoğan takes the same approach as Abdulhamid II when responding to internal and external threats. Abdulhamid II, who ruled for thirty-three years, favoured Muslim unity during his reign because the Ottoman Empire was in decline and for him, this could be stopped by being united. This raised criticism at that time because elites, such as the Young Turks[38] and Ottoman Committee of Union and Progress (CUP) – which according to Hanioğlu[39] is 'an outgrowth of the Young Turk movement' inside of the caliphate[40] – favoured modernization, not just militarily, but also ideologically. The similarities between Erdoğan's and Abdulhamid II's use of political discourse encourage a comparison between the leaders, as Erdoğan is placing less importance on pluralism over time.

The change in political discourse is dependent on political survival as stated by JO4. Given that more than 90 per cent of the country is Muslim, the needs of this majority need to be addressed. Although this might be called 'Islamism' in the West, Erdoğan personally views it as a feature of 'national struggle', a term favoured by populist leaders across the world. Moreover, JO4 claims it is only 'rhetoric' that associates what a national struggle is with 'Islamic concepts'. This view is mirrored by that of AC2 who summarized Erdoğan's approach as a 'national reflex'. In other words, many of the interviewees agreed that Erdoğan's discourse arises from political clashes, both internal and external, rather than from the desire to develop a unique ideology.

The foregoing discussion implies that a shift in the AKP's political messages is apparent in last decade. However, when discussing this, the majority of the interviewees focused on Erdoğan's discourse rather than on that of the AKP. To argue that Erdoğan determines the AKP's discourse and that what he believes automatically becomes the official discourse of the party is in by no means controversial. Moreover, data suggest that a combination of internal and external struggles led Erdoğan to develop the party's message to a populist Islamist discourse.

Populist leadership and media relations in Turkey

The reason why Erdoğan is framed as a 'populist Islamist' leader in this research is mainly because of his approach of portraying himself, speaking in the name of the majority of the religious conservative Turkish people, as being in a struggle against 'the elite'[41] or 'the oligarchy'.[42] According to PO8, a high-profile at the presidency's communications office, who met me in a funky cafe in Istanbul's hip district Karaköy, the elite comprises, in the AKP's context, Kemalism and its institutions that has transformed the country with its anti-Islam policies after the birth of the Turkish republic. Owing to this fact, populism can be defined as a class struggle; in other words, the people of a country are sovereign and above their rulers.[43] But while populist leaders advocate this idea, they only favour people of a thin-centred ideology who are aligned with their Weltanschauung while undermining the rest. Another fact is the direct relationship between the people and their governments; this overlaps with Erdoğan's discourse as he constantly repeats that, during the AKP rule, the walls between the people and the state have been removed. He supports this argument with the new presidential system. This is reflected in the fact that Erdoğan proposed implementation of direct election of the president since 2014 – that is, not being appointed by the parliament anymore, but rather elected directly by the people.

'Mediatization' is another important element of populist leaders. It starts by 'simplifying the problem so that even less-educated average minds understand the perspective.[44] Then 'polarization', between 'us' and 'them', differentiates to make it even simpler to digest and realize who the enemy is, in other words, 'prioritization of conflict'.[45] 'Emotionalization'[46] needs to be considered when analysing populist leaders. Erdoğan's poems, emphasis on the Ottoman past and moreover his victimhood since he has been jailed in 1997 play a key role in influencing Turkish society because Turkish people prioritize victims over the elites and powerful. Furthermore, populist leaders prefer 'focussing on scandals'.[47] Similarly, Erdoğan cherry picks the scandals and dishonourable actions of the opposition candidates or parties very carefully and is hence able to change the agenda very quickly. In addition, he turns it to symbols, in other words 'privileging of the visual',[48] to dramatize and simplify in order to present it in an effective way. In the 2014 elections when the opposition candidate Ekmeleddin Ihsanoğlu mixed up the national anthem, Erdoğan turned this into a symbolic act by highlighting, in every single rally, the fact that a presidential candidate is not even able to remember the Turkish national anthem.

The relationship with the media is the final important aspect regarding populist leaders' attitude. In fact, populism does not leave a room for criticism; in other words, media is not seen as a checks and balance system for populist leaders. When populists do not agree with certain media platforms' perspective, as Waisbord[49] argues, they attempt changing the media system. Indeed, Turkey stands out when journalism is discussed. Some of the large media outlets in Turkey were in support of the AKP's liberal politics when the party was founded. However, Erdoğan was never satisfied with their attitude as the media were critical of the party from time to time. When he drifted away from the EU, and towards the Muslim world, the established media in Turkey, in particular the media outlets of former media mogul Aydın Doğan, who owned major news outlets like Hürriyet, CNN Türk and Kanal D, followed a critical editorial line. Following the Gezi Park protests in 2013, Turkey's media landscape started changing along with AKP's direction. Erdoğan mobilized the business world to acquire TV channels and newspapers. As a result 85 per cent of the current media landscape in Turkey is controlled by pro-government sources according to Önderoğlu, Turkey's representative for Reporters without Borders.[50] The post-coup attempt in 2016 has increased the control of media outlets when more than 100 of them were shut down and journalists were jailed.[51] Due to the restrictions on freedom of speech, digital media, along with few media outlets like Fox TV, purchased by Murdoch in 2006, and *Sözcü* newspaper are the main opposition sources. Fox TV is the leading popular TV channel in Turkey, both in news and in entertainment.[52] Furthermore, the polarized media landscape as well as the lack of information access to critical perspectives have enabled foreign news outlets like BBC, Independent, Deutsche Welle, Sputnik, VOA, Euronews and Chinese CRI to establish in Turkey.

Framing Erdoğan with Weber's charisma theory

According to JO1, a strong populist leader is necessary in Turkey because Western countries are deeply institutionalized, whereas Eastern societies rely on strong leaders. Despite his critical role as head of a popular newspaper backing the AKP, JO1 did not hesitate to criticize the de-institutionalization within Erdoğan's party. While doing so, he also observed that Turkish society is known to prefer a charismatic leader and always seeks out a hero. There is little doubt that this sentiment has been inherited from the Ottoman era, and it is one that is respected among the conservative majority in Turkey. Strong and charismatic leadership requires self-confidence, and JO1 notes that Erdoğan's initiative has enabled him to change the political landscape in Turkey.

> There is no other charismatic leader who can challenge him. Hence Turkish society is following Erdoğan. If another leader would appear, we could maybe see a competitor. If you look at the political arena in Turkey, you cannot see another leader who has the same charisma and power to influence.

The lack of an opposition party in Turkey has been an important advantage for Erdoğan, who distinguishes himself from other leaders. However, the victory of CHP's Ekrem Imamoğlu in Istanbul's and CHP's Mansur Yavaş in Ankara's 2019 mayoral elections poses a future challenge for Erdoğan in the next presidential elections.⁵³ According to TT3, former pro-AKP think tanker who now works for an international research centre in Istanbul, the rise of Imamoğlu and Yavaş has encouraged hundreds of thousands: 'Both used a positive tone when they delivered their message and did not go into any polemics with Mr Erdoğan which enabled them to secure votes of AKP sympathizers.' Interestingly the 1994 local elections, in which Erdoğan was elected as the mayor of Istanbul, were a turning point in his political career as it marked the beginning of his rise and popularity. Similarly Imamoğlu's victory was compared to that of Erdoğan as he defeated the AKP opposition candidate to win in both elections – first in March 2019 and then in repeat elections in June 2019, with a victory margin that rose from 13,000 in the first election to 800,000 in the re-run. Nevertheless, it would be wrong to state that Erdoğan's charisma alone is the reason for his appeal as this would mean overlooking the reality of religion and ideology. Weber claims that those perceived as charismatic leaders are not bureaucrats or officeholders, but members of the crowd.⁵⁴ The natural leader who emerges from among the masses is often the most effective. Therefore, Erdoğan's past needs to be examined carefully to understand how his appeal became consolidated. When he was 15, he joined a religious and activism-driven youth movement called the MTTB which played a key role in shaping his Islamist ideology. By joining Erbakan's party at a young age, he strengthened his Islamist foundations, and was influenced by populist poems and writings of Necip Fazıl Kısakürek, Nurettin Topçu and Sezai Karakoç. His political ambitions resulted in his rise to prominence within the ranks of the Milli Görüş, and he assumed critical positions, including the mayorship of Istanbul. TT1 argues that Erdoğan became enshrined in people's hearts as a consequence of his religious sensibility and his passion for serving the people of Istanbul – both of which added to perceptions of Erdoğan as a charismatic leader. Despite confirming the importance of leadership in Turkey, JO2 argues that strong leadership is less important now than it was ten years ago, as the level of education within society is changing as Turkey becomes more integrated into the global economy. As a consequence, threats are fewer and so the perception that a strong leader is essential is diminishing. Another journalist, JO1, claims that charisma is still an important factor in Turkey, possibly being the most crucial attribute behind Erdoğan's success:

> You can plan election songs, mobilize the TV, mass and social media coverage; however, this does not mean achieving success. Erdoğan's message is hitting its target, because he knows his audience very well. If another politician were to

give the same message, the language and discourse would not fit. Why? Because he is a tough guy. Turkish people love this kind of character.

JO1 highlights Erdoğan's charismatic leadership style, referring to his 'message', his understanding of the audience as well as his 'brave political programme', adding that 'Turkish people do not like cowardly politicians who always step back.' Apart from the message that is being put forth, PO1 also emphasizes the importance of strategy and politics. For him, charisma is of value only when combined with a desire to provide 'multi-lane highways, health service, schools and improved living standards'.

Erdoğan's one-man leadership limiting freedom of speech

The AKP's post-Erdoğan term is expected to be fragile according to JO1. He insists that the ruling party must urgently begin institutionalizing its processes to prevent problems arising after the departure of Erdoğan. Institutionalization is a crucial step in order to establish an agreed party discourse and align political strategies. JO1 stresses that Erdoğan embodies 'personal institutionalization', in that he has learnt how to govern and lead, and has created a system based on his management style, which only functions with him at the head of the party. Certainly then, if Erdoğan takes responsibility for determining the institutionalization process, whoever follows him must continue with the same discourse, which will create the much-needed continuity, according to JO1. When asked whether any party in Turkey is adequately institutionalized, the interviewee mentions the CHP, founded first as a resistance organization in 1919, then as a political party in 1923 by Mustafa Kemal Atatürk. From his perspective, the CHP is a party that is naturally institutionalized. When questioned whether corporate institutionalization could be effective during Erdoğan's tenure, AC2 suggests it might not be, as Erdoğan's leadership and character is so strong that it cannot be controlled. Moreover, it is unlikely that a new institutionalized mechanism would satisfy Erdoğan as its remit of responsibilities might curtail his freedom to manage the AKP without hindrance. This lack of checks on Erdoğan was mentioned by AC2 when he was questioned about the inability of civil and military mechanisms to control his leadership – this is a new first in Turkey's history.

Portrayed from this perspective, the de-institutionalization is an advantage for Erdoğan, who, according to JO1, prefers individualization of communication, an important aspect of personalization. The significance of political parties appears to be reducing, in part due to their lack of distinctiveness, which accentuates the role of personalization. Langer calls this the 'politicisation of the private persona',[55] a phenomenon which has played a central role in politics since the Americanization of political communications in democratic countries. Yet, whereas the application of personalization in democratic countries means that the leader is more in the foreground than the party itself, it does not mean undermining other institutions and their values that create democratic accountability. But the 'democratic' description is not wholly applicable to Erdoğan, because, for him, the de-institutionalization provides an opportunity to create a personal political landscape reliant upon authoritarian leadership. According to JO2, Erdoğan's aim of one-man leadership is the principal cause of the limited freedom of speech in the country. This is because populist leaders do not want to be challenged, and freedom of speech for journalists in particular means – if necessary – criticising the government. The report of Freedom House in 2020 supports JO2's opinion, as the country was ranked 32nd out of 100.[56] However, the majority of the party members were uncomfortable when I asked them about freedom of speech affecting journalists in Turkey; JO2 was the most open during my interviews.

Surpassing opposition voices within the party

When I asked TT1 if the Gezi Park protests in 2013 were a failure of Erdoğan's management and communication, in particular when he referred to the protesters as *çapulcu* (which means marauders in English), he defended Erdoğan's handling of the public's perception:

> If someone like Abdullah Gül [former president] or Bülent Arınç [former speaker of the parliament] had been the leader during the Gezi Park protests, we might have faced civil war in Turkey.

Here he distinguishes between Erdoğan and his former colleagues. Gül and Arınç were key personalities within the AKP whose prominence was ultimately cast into the shadows by Erdoğan. Their different approaches to critical issues, such as the Gezi Park protests or the 17/25 December 2013 corruption scandal, revealed the more tolerant and moderate voice within the ruling party, a voice which considers the entire population. TT1 emphasizes that had either the Gezi Park protests or the 17/25 December 2014 corruption scandal been managed by someone other than Erdoğan, many high-ranked AKP supporters, including Erdoğan himself, would be in prison now. Interestingly, JO2 thinks that those within the AKP who disapproved of Erdoğan's dismissive language are in the majority, but they had been unable to speak out. It was particularly after the local elections in 2019 that criticism within the party increased tremendously. The AKP's former Istanbul MP Mustafa Yeneroğlu, a religious conservative lawyer by profession who left Germany to join the party upon a personal invitation of Erdoğan in 2015, resigned four years later and joined Babacan's DEVA Party. He spoke out on justice system and human rights in Turkey at the parliament in April 2020:

> 'Where liberty is, there is my country', Benjamin Franklin once said, to which Thomas Paine replied, 'Where liberty is not, there is my country', 300 years ago. Although I feel ashamed to build the same sentence in the twenty-first century, 'Where there is no freedom, where there is no justice, there is Turkey.'[57]

These words of a religious conservative MP summarize AKP's turmoil regarding freedom of expression in the country. This situation began to change when Ahmet Davutoğlu became chairman of the AKP and prime minister of Turkey in 2014. Indeed, the AKP was split before Erdoğan forced Davutoğlu to resign, according to JO2, with one group operating along the same political lines as Erdoğan and the other willing to engage in a more moderate form of governance. When Erdoğan became president of Turkey in August 2014, he was required to resign from the AKP and the position of prime minister. Consequently, after a long discussion, he appointed Davutoğlu, his former foreign minister and advisor as prime minister. Certainly there was initially no sign of differences between the thoughts and actions of Erdoğan and Davutoğlu, but during crisis periods, disagreements arose.

Erdoğan less favourite among generation Z

When considering the above relationships, it is useful to look at the allegations made by social media trolls supported by the AKP who are responsible for posting provocative messages on social media sites to cause disruption. JO2 claims that these trolls are paid by the AKP through unofficial channels. In one 'troll campaign', as he notes, they claimed that Davutoğlu was associated with a 'German school of thought'[58] and had signed a secret agreement with Germany to overthrow Erdoğan. In addition, both Davutoğlu and former president Abdullah Gül were accused of being 'controlled by the Queen', because they had studied in the UK. PO4 argues that the campaign to malign other individuals is a crucial aspect in maintaining the perception of Erdoğan as the only plausible wholly charismatic leader.

Despite the use of social media as a propaganda tool here, JO2 accentuates that patriarchy in politics is old school and not sufficient to convince the generation Z. Thus, even the children of conservative religious AKP supporters are not impressed by Erdoğan's discourse. The charismatic leadership style exhibited by Erdoğan lacks appeal for the younger generation – a fact that became apparent in the June 2015 general elections. The most preferred party among youths was the HDP, followed by the MHP, the CHP and finally the AKP. This finding, which was not released into the public domain, was reportedly an outcome of a poll developed by TT1 for the AKP.

However, Ünal does not agree that the significance of the role played by Erdoğan's charisma is decreasing. On the contrary, he stresses that Erdoğan's charismatic leadership style is a principal tool in the AKP's political communications armoury. He reveals the findings of a poll that examined the role of propaganda during the 2014 Turkish presidential elections, which found that just '3 per cent of Erdoğan's supporters were influenced by the propaganda' and that the key consideration was economic development; although, he does add that the success of the economy partly also depends on the presence of a charismatic leader. Yet none of my interviewees could share a percentage for 2018 and 2019 elections. But PO6, who became an MP in 2018 elections, underlined that despite economic failure of the AKP, it is Erdoğan's charisma which brought success in 2018 and 2019, 'otherwise the outcome would be much worse'. JO2 acknowledges the fact that despite the limited appeal of Erdoğan, his charismatic leadership style is highly influential: '15 per cent of the 50 per cent of voters who support the AKP only do so because of Erdoğan's charisma, not because of AKP's politics.' To some extent then, personality is the path to credibility, as Bruce[59] accentuates. The credibility conferred on Erdoğan and the AKP by their supporters fuelled economic prosperity, as JO3 notes. Moreover, there was a need for a strong leader to manage economic development in 2002, stating that at the time Erdoğan was the main symbol of hope: 'if you take Erdoğan away, there is no hope in Turkey'. When I asked JO3 about the de-institutionalization in Turkey, and within the AKP, his view echoes that of JO1 given above:

> There is definitely a de-institutionalization. That is the reason why there is an incredible support for a charismatic leader such as Erdoğan. Because people say 'if Erdoğan goes, everything will end'. This is also the reason why Erdoğan has won so many elections in a row, despite the military, judiciary, Gülenists etc.

Turkish society knows that Erdoğan is a human and has faults. However, they realize that there is no institutionalization in the country. This is the reason why they are supporting Erdoğan.

This statement questions whether Erdoğan's charisma is really the reason he was able to prevent the military and judiciary from intervening to oust the AKP from government. Furthermore, not only the 17/25 December 2014 corruption scandal but also the 2016 coup attempt represent another important turning point when assessing the achievements of Erdoğan's leadership. PO1, a former interior minister and founding member of the AKP, argues that Erdoğan's charisma is a feature that results from his Islamically motivated activist roots as a member of Erbakan's movement. He asserts that Erbakan's political approach as an academic differs from that of Erdoğan, whose knowledge is practical rather than theoretical. In order to succeed, according to PO1, in the political landscape, a leader's advisors need theoretical knowledge, whereas a leader needs know-how and relevant management skills.

The information collected implies that perceptions of Erdoğan's charisma in the early years were mainly linked to the recognition he gained for his work as the mayor of Istanbul. His Islamist background and his ambitions to serve the population of Istanbul amplified his popularity. Indeed if we trace the development of Erdoğan's charisma as progressive, we can note a clear transformation after 2009, as confirmed by the majority of the interviewees. The pro-Palestinian cause can be analysed as critical moments in Erdoğan's political career, as they led to his being widely regarded as 'the charismatic leader of the Muslim world'. Thus, 2009–10 marks the date from which the popularity of the Turkish leader was deemed influential on 'Arab streets' and beyond.

Americanization as a communication model of the AKP

'Persuading people' something is true is fundamental to public relations, as Bernays[60] observes. In the domain of politics, truth is communicated to the public within a strategic 'political' framework, intended to produce 'influence' and benefit 'reputations'. Olçok, Erdoğan's spin doctor and campaign manager, worked for both the AKP and Erdoğan; he underlines that the AKP follows a policy of constant communication – a strategy which distinguishes it from other parties, and Erdoğan from other political leaders. He explains that 'constant communication' refers to 'uninterrupted' communication; that is, the party not only communicates during elections or crisis periods but continuously. When the in-depth interview with Olçok took place, it was December 2014 and so there were seven months to go before the general elections in June 2015. At this time, Olçok commented on the fact that nobody was questioning who would win; he said: 'The only question people and media ask is "how many votes will the AKP get?"'

He noted that he used the brand 'Erdoğan' as evidence upon which to base communication strategies designed to increase the party's impact. He explains modestly that although fifty people comprise Erdoğan's Strategy Team, 'success belongs to the leader'. He asserts that Erdoğan has conquered the hearts of the people during his forty years in the political spotlight, through his discourse, actions and attitudes. To explain the longevity of Erdoğan's charisma, Olçok refers to the time the leader spent working for Erbakan's party and then as mayor of Istanbul, when he achieved remarkable success as an energetic mayor delivering services to 'nearly every household' – an efficiency never before witnessed in Istanbul. As an example, he solved the water crisis in Istanbul; overcoming this major challenge won him the support of many who were then willing to overlook any ideological differences.

In the 1994 elections, around 4.08 million people voted, and Erdoğan received more than 973 thousand votes, a quarter of the vote. At this time Erdoğan emerged as a natural leader, standing up from the centre of the silent majority – a man who sold lemonade as a boy to support his family, Erdoğan overcame hardship in his youth to become a figurehead, an inspiration for others like him. This history explains why Erdoğan's personal success has been at the crux of the AKP's political communication. Olçok continues that Erdoğan's presence at the head of the party is sufficient in itself to persuade the public to vote for it. Olçok emphasizes the central role of his own agency, which has served the AKP since its establishment, seeking to convey the impression that all important work is based on the outcomes of his agency, Arter. TT1 explains how Erdoğan's Strategy Team works below:

> Immediately after the presidential elections, I was invited for a meeting. This was a strategy meeting. This is one example that shows how professional and determined Erdoğan is. In this meeting we discussed what discourse and terms should be deployed for the election. Collecting, discussing and analysing are the jobs in the beginning preparatory phase. We look at previous elections in terms of discourse, slogan, election promises, etc., and work on new strategies and ideas. By the time the main opposition party starts preparing their election campaign, the AKP has already decided everything, such as slogans, music, election manifesto, etc. in draft form. We then send the plans to a smaller team to revise and decide on the details. When they finished their work, we come

together for a two-day camp, at which the chairman and all the other party members are present. This meeting means 'we are ready', and covers 'who is doing what?' The party has been victorious in all of the elections to date. This is the difference between the AKP and the opposition parties.

TT1's foremost emphasis is on the party's professionalism, and the significance of its adapting to the 'changing nature of technologies of communication'.[61] After the 2007 general elections, TT1 explains, things became more professional and digital technology was more fully incorporated into the party's communication strategies. Yet when the new presidential system was introduced with the 2018 presidential elections, Erdoğan decided to form a new directory to control the communication and PR of the government. He called it 'Communications Directory' and was modelled after the White House Communications Office. This department started managing the internal and external communication, PR, advertising and press releases, public-funded broadcaster TRT, Turkey's state agency, Anadolu, public diplomacy. One thousand people are working for this office in Turkey and five hundred abroad. JO7, an anonymous journalist working for the Ciner Media Group, mentions that 'it became professionalized and more organized'. When I asked her if this new office has also increased the one-man dominance, she nodded and agreed.

During the interview, I asked Olçok if the party uses their status in government to assist with campaigning, because during the 2014 presidential elections I saw many more campaign posters of Erdoğan on the streets of Istanbul and Ankara than of both opposition candidates Ekmeleddin Ihsanoğlu and Selahattin Demirtaş. Olçok explains that regulations forbid this and emphasizes that they are adhered to. However, he explains they employ a clever promotional technique:

> During the election period, we received hundreds of phone calls from people who are interested in hanging up a poster of Erdoğan in their own homes, shops, offices etc. This is a civil initiative. That is the reason why people feel that Erdoğan is using the power of government. In addition, I must say that Ihsanoğlu received support from thirteen different parties. Seven of these parties have approximately 6,000 offices in Turkey. If they were clever, they would use this opportunity, and use their office spaces to campaign for free.

For the 2007 general elections, volunteers were trained for fifteen days by the party in order to prepare them for successful political communication campaigning. Both examples show that the AKP is using its support base when campaigning. However in the 2018 and 2019 elections, although volunteers took part in the election campaign, professional companies were more in the foreground, according to PO6. Yet, she underlines that in the 2019 local elections in particular, three different groups managed the whole process which resulted in a critical defeat. PO6 was part of the Communications Team in Istanbul and witnessed different meetings where she worked closely with Yıldırım, AKP's Istanbul candidate in 2019 and former prime minister. Yıldırım had a PR team while the party headquarters worked on the communication with the president's Communication Directory on board. However, PO6 argues that the interference of the party and presidency led to the mismanagement of the whole process which led to AKP's defeat in Istanbul.

PO1, who is part of the AKP's Strategy Team, claims that the party's political communication strategy is to focus solely on the leader. Unlike Olçok, who did not share the details of the members of the Strategy Team, PO1 disclosed that ministers, MPs, research centres, think tanks, political scientists, PR and advertising agencies are all part of the team, thus highlighting the fact that the communications produced are the product of a 'collective': 'Despite differences in ideas and strategies related to our communication, we act with a collective mind.' Undoubtedly, 'exchanges, negotiations, decisions, and conflicts' take place from within this collective whole,[62] but ultimately, according to AC2, it is Erdoğan who sets the agenda, not the Strategy Team. To this end, the role of a social movement is crucial. Although Erdoğan sets the agenda, he also wants to act in a way that consolidates collective identity, as AC2 highlights. This approach forms the basis of the 'establishment of a new order'[63] and the forging of a new national identity.

When AKP officials spoke about political communication during the interviews, they mentioned only Erdoğan and not the party. This provides further evidence of the institutionalization problem and identity crisis. It also promotes authoritarian governance as pluralism disappears systematically when replacing collective party identity with one-man leadership. It is important to mention here that in order to have a successful social movement it is necessary that five components are met: 'interest, organization, mobilization, opportunity, and collective action itself.'[64]

Obama and digital political communication

As set out earlier, the Americanization of political communications is an important lens through which to observe the AKP's communications. When I consulted political communication advisor Olçok about whether the AKP utilizes American-style campaign strategies, he admitted that the team responsible for managing public relations, media and communication affairs closely observes the conduct of election campaigns in the United States:

The United States is the centre of marketing, advertising and public relations. Furthermore, it is one of the most important countries where political communication principles, theories and practices are applied.

However, different dynamics, and historical as well as sociological frameworks, prevent wholescale imitation of the US model in Turkey. According to the communications guru Olçok, the problems effecting Turkey and the United States differ, necessitating the development of a unique political communication campaign for Erdoğan, which is only 'inspired' by techniques used in the United States. Here it is important to point out that, due to his position, Olçok was naturally unwilling to suggest replication of US strategies as this might risk damaging the party's or Erdoğan's image. Moreover, chastening the approach of Western nations, specifically America, is a common approach in Turkey among conservatives, as I have observed during my fieldwork. The wars in Iraq and Afghanistan after 9/11 poured oil on flames, magnifying the negative image of the United States in the eyes of Turkish society.[65] Trump's fluctuating relationship with the Erdoğan administration, his unlimited support for Israel as well as the US policy on Syria have played key roles in recent years on Turkish people's attitude towards the United States. Kadir Has University's research delineates the reality on the ground. According to their poll, 81.3 per cent of Turkish people see the United States as a threat to Turkey.[66] Despite this perception and religious conservatives' sensitivity towards the United States, the AKP has not hesitated to look to the United States regarding communication strategies. A crucial reason for this is the image created by the US politicians during the campaigns; Olçok explains thus:

> I was very impressed when I followed Obama's 2009 election campaign. Concentrating on the leader was something we could implement as we have a leader like Erdoğan, strong and charismatic. Hence, we prepared the 2014 campaign according to similar principles.

AC2 notes that the AKP started the process of Americanization in Turkey using professional spin doctors, advisors, advertising agencies and research centres, as well as think tanks. He refers to Erdoğan's Strategy Team as adopting 'Americanized processes of political communication'. Although the AKP was not professional in its campaigns during its early years, over time it has invested more money in political communication. The use of digital communication is an aspect to consider in particular after the foundation of the Communications Directory. PO8 from Erdoğan's Communications Team explains that Twitter handles @iletisim ('communications' in English), @communications and @kommunikatsiya (which is the Russian word for 'communications') were acquired when Fahrettin Altun became the first director of the Communications Directory. After this, short explanatory videos were produced and social media platforms were used effectively to 'not only reach the public through traditional media, but through modern tools which are more important to the younger generation who consume more digital media than traditional TV or newspaper'. PO8 explains how they produced videos during the 'Olive Branch' and 'Peace Spring' operations in Syria in 2018 and 2019, and during the Libya operation in 2020 to 'inform the public'. Similary, Erdoğan's Communications Chief released a video in August 2020 with mainly Islamist, nationalist, cultural and neo-Ottoman images. From fighter aircrafts to drill ships, from the Green Dome in Medina where Prophet Muhammad's tomb is located to al-Aqsa Mosque in Jerusalem, with an upbeat music in the background and slogans such as 'Allah (God) is great', the video emphasized how Turkey is protecting the oppressed across the world. There are scenes from the Hagia Sophia and Erdoğan citing verses from Surah al-Fath (The Victory) from the Quran; 'Indeed, we have given you a clear victory. Allah may help you with a mighty help.'

Although the 4-minute long propaganda video, which included Alp Arslan, second Sultan of the Seljuk Empire, Sultan Mehmet II, also known as Sultan Fatih, who conquered Istanbul, and Erdoğan, it did not include footages from Atatürk which was later a discussion topic on social media. However, AC7, who knows Altun and his personality very well, believes that this is pure propaganda of Erdoğan to justify his war decisions; more importantly, it is a tool to increase his popularity 'every time when it starts falling', particularly since 2019. In fact, 'digitalization of culture and communication enables convergence and transmission' across different platforms.[67] In the context of the work done by Erdoğan's communications office, it is important here to highlight the impact of traditional media on consumers. According to AC6, who was quite suspicious before our meeting at a cafe near the Süleymaniye Mosque, which was commissioned by Suleiman I, also known as Suleiman the Magnificent, and designed by Mimar Sinan, but opened up during our interview, traditional media reaches out to a certain audience that does not include the millennials and generation Z. Hence digital communication is a more effective way to garner support of AKP members on the one hand, and the AKP troll accounts on the other, in order to create Top Tweet (TT) campaigns regularly. Ever since the Communications Directory has been established, Twitter campaigns have increased. It is not surprising that these campaigns mainly focus on Erdoğan, such as by posting a picture of him on Twitter, or campaigning for the reopening of Hagia Sophia as a mosque to build 'public awareness and public support' before

Erdoğan decided to turn it to a mosque. When it comes to social media use, Erdoğan's Communications Team uses a combination of Obama's and Trump's strategies in the context of Twitter: while Obama used the networking site professionally, Trump utilized a more guerrilla-like strategy, which disregarded accuracy, for his tweets.

AC2 states that Turkey will focus more on Americanization, which usually concentrates more on the media, indoor meetings, soft advertisings, digital and print media and various other persuasion techniques. However, '[w]e do not have specialists who know this process very well. When the country is developed and normalized, this will have an impact on the political communication too'. In fact the implication that AKP's communication strategies are based on the US campaigns confirms AC2's approach which considers professionalization as a sub-area of Americanization. Negrine[68] summarizes three aspects of professionalization: '[the] changing organizational structures of political parties, the changing nature of technologies of communication, and the place of spin in modern politics.' According to Olçok, the AKP is implementing all three. Whereas organizational change is based on the work with advertising agencies and think tanks, he explains that changes to communication technologies involve the implementation of the Americanization model.

AC2 underscores that development and normalization are central to the introduction of Americanization as a model for political communication. In fact, the way Americanization developed relates directly to AC2's comments. That is, after the Cold War, the impact of popular culture became amplified and America's domination beyond its borders increased, leading to the transformation of many societies. This process is closely related to the intensification of capital expenditure as it leads to economic growth and fuels development in the form of improved socio-economic conditions. This development then enables a country to adopt modern and current strategies and tools and use them proactively. In addition, for AC2, there is a tool which is 'more effective than Americanization' – something that is not widely used in the West – namely outdoor campaigning:

> No other leader in the West in the twenty-first century has been able to bring one million people together for a rally as Erdoğan does. This is more important than Americanization. It is the reality of Erdoğan.

AC2, who prior to the interview agreed to allow me to disclose her name, later, before the interview started, decided to stay anonymous, points out that direct communication is crucial to Erdoğan's success; the message plays a key role in direct communication, strengthening the impact on the electorate. Whereas indoor meetings with small numbers of people is standard practice in American contexts, the aspect of rallying with millions of people like in Turkey is not a major part of standard Americanization communication. It can be recognized as a local factor within the context of the AKP's use of Americanization.

Contradicting the view espoused by AC2 that the AKP's communications were not professional in the early years, JO4 states that the party's communication strategy has deteriorated since the Gezi Park protests in 2013. He claims the AKP's political communication strategies were very effective until that time, as they were 'systematic, disciplined and conceptualized clearly, resulting in strong slogans'. Furthermore, JO4 cautions that Americanization is not necessary in Turkey, as Erdoğan's place at the epicentre of the political landscape says more than any campaign strategy ever could.

Erdoğan's body language

According to JO1, another aspect of Erdoğan's charisma is his capacity to forge an emotional bond with his audience. Here, the interviewee focuses on Erdoğan's use of body language and poetry, observing that whether Erdoğan is speaking about highways, hospitals or Gross Domestic Product (GDP), the audience listens and responds with great emotion. This interviewee, an experienced journalist, comments that some people even shed tears when Erdoğan is addressing the crowds. In fact, I personally witnessed this during my fieldwork at AKP rallies in 2014, 2018 and 2019. This level of emotion discloses the strong relationship between the leader and his supporters. It is the result of years of employing a candidate-centred campaign policy, which can be described here as personalization. JO1 notes thus:

> Anti-Erdoğan campaigns never succeed because the people who love Erdoğan are loyal to him. There is an emotional relationship. Consequently, as long as this relationship endures, all anti-Erdoğan campaigns will fail. Erdoğan is successful despite media bias, because he is a direct communicator and reaches society directly. Even if you create an anti-campaign using mass media tools, you cannot touch these supporters. Therefore, emotional loyalty can be seen to be very important in political communication.

'Emotionalization'[69] is a key word when analysing populist leaders' attitude. Erdoğan's over-emotional attitude is in this sense crucial when analysing his impact on the audience. He can dramatize even simple issues to get attention from the audience as well as media outlets. Furthermore, Erdoğan uses body language and gestures, in other words, non-verbal communication, very effectively. 'He is a natural born leader; he has not attended any body language diploma programmes; rather it is all based on his long career in politics', according to PO6, whose emotional relationship to Erdoğan has been quite influential in his decision to join politics today. The Turkish president's use of voice needs to be considered when analysing his overall charisma as he knows how to use his voice – that is, how to modulate as well as how to intonate – to produce maximum impact on the audience. This all has a direct relationship to his Islamist background as most of the religious conservatives who study at Imam Hatip schools learn how to read poems and make public speeches at a very young age. Erdoğan was in fact one such student who was always keen to read poems from ideological role models like Kısakürek or Karakoç.

The use of opinion polls in communication

Opinion polls, another Americanization technique, is an important tool when designing a communication strategy. Political communications professor McNair[70] summarizes this relationship in Figure 1, including it in his elements of political communication. Typically, opinion polls collating the views of citizens are conducted by research centres; however, the results of these polls are fed back through the media to political organizations. Olçok explains, 'Opinion polls are an important part of our success. Through measuring the pulse of the public, we see how the land lies and develop our strategy.' He also explains how the process works as follows. First, the Strategy Team determines the focus of the polls and their target audience, and then the research centre defines the questions including details relevant to the chosen audience. When the poll has been conducted, the results are delivered to the research centre, where they are analysed by specialists and the findings presented to the Strategy Team, which sets the election agenda accordingly. PO8 explains that in the 2019 local elections the presidency's Communications Directory was in charge of opinion polls, while AC7 argues that the AKP does less consider opinion polls since 2018, which is the reason why they had a dramatic fail in 2019 elections.

AKP's political communication inspires Islamist parties

Olçok highlights that Erdoğan's Communications Team is in the process of transferring its experiences of this 'new kind of political campaigning' to other Islamist parties and movements in the region. When asked which parties these are, Olçok mentions the MB in Egypt after the revolution in 2012 and the Ennahda in Tunisia. Olçok notes that he went to Egypt and Tunisia personally to work with these parties. More importantly, Olçok disclosed that Erdoğan had assigned this job directly to him, which basically demonstrates the direct relationship in terms of campaigning between the AKP, and the MB and Ennahda. Thus, while the political communication strategies of the United States offer inspiration for the AKP, the party's communication strategies inspire other Islamist parties in the region. Indeed, the relationship between religion and communication style is critical when preparing a unique model that reflects local dynamics. For example, in contrast to the AKP, the Americanization of Morocco's PJD concentrates on professionalism, such as 'political consultancy and spin-doctors'.[71] Thus, 'American electioneering' coincides with the realities of society, as illustrated by the fact that while appearing with family members is a sensitive issue in Morocco, it is viewed as a positive move in Turkey because of the country's laïcité understanding. Thus, the reality that what works in one country may not work in another and what works in one election may not work in the next should not be ignored. In addition, Americanization can be viewed as a form of cultural homogenization, which transforms traditional societies, assimilating them with others, and standardizes the campaign strategies of different countries and parties. That the AKP is assisting other Islamist parties clarifies that the Americanization process is now entrenched within the AKP, with the result that it now has its own technical experts and professional advisers. JO2 explains that Erdoğan's willingness to innovate in the area of communications makes the job of the Communications Team easier when drawing on models from Western countries.

JO1 explains that part of the Americanization process of the AKP is the emphasis placed on introducing key 'family figures' to the electorate. By making an appearance with his wife during rallies and all public events, Erdoğan conveys the message that all his supporters, regardless of their hierarchy, are part of one big family, according to JO2. Clearly the practice of appearing with a partner is not widespread among conservative politicians in Turkey. JO1 argues that it symbolizes confidence when a leader appears with his family, which is the tradition in the United States; 'this is how we know Michelle Obama, Laura Bush and Hillary Clinton'. Yet in a religious conservative context such as in Turkey, the place of women in society needs to be discussed to understand why Erdoğan and other AKP figures attach importance on appearing with their wives on public events.

After the postmodern coup in 1997, women wearing headscarves were marginalized from all walks of life. They were not allowed to enter universities or military premises to visit their husbands, sons or other family members. Moreover, in 1999, Merve Kavakçı – the first woman to be elected to the parliament who wore a headscarf – had to leave the Turkish parliament as Prime Minister Bülent Ecevit and opposition voices protested when she entered the premises; she was, however, later rewarded by Erdoğan, by being appointing as an ambassador to Malaysia. In short, religious conservative women had a negative image as being uneducated, as having a lifestyle that is incompatible with the Kemalist laïcité and as second-class citizens. The postmodern coup period prohibited women with headscarves from playing an active role in state institutions, such as by becoming lawyers, teachers or doctors. When the AKP came to power, Erdoğan, for a long period, had not concentrated on this particular problem in society, as explained earlier, but Erdoğan's appearance with his wife, and in later years with his daughters, in public events was the first step in changing the image and perception in Turkish bureaucracy. Hence family portrayal in the context of communication plays a key role within the dynamic of populist Islamist agenda.

Erdoğan's polarizing discourse

Professor Ismail Kara, a scholar of Islamic philosophy, explains that the AKP makes Islamic references in its political activities, which to him reflects its confidence as an established party. He states that this move does not then represent a shift in the main direction of the party. Erdoğan's discourse is undoubtedly that of the AKP, and this is a crucial point to take into consideration for my interviewee, who has a vast archive on Islamism and Political Islam. Erdoğan controls the AKP, and so sets the discourse and its agenda. Although Kara criticizes this, he underlines that this is a successful strategy and credits Erdoğan for it, as it is not easy to manage such a large party, with nearly ten million members. Nevertheless, as discussed previously, Kara admits that it is in part a consequence of the expectation in Turkey that the leader chooses the direction of the national political discourse.

Kara also believes that Erdoğan's discourse has served to polarize Turkey increasingly since 2011. This has generated uncertainty and is risking a division between the different social groups in Turkey. That is to say that the interests of parties, secularists and conservatives are increasingly polarized.

> Actually, this is one of the main problems related to the Westernization in the Islamic world. Two things which are philosophically opposite are expected to function together. If you conduct a philosophical analysis, both push each other away. The AKP has increased this parallel position. So, the answer to the question 'is Turkey becoming more secularized' is 'yes'. But to the question 'is Turkey becoming more religious', it is also 'yes'.

Kara, analyses the processes in Turkey by examining the nature of change in society. Erdoğan uses inflammatory rhetoric not only regarding issues related to politics but also when passing judgement on the lives of people, such as by introducing new regulations on alcohol and issuing abortion restrictions. On 24 May 2013, the Turkish parliament approved a bill which banned the sale of alcohol between 22:00 and 6:00 hours. Erdoğan justified these actions by citing examples from European countries; however Kara believes that the decision to limit alcohol availability is driven by Erdoğan's Islamist ideology. In fact, as Erdoğan emphasizes, the alcohol ban is similar to that in the West, and referencing Turkish youth, he also cautions against allowing the emergence of a drunken generation.

According to PO1, this is an obvious introduction of religious prescriptions into politics. He adds that the AKP's policies to date have made Turkey more democratic, expanded freedoms and developed the country economically. During the discussion on this issue, PO1 emphasizes that he has always worked towards achieving modernization. What is more, his tone suggests there is a conflict within the AKP, and that he disapproves of Erdoğan's policies. Similarly, he argues that universal values were at the epicentre of the AKP's policies in the first two election periods, 2002–7 and 2007–11, revealing a contradiction with the views of the other high-profile AKP officials who were interviewed. In fact, the AKP's main intention in the first period was to raise the living standards of people in Turkey but also altering negative perceptions of the country globally to attract investments from abroad. Thereafter, economic as well as social initiatives were included on their agenda. Intending to join the EU, the AKP introduced the Copenhagen criteria, which emphasize freedom of thought and expression, and freedom of economic investment. AKP's successful management of the economy in the first two periods brought average working-class conservative men and women to the epicentre of the political agenda, introducing a politics that focused on them rather than on the elite, who previous governments in Turkey had targeted.

AKP's identity crisis

During our interview at a fancy cafe in an upscale neighbourhood in Ankara, Ünal confesses that there is an element of chaos concerning the AKP's identity, which is apparent in the party's rhetoric and discourse. Analysing this internal conflict from a broader perspective, he likens it to Turkey's 200-year long struggle with the Westernization process. Mehmet Akif Ersoy, author of the Turkish National Anthem, stated, after visiting Germany, that Turks should compete with the science of the West, adopting the necessary tools to do so. However, he discerns that not Western science but its 'immoralities' were adopted.

As analysed in the previous chapter, the modernization process was started by Sultan Selim III who marked the commencement of an era of retrogression in the Ottoman Empire, which led to the establishment of the Turkish Republic. Both Sultan Selim III and his successor Sultan Mahmud II introduced new policies in the fields of military, education and society to benefit religion and state, halt their country's fall and modernize the empire. These motivations caused the identity of society to become fractured, according to the former Milli Görüş member. Ünal states that Erdoğan is trying to set a new agenda to advance Turkish society, but due to the turbulent past, many questions remain unanswered:

> Where do we live? What kind of Muslims are we? What kind of democracy do we defend? What form of government do we desire?

Answering these questions is fundamental, according to Ünal, in order to establish a consistent discourse that will endure regardless of one-time events or changes in leadership. It is the lack of identity that is causing the people in Turkey to be confused politically. On the topic of Erdoğan's rhetoric, his former speechwriter does believe that it has changed since 2009, as summarized below:

> Erdoğan is dreaming of a young pious generation, which holds the Quran in one hand, and a computer in the other.

This sentence alludes to Ersoy's words, as mentioned above. The inclusion of the metaphor of the Quran is a clear sign that Erdoğan is confident about discussing religion, but it also suggests that his vision is one that can embrace and combine both faith and advanced technology. As expressed by Ünal here, this is a recent vision:

> When Abdullah Gül became president in 2007, and when the AKP survived the closure trial in 2008, this was the time for Erdoğan to begin challenging the secular establishment.

Ünal purports that the confusion surrounding the language and discourse used by the AKP and its supporters relates to the party's failure to institutionalize its position. More importantly, Ünal does not accuse Erdoğan, his advisors or AKP officials of creating this situation, but rather the academics and social scientists, noting that subscribing to an 'Anglo-American syllabus' based on the West prevents the development of unique Turkish theories and discourses in politics, sociology and science because it offers a 'different paradigm'. He further explains that many problems arise as a result of alternative education systems employed in Saudi Arabia, Egypt and other countries. He considers the emergence of the Islamic State of Iraq and Syria (ISIS) and al-Qaeda as part of this problem, adding that he cannot see any solution in the near future. 'Whether the education system in Turkey offers an alternative to the West' is a reasonable question to ask.

Neo-Ottoman identity

Erdoğan's longest serving speechwriter clearly underlines that the AKP does not have a unique discourse, but that Erdoğan is seeking to introduce a local and native discourse that references history and literature, while encompassing the intentions of great political and religious leaders. According to Ünal,

> Erdoğan is a leader who quotes from Ahmed-i Hani, Kurdish poet and historian who lived in the seventeenth century, whose name was unknown until 2009 as nobody was brave enough to mention him in speeches. Furthermore, he refers to Yunus Emre, a Turkish poet and Sufi mystic who lived in the thirteenth century. He reads poems by Mehmet Akif Ersoy courageously. He talks about Abdulhamid II, one of the most important figures in the Ottoman Empire, who is known as an 'Islamist sultan', Fatih Sultan Mehmet, Ottoman sultan who conquered Constantinople, and Alp Arslan, second sultan of the Seljuk Empire. Furthermore, he does not hesitate to point to Saladin's Kurdish Identity.

Ünal acknowledges that Erdoğan draws on concepts introduced by certain key figures, but states that it is his reflection on history that is significant. The extract above portrays how Erdoğan associated his ideology with the Ottoman and the Seljuk Empire. Referencing both empires and relating to sentiments expressed by key Islamist thinkers is a sign that he is pursuing a sense of collective identity, which 'is a product of conscious action'.[72] The idea of collective action in the context of Erdoğan's relationship with both empires is one that communicates a 'native and national' vision, as elucidated by Ünal earlier, and can be interpreted as an interest in looking at lessons from history from a modern viewpoint. This explains why the term 'neo-Ottoman' is occasionally used to characterize the position of the AKP in academic journal articles and conferences and the media.

Collective identity is an essential aspect of social movement theory; one that focuses on the unification of social, political and economic conditions. According to Professor Kara, Erdoğan's references to history suggest that he is trying to develop a social movement similar to the Milli Görüş movement in order to ensure he leaves his imprint behind. Social movements mobilize the masses and bring about change in society. Arguably, without any clear identity, discourse or political institutionalization, as highlighted earlier, the AKP's message is not sufficiently meaningful to establish a de facto collective identity. Thus, as power 'lies in the images of representation', as Castells[73] highlights, maintaining an imprint after the death is achievable only by forging an enduring image based on a legacy of power. When delivering his final speech at the AKP group meeting before becoming president in 2014, Erdoğan asserted that his aim was to leave a meaningful imprint behind. According to Kara, this refers to Erdoğan's intent to make a positive contribution to the country – one that will endure even after his political career ends. However, Kara thinks this is also reflective of Erdoğan's Islamist ideology because the meaning of 'Jihad' is to fight and die for the sake of God: 'A true Muslim believes in Jihad and desires to change the society when necessary.' Hence, Erdoğan's main aim as a leader is 'to fulfil his duties as a real Muslim'.

Reconversion of Hagia Sophia as part of Erdoğan's populist politics

The reconversion of Hagia Sophia into mosque in July 2020 is a critical turning point in this regard. By ordering a presidential decree, Erdoğan, once again, used a symbolic step to highlight that he is the one who has the last word even on topics that have a meaning for non-religious conservatives. No doubt that this was not only the dream of Erbakan but of Turkey's Islamists.

Hagia Sophia was built by Byzantine Emperor Justinian in 532 CE to serve for the Orthodox patriarchy. When Sultan Fatih conquered Istanbul in

1453, he added four minarets and turned it to a mosque. When the caliphate was abolished and the modern Turkish Republic was found, Atatürk decided in 1934, as has Erdoğan, with a decree, to turn the historic building to a museum. Finally, Erdoğan, who sees himself as the founder of 'New Turkey' decided to turn it to a mosque on 24 July 2020, on the anniversary of the Treaty of Lausanne, which was signed in Switzerland by the Allied powers and Turkey, defining the borders of the modern Turkish Republic. Symbolically, Erdoğan highlighted that he does not accept the Treaty of Lausanne and Atatürk's secularization policies. Whereas internally it is seen as consolidation of his power during a time of economic recession and emergence of new parties and political figures. Furthermore, it is the crème de la crème of his populist Islamist policies. Professor Oliver Roy, political Islam expert, summarized Erdoğan's symbolic act of Hagia Sophia with the following words:

> The botched coup dealt both a psychological and political blow for Erdoğan … The reprisal of Erdoğan in the aftermath of the coup against religious and political networks also meant that he lost the grip of even the Imam Hatips and mosques … even though it tries hard. Besides, Erdoğan lost his grip on the economy. He lost the technocrats like Ali Babacan and the liberal wing. The AKP could not fulfill the Islamists' biggest promise about being against corruption. Exactly for these reasons, Erdoğan is only left with symbols as tools for consolidating the electorate. In that sense, what better symbol than converting the Hagia Sophia to a mosque. Erdoğan could not Islamize minds, so he is trying to Islamize stones.[74]

It was Erdoğan's government who stood for minority rights for Kurds, Alevis, Armenians and Romani people. However, since post-Gezi Park protests and post-July coup attempt, it is the same government that does not stand for pluralism but assertion of Islam in the public space, a gradual toning down of secularism. Whereas Erdoğan's dream of 'pious generation' has failed considerably after two decades of governance, he is focusing on top-down policies with symbolic acts like the converting Hagia Sophia to a mosque; building new mosques like the biggest mosque of Turkey, Çamlıca, which is also known as 'Erdoğan mosque'; or remodelling Taksim square, known for the protests in 2013 and gathering place of secular Turks; banning Pride marches and queer-friendly events despite supporting gay rights when he came to power; removing evolution from the official curriculum at school; introducing new religious schools; and implementing further initiatives based on this objective as well as playing by his own terms.

During the reopening ceremony of Hagia Sophia, Erdoğan recited the Surah al-Fatiha from the Quran which means 'the opening', to mark his 'New Turkey'.

He framed his decision from a wider point of view which embraces his Palestine cause and ambition of reaching out to the Muslim world:

> Today, Hagia Sophia is having another resurrection, many of which it has witnessed since its construction. The resurrection of Hagia Sophia heralds the liberation of the al-Aqsa Mosque. The resurrection of Hagia Sophia is the footsteps of the will of Muslims across the world to come out of the interregnum. The resurrection of Hagia Sophia is the reignition of the fire of hope of not just Muslims, but – together with them – of all the oppressed, wronged, downtrodden and exploited.[75]

Obviously, just as Atatürk's decision to turn Hagia Sophia to a museum was a result of his authoritarian one-man policies, similarly, after eighty-six years, so has Erdoğan's act followed the same path using the same tools. However, both decisions are based on revenge – acts that will never provide a healthy environment for upcoming generations to discuss politics and religion in the years to come.

Despite these steps, when Erdoğan visited Egypt immediately after the Egyptian revolution in 2011, he recommended that the MB follow a secularist line, which caused the MB members to react solemnly. This exemplified his pragmatic side, or for some, *taqiyyah*,[76] as it was analysed for a long period of time, as AC5 underlines.

PO4 analyses the use of religion as a political communication tool, viewing it as a commonplace practice in politics. When there is a shared base and common identity among an audience in terms of religious affairs and values, it is logical 'to use this opportunity':

> If you see a benefit you can reference religious things. This is also mentioned in the Quran. Erdoğan is not addressing everybody. He is focusing on the members of his audience who believe this. He is not saying anything to those who do not believe him.

Certainly this approach contributes an element of othering to society, also clarifying how interpretations of religion, despite not being able to cite a specific verse from the Quran, can be easily legitimized.

Populist Islamist discourse after the Egyptian coup

TT2 has a different reading of the process than PO4. He claims that Erdoğan's discourse, and that of the AKP's Communications Team, relates to the demands of society. While the need in 2002 was to address issues related to economy and development because of the economic crisis in 2001, after the AKP's economic success and prosperity, the demands imposed on it by society started changing. Hence Erdoğan started to include references to religion to fulfil a sociological and psychological need within Turkish society. TT2 adds that while a lack of self-confidence led Erdoğan to avoid using religious vocabulary in the early days, over time, and after losing faith in the West, he altered his narrative:

> In particular after the military coup in Egypt in 2013, Erdoğan's discourse became more Islamized. Erdoğan saw clearly that Western countries are not sincere in their support of the Islamic World's democratization process. He considered the coup d'état in Egypt as a threat to himself.

According to the interviews conducted with TT2, JO2 and Ünal, Erdoğan's reactions to domestic and international issues started changing after the West's reaction to the military coup in Egypt in 2013 as well as the Gezi Park protests in Turkey in the same year. TT2 states that neither of the events was condemned by Western capitals properly, or in a timely manner, which 'aroused Erdoğan's suspicion' of the West. What these suspicions are is unclear, but he did cite a biased attitude in terms of the case of the EU. After the Egyptian coup, Erdoğan perhaps began to suspect that a similar coup might happen in Turkey, according to JO2. The above interviewees (TT2, JO2 and Ünal) all agreed that the 'West's main problem with Erdoğan has been what it characterizes as his so-called Islamist ideology', which it suggests developed after the above-mentioned events took place. Nonetheless, the evidence presented clearly indicates that mutual interactions between Erdoğan and the West led both to profoundly revise their political messages.

A closer examination of the data indicates that Erdoğan's primary aim when his party was first elected as the main party in 2002 was to focus on the economy and its development in order to strengthen Turkey's image internally and globally. At this time, Erdoğan never associated himself with an Islamist ideology, message or discourse. As a result, he was viewed as a moderate in his religious affairs, and was characterized as pursuing a liberal approach, supporting the free market and advocating political democracy. Consequently, reversing the headscarf ban in universities and Imam Hatip schools was not on the agenda of the self-governing party in the first period. In other words, the development process enabled the AKP to realize a 'silent revolution' in Turkey, according to AC2, which influenced Erdoğan's discourse and the party's communication.

There is little doubt that the development process meant the AKP could control every institution in Turkey, which led Erdoğan to become more self-confident as a leader. In fact, not only the crisis at the World Economy Forum and his support of the civil initiative Mavi Marmara, but also the coup d'état in 2016 reflected his growing self-assurance. The majority of my interviewees from the domains of politics, media, academia and government think tanks and research centres opine that these events repositioned Turkey in the region, as Turkey distanced 'itself from Israel with a turn on Islamist agenda'.[77] The available evidence seems to suggest that Erdoğan's authoritarian style of governance developed from self-confidence, which grew after he became the president in 2014. It is the same period when of the rise of populist leaders across the world increased its dominance.

The results of the in-depth interviews provide confirmatory evidence of the use of religion as a key political communication tool: the majority of the interviewees were of the impression that it was in 2009/2010 that change occurred. In fact, the identity crisis, de-institutionalization and a control mechanism as well as the elimination of opposition voices enabled Erdoğan to create his own style of discourse, which had a moderate and secular tone in the early days but evolved to a rigid, more religious nationalist populism over time. According to PO1, the 'successful management of international political communication' led the AKP to negotiate to a large extent with the EU in the early days. Notwithstanding, AKP-affiliated interviewees (composed of high-profile AKP ministers and party officials) agreed that subsequent actions by the West, in particular the stance of the EU towards the AKP's governance, influenced Erdoğan to develop a reactive stance. JO2 notes that in 80 per cent of the cases, the AKP is reactionary. Furthermore, featuring religious values and referencing them is seen as a reflection of his Islamist ideology, which he uses as a populist tool to win the support of his base on the one hand, and change old Turkey's laïcité habits on the other. In fact, he integrates religious nationalist populism into a secular framework.

5

Communicating religion

Power is the most fundamental process in society, since society is defined around values and institutions, and what is valued and institutionalized is defined by power relationships. Power is the relational capacity that enables a social actor to influence asymmetrically the decisions of other social actor(s) in ways that favor the empowered actor's will, interests, and values.

– Castells[1]

The year 2014 was a critical turning point in Turkey's history as it was the first time that a president could directly be elected by the people. Turkish diaspora were permitted to vote in these elections for the first time by visiting Turkish consulates in their place of residence. This enabled the AKP to mobilize sympathizers across geographical borders, particularly in Europe, to expand its influence. Similarly, it was a historical moment for Erdoğan as he reached the peak of his political career by becoming Turkey's first directly elected president who would later change the constitution and become the strongest politician in modern Turkey by abolishing the position of prime ministry. Being both the founding chairman of the AKP and prime minister since 2003, Erdoğan's election to the presidency represents the apex of his achievements to date.

By witnessing these critical turning points in Turkish history, and viewing the presidential election period and its aftermath through the lens of non-participant observation, my intention is to provide an ethnographic insight into the AKP and its leader. Investigating the realities behind the ascendancy of one of the most criticized leaders in the mainstream media since the Gezi Park protests in 2013 required a comprehensive appreciation of the AKP's extensive communications network. Cognizant of Erdoğan's increasingly authoritarian policies, this chapter envisions how religion is used as a communication tool, and how Americanization informs the discussions that took place when drawing up the party's political communication strategies. As a result, the shift to candidate-centred campaigning by personalizing Erdoğan's public image and emphasizing his charismatic leadership style and appeal as a man of the people will form a significant focal point of this work. The perceptions of activists working at the AKP headquarters, voluntary members on the ground, Erdoğan's Communications Team, Strategy Team, the AKP's Publicity and Media Department, Youth Branch as well as Erdoğan's current and former advisors will prove to be significant resources for conducting a healthy analysis of the communications perspective.

Direct or face-to-face communication remains one of the most effective modes of political communication for Erdoğan. Organizing outdoor election campaigns, in which a party sets up a stand at a well-known central point, and rallies in different cities and districts are influential ways to achieve direct communication in Turkey. From East to West, and from North to South, every rally provokes a different dynamic response that reflects the specific local political atmosphere.

Mobilizing religious conservatives at mosques

The use of election booths is a long-held tradition in Turkey. Each political party installs booths in significant and populated city districts throughout the country, and campaigns from these venues for the forty-five days running up to the election. The use of booths cannot be classified as an example of the Americanization of political communication, because in the United States, gatherings take place principally in indoor halls and in front of small groups of people, with parties attracting attendees via the Internet and social media. Nevertheless, it is still an important communication tool, renowned for its effectiveness in Middle Eastern countries and societies like Lebanon and Egypt, where I personally witnessed this method being used during the 2012 presidential election campaign in Cairo when the 'Arab street' was mobilized.

During my research, I observed outdoor campaigns conducted by the AKP, visiting three election booths in Istanbul's Eyüpsultan, Fatih and Üsküdar districts. These three districts have the highest percentage of religious conservative individuals in the population, and can be considered AKP hubs that provide key resources and support to the party. In Eyüpsultan district, the election booth was located next to the Eyüp Sultan Mosque, where Ayyub Al-Ansari's tomb is located. Al-Ansari, a companion of Prophet Muhammad, is one of the religious figures associated with the history of Istanbul. He fought during the second siege of Constantinople in 669 CE and died during this battle. Hence, the Eyüp Sultan Mosque is one of the most popular places for tourists and locals to visit at weekends in particular; people come to pray in the mosque and visit the tomb of Al-Ansar, a traditional mode of burial in the Ottoman tradition, which is located inside the mosque yard. The AKP located its campaign booths close to mosques where the conservative community spends much of their time. Doing so enabled the party to draw on the notion that it is part of a social movement, emphasizing that it prioritizes developing Turkey's collective identity. Although the AKP is not an Islamist movement, unlike the MB in Egypt, many of the AKP's members are former supporters of Erbakan's movement, and as such are personally religiously oriented like Erdoğan. This explains their relationship with mosques and holy places, such as tombs or historic buildings inherited from the Ottoman era. Notably the AKP uses its background as a social movement to influence people and their collective identity. It is important to note here that the role of a social movement is to act in a manner that is conscious, collective and well-organized, as that is the impression given by the election booths run by the AKP.

The AKP's strategy is also intergenerational: while middle-aged party representatives and volunteers were handing out leaflets and flyers, and campaigning with banners and large screens in Eyüpsultan, younger party members were recording interactions on the streets and conducting short interviews to boost their social media presence. The majority of the representatives of the AKP were noted to be religious in appearance – men sported beards and women wore headscarves. Despite the religious attire of the women representatives, they were still observing stylish trends, such as wearing colourful headscarves, using heavy makeup and carrying kitsch handbags. Unveiled women also participated, but they were dressed more modestly, with clothes that covered their arms and in long skirts. Having representatives displaying different levels of adherence to religious customs conveys an impression of 'diversity and openness', as one of the organizers explained. It was nevertheless apparent that the definition 'conservative democratic' was visible in the party's image. In Turkey, political parties do not prefer to use religious motifs in their official booths or materials because of the separation of religion and state in the Turkish Republic's constitution. However when visiting the AKP's booths, their location and the external appearance of the local party representatives make it clear that the party appeals to religious conservative people in the first place.

The election booth in Fatih, another conservative district where thousands of Syrian refugees are based and where the streets have many shops, cafes and restaurants with Arabic signages, was also located beside a famous mosque, the

Fatih Mosque, which was constructed after the conquer of Istanbul. Free tea was offered to those who had finished their prayers as they left the mosque while the AKP representatives explained their projects and goals to those who were interested. Most of the questions asked by voters related to the presidential system itself, as this created a dilemma for the potential voters with whom I spoke. One of the main promises by Erdoğan in 2014 was that he would aim to increase the executive power of the presidential office, implemented with 2017 referendum, with the aim of more economic investment and political development.

On some occasions I witnessed MPs visiting the election booths to speak with visitors. Some of the visitors took selfies with the MPs to share on social media. Some MPs also asked their advisors to take pictures while they were speaking to the people so that these can be shared on various media. When I asked one of the advisors why the AKP members used social media to share every single activity, he replied that it is important for them to show Erdoğan and the party officials how hard they work, as this is a way to display loyalty and earn credibility. One member of the AKP's social media team explained that every single MP is required to have a social media account, in particular Twitter and Facebook, and a presence online. She explained that social media is an important tool that enables the party to interact directly with the public. When I conducted interviews in 2019 and 2020, I recognized that Instagram was added to the 'to do list' of MPs and AKP officials to reach out to generation Z. Digital communication is an important tool of political communication which expands its impact every single day. Ministers, MPs, party officials and advisors use their social media platforms effectively as their main propaganda tool. It is the norm today to be on digital platforms. In fact, with the objective of removing prejudices against them, even the MB was engaged in digital activism in their dialogue with the West until the military coup in Egypt in 2013.[2] The use of digital media by the AKP members is based on the same principle, but is directed towards a domestic audience rather than a foreign one. Yet the communications director or chief advisors of Erdoğan use digital platforms in English and occasionally other languages such as Arabic when it comes to themes related to the Arabic-speaking world, or in French and German when political developments with the related countries are on the agenda. 'Their use of social media is not just election based', says the same source, but rather a long-term goal. She underlines that the use of social media is important from a psychological point of view: 'The more we tweet, the more control we have.' However, the yardstick for the AKP social media team is to increase the sharing, not the impact it has on the followers online. According to the pro-AKP think tank chairman TT1, their use of social media is not reaching the younger generation in an impactful way. 'Young people, in particular the generation Z, are keen to live on the edge; hence whatever the AKP is offering, it does not have an impact on them', he says.

Many Erdoğan flags, banners and posters were displayed at the election booths in Istanbul. The presidential election and candidate-centred campaign was nearing its peak at this time. It was the first political communications feature that appeared to imitate the American style of campaigning as it was a presidential campaign and electorates were allowed to choose the president directly for the first time. I asked one of the volunteers at the booth in Istanbul's Fatih district why the leader was in the foreground in all communications rather than the projects and policies he was promising to enact. I was prompted to do so because the printed materials and conversations at the AKP's booth concentrated on messages relating to Erdoğan personally and to the proper leadership of Turkey. I was told that people want to see Erdoğan, because they associate 'confidence' with him. This suggests that traditional ties between voters and parties, which are usually effective, are weakening in Turkey in favour of interest in personalities. However, the same strategy had a negative impact in the 2019 local elections because, according to JO5, people were more interested in the local initiatives of all parties rather than seeing their leaders on billboards. Association of 'confidence' with the leader has not helped the AKP as Erdoğan was not only seen on billboards, newspapers, TV and digital media advertisements, but he was also present in rallies across the country, and particularly in Istanbul, as noted earlier.

The AKP's election booth in Üsküdar was not only positioned centrally, at one of the main transit centres of buses, metros and ferry, but also situated next to two historic mosques, Mihrimah Sultan Mosque and Yeni Valide Mosque. As it was a central location, the main opposition parties were also present. From a professional perspective, the AKP stood out from other parties as it had larger screens and a modern vehicle instead of a traditional booth stand. The impression created by the party of 'active use of public space', drawing on the 'art of presence', consolidated the image that the AKP's was the leading campaign.[3] Financial sources of the AKP were another reality that build this image and differentiated itself from opposition parties.

Dawah as a source of motivation

When I asked a 68-year old woman about her motivation for becoming involved in the campaign, and why she was working to convince her peers to support the ruling party, she summarized in an interesting sentence: 'For the sake of

God.' This was not the first response of this type I received while talking to party officials and volunteers. This is an important indicator that people who are religiously adherent are attracted by the collective identity of the party. These individuals are mostly volunteers, working at the bottom of the party hierarchy, and, as this research figures out, religion is the main factor motivating their involvement on behalf of the party. This situation differs from that during the 2002 and 2007 elections, as one of AKP's Üsküdar branch members emphasizes:

> Erdoğan's emphasis on Islam, in particular his Middle East politics after the Mavi Marmara flotilla, was a turning point, encouraging me to support the AKP. Personally I think that being involved in AKP is a must because it is a *dawah*.

The word *dawah* is best described as 'the act of inviting a person to the faith'[4] – a term from Erbakan's ideological tradition that is used to describe political parties in this manner. Specifically, in the early days of the Milli Görüş, Mehmed Zahid Kotku, an Islamic scholar, advised Erbakan and his friends to found a party in the end of 1960s to 'protect' society to retain the 'core identity and character of Islam' as the 'main heritage of Islam and Muslims'.[5] Hence Erbakan's entry into politics was based on an indirect description of *dawah*, intended to restore the Ottoman-Islamic identity. The understanding expressed above is that the party defends Islamic ideology at a discoursive level. Furthermore, as discussed in the previous chapter, it suggests an evolution has taken place in the party politics and in the message that the AKP is trying to convey. When asked what he understands by the word *dawah*, the informant replies as follows:

> I was a staunch supporter of Erbakan *hoca*.[6] His Milli Görüş ideology taught us that we need to stand for something, otherwise the world is meaningless. We need to find a solution for injustice, oppression, and spread peace. This is called *dawah* for me as Erbakan *hoca* taught us.

It is clear that motivating party members through the use of religious ideology is one of the strategies used by Erdoğan to consolidate his supporter base around a common identity so as to strengthen his position as well as gain success. It is a method he has adopted from his political master, Erbakan.

The voice of the oppressed

The AKP organized a presidential election rally in Aydın that drew massive attendance. This was despite the fact that the majority of Turkey's cities that are located in the Aegean Region of western Turkey are thought to be more secular, with CHP's influence and success rate being higher than that of the AKP here. The euphoria started from the moment the AKP's presidential election song was played. The song hails Erdoğan, his politics and his mode of leadership:

> He is the voice of the oppressed,
> He is the voice of the silent world,
> He is the one, who is what he believes,
> He is the one, who gets his support from his people,
> Recep Tayyip Erdoğan, Recep Tayyip Erdoğan.

During the riotous song, people murmured along, suggesting most had memorized it; either because they liked it as it was a catchy, appealing emotional or because it was being continuously played everywhere: namely on the TV, radio, social media, on the streets broadcast by campaign cars and the like. In the 2018 and 2019 local elections, this song was used in some AKP rallies across Istanbul which demonstrates that a better song could not be composed since 2014. The lyrics communicate their message by summarizing perceptions of Erdoğan through the eyes of his supporters. He is seen as a hero and the voice of the voiceless, creating the sentiment that 'he is the last beacon of hope for Muslims', as one of the participants told me when I asked what Erdoğan means to her. She explains it is necessary for the Muslim world to have a leader like Erdoğan because 'the world is approaching a dead-end regarding injustice':

> He is the only leader who raises his voice against injustice and oppression in Palestine, Iraq and Afghanistan.

Many religious conservatives in Turkey consider the situations in Syria, Palestinian territories, Iraq and Afghanistan collectively, and also keep them in their prayers. Yet PO6 highlights that the same Erdoğan who says 'the world is bigger than five' – when he talks about the injustice of the international system, or about the status of Palestinian territory – has neither done anything about long-term investments to the people of Gaza that are needed to build job opportunities and to help them economically nor change the Israel-Palestine narrative in the media or academia. 'Erdoğan's approach towards the Muslim world is mainly based on rhetoric. Except humanitarian aid, Turkey does not do much', she underlines. In other words, Erdoğan uses the Palestine course in his communication to show that the AKP is one up on the opposition parties who do not have this issue on their party agenda.

Returning to Erdoğan's song, the messages it espouses strengthen the impact of the party's communications. As in Americanized media campaigns, the lyrics place the personal image of the political leader in the foreground rather than the corporate image of the party. When Erdoğan's presenter announced Erdoğan on stage with an excited, enthusiastic and strong voice at the Malatya rally, the audience began shouting slogans such as 'the leader, the commander' and started chanting Erdoğan's name, 'Recep Tayyip Erdoğan', rhythmically. When Erdoğan stepped on stage, I observed some people crying, showing great emotion and loyalty to their leader. Erdoğan is seen by his supporters as pious, humble and modest, which increases his popularity, as one participant summarizes: 'He is one of us.' What makes Erdoğan different from other political figures in Turkey is that he is an average person, someone from a religious conservative working-class family. His outfit on stage was modest; black trousers and a white shirt, with no jacket or tie. This modesty is symbolic and important to voters. In fact, in the summer of 2015, after the June 2015 elections when former prime minister Ahmet Davutoğlu was running for prime minister, as one of his advisors recollects, it was impossible to convince Davutoğlu to take off his cufflinks for speeches, despite telling him that wearing them 'created a wall between the leader and the public' as they are not usually worn by working middle-class people in Turkey.

Spouse as part of communication

An obvious candidate-centred election strategy at all rallies was the appearance of Erdoğan's wife. When Erdoğan arrived on stage, he would appear with his wife, Emine Erdoğan, who would also greet and wave to the crowd. Likewise, when he finished his speech, his wife joined him on stage for a final ceremonious waving of hands. This strategy portrays the leader as a family man and is one commonly used in American-style campaigns. Sometimes, at the end of a rally, Erdoğan and his wife would throw flowers, usually white, and T-shirts bearing Erdoğan's presidential logo to the crowds. When I asked a member of AKP's Publicity and Media Department about the meaning of the T-shirts later, he explained that people attach importance to gifts from political leaders, and they will cherished as souvenirs. According to my source, the gesture of using flowers of a particular colour carries a specific message: for example, white flowers as a symbol of 'peace', and red flowers as one of 'love'. In this manner, even the election gift symbolizes personalization of the AKP's political communication. My anonymous source explains that it is not uncommon in Turkish politics for the wife of a politician to appear on stage. This was also highlighted by other members of the Communications Team. During our interview, while discussing the Americanization process of the AKP, one of the examples my source gave was that of family portrayal: family, personal appearance, private lifestyle and religion are more important in the personalization of political communication. The desire to show a personal side to Erdoğan is also one reason the mass media close to the AKP and its social media trolls generate PR opportunities based on Erdoğan's personal life. As one committed PR expert for the Publicity and Media Department explains:

> Nowadays people are more focused on the personal lives of other people, but more importantly, that of politicians. People do not feel themselves affiliated to a party but to a person. As we have observed this for a long time, we have started using our voluntary supporters on the ground to share details about Erdoğan on social media. These can include recitations of the Quran in mosques, or visits to a martyr's family, or an emotional moment when he is attending a special event.

As a result, amateur videos recorded by Erdoğan's advisors, ministers or MPs, in particular those with religious motives, can be frequently found on AKP's social media and WhatsApp groups, which have a wide reach in Turkey. This reflects Erdoğan's personal side and presents him as someone with a strong faith. It is an 'impressive way of communication' especially when appealing to the conservative roots of the AKP, as the PR expert revealed. From a propaganda perspective, this type of action can help persuade people and integrate them with the party, as they share the same conservative concerns. In addition, this method of communication makes people feel like Erdoğan is 'one of them'. In this regard, one of Erdoğan's advisors recalled that when on a trip during Ramadan he had witnessed Erdoğan reading the Quran with his family members in the private cabin of the plane as well as fasting despite the long journey. When the advisor excitedly relayed this story, he emphasized that he had never seen a person as committed to religion as Erdoğan is. Similarly, in 2020, during the month of Ramadan when the country was facing the COVID-19 pandemic, one of Erdoğan's advisors tweeted a video footage of Erdoğan reading the Quran with his advisors at one of the presidential mansions in Istanbul while managing the crisis.[7] Both stories show that in addition to the impression that people have of Erdoğan as a person, his actions also fascinate those around him, motivating them to support the 'most important man' in the world, as the young UK-educated advisor states. He notes that it is an honour to serve Erdoğan. During my fieldwork at the AKP headquarters, I heard similar stories through the grapevine. It is not difficult to imagine these anecdotes reaching the public and influential members on the ground. For example, I met a 41-year old taxi driver who voted for Erdoğan because of his 'personality, religious ideology and political stance against the establishment'. This shows that the personalization of the AKP's political communication has a considerable influence in terms of attracting middle-class voters in the 40–45 plus age group.

Observations from Erdoğan's rallies

After the Konya rally, one of the organizers explained that other parties had begun organizing outdoor election rallies because of the impact Erdoğan has in these events. Had the AKP not organized such 'massive rallies', the opposition parties would have conducted theirs indoors with fewer attendees 'as in most European countries'. However, Erdoğan's popularity flourishes after these rallies, because he is skilled at communicating directly, just as former US president Barack Obama in 2008 and 2012 US elections, and later Trump in 2016 US election proved to be during their campaigns. However, the difference between the US presidents and Erdoğan is that the former use mainly digital media, whereas the latter prefers one-to-one communication on the ground. Erdoğan's advisor told me that during a meeting with German Chancellor Angela Merkel in Germany, Merkel asked Erdoğan how he managed to bring more than one million people together for a rally, as it would be impossible in Germany. Erdoğan's advisor does not say what the reply was, but explains with great enthusiasm that even 'foreign leaders are impressed by Erdoğan's communication'. According to this passionate advisor, no other leader would be able to bring such a crowd together, regardless of pouring rain or scorching heat. During the rallies in Turkey, I have personally witnessed people participating enthusiastically despite the searing weather conditions. Undoubtedly, Erdoğan's charismatic leadership style makes a strong impression among the religious conservative middle-class grassroots. When I spoke informally with attendees at rallies and events, and with AKP supporters on the streets of Istanbul, Ankara, Malatya, Konya and Aydın, I learnt that the majority are proud to have such a leader. For them, strong leadership had been lacking in Turkey for too long, and, as a middle-aged Anatolian man[8] in Konya explains, it is the first time the conservative majority feel as if they are a part of the society. Not only in the 2014 election but also during the 2007 general election campaign, Erdoğan's character and his public appearance played a key role in achieving success. However the economic and social problems of people at that time were foregrounded in Erdoğan's campaigns. This was an aspect that distinguished his earlier election campaigns from the more recent ones in which his personal charisma dominated rather than projects and policies. Erdoğan's impact in the 2019 local elections seemed to have diminished when compared to that in the 2014 elections, according to PO5, because the currency and debt crisis in 2018, which 'affected millions of people directly', played a far more significant role on the outcome, particularly in larger cities.

Poetry as a means of Erdoğan's Islamist communication

In one of his speeches, Erdoğan recited the lyrics of the Turkish singer Aşkın Tuna's poem 'We Walked Together', which has been known as 'Erdoğan's song' since he was jailed in 1999:

> Memories wrapped up all around me,
> Wherever I look it has your imprint,
> Everything reminds me of you,
> We walked together on this road.
> Together we got wet from the falling rain,
> Now all the songs I'm listening,
> Everything reminds me of you.

Thousands of supporters gathered outside the prison in Istanbul and escorted Erdoğan, and when he arrived there he quoted the above lyrics together with the crowd. This song signifies that he considers his path to be an extraordinary one. As 'collectiveness' is a key theme of social movement theory, it is important to note that a crowd singing a song in unison symbolizes togetherness and stands for the collective action of the party, as the lyrics bring people under the same umbrella.

Poetry has held a special meaning for Erdoğan since his youth because of his fascination with Turkish poets who embrace Islamist ideologies, as elaborated in the previous chapter. For this reason, Erdoğan has read poems and songs from these two poets frequently during rallies or large gatherings. He told the *New York Times* in 2003 that he uses poems as an 'attention-getter to make the people spirited'.[9] This is also something Hezbollah's Hasan Nasrallah does. Nasrallah recites the work of Palestinian poets in order to motivate his supporters in their resistance against Israel. Some of these poems have even been made into songs and video clips portraying images of Nasrallah and other historic Shiite figures. According to my source at the AKP headquarters, the poetry excerpts from Erdoğan's rallies are used to prepare short video clips which are then shared on Twitter, Instagram and YouTube in particular, as well as on WhatsApp, though not professionally, in order to raise awareness through amateur, guerrilla-style campaigning.

Erdoğan's logo versus Obama's logo

In addition to Erdoğan's election song, his election logo has played an important role in representing an image. As the significance of the role of religion in political communications is one of the focal points, it is important to cover occurrences of the use of religion as a political communication tool. When Erdoğan's logo was first announced, Turkish newspapers enthusiastically discussed it, likening it to Obama's 2008 campaign logo. However, later, the former minister of finance Mehmet Şimşek clarified from his private Twitter account that Prophet Muhammad's name was included in Erdoğan's logo in Arabic calligraphic style. An official announcement from either the AKP or Erdoğan's office was never made regarding the logo. However, the logo did appear to be an example of the use of religion as a symbol in the art of Islamic calligraphy. Meanwhile it was also a clear example of Americanization guiding the AKP's political communication strategy, because it was designed to focus on the candidate directly as the central actor in the election campaign. To that end, it reflects Erdoğan's personal characteristics and personal life, including his Islamist ideology. During my fieldwork, when I asked about reactions to the logo, I learnt that most people were unaware that the name of the Prophet Muhammad was included in calligraphy form. When I consulted Erdoğan's Communications Team regarding what motivated them to allude to a religious figure in the logo, a high-ranking member of the Strategy Team denied the use of the word Muhammad and claimed that the logo depicts 'a route to the sun, in other words to the future'. Erdoğan used the same logo in 2018 presidential elections and in the rallies, he attended in 2019 local elections.

AKP's name and logo adapted from Morocco's Islamist party

JO7 emphasizes during our interview in a pretentious cafe in Bebek where we overlooked the 'Erdogan mosque', which was built for $100 million, that AKP adapted its logo and name from Morocco's PJD, 'a clear sign that the founding members of the party were closely analyzing other parties before they found the AKP', she underlines. Although there were some news articles that talked about how the AKP imitated PJD's logo and name, official comments were not made. The PJD's gas lamp as a symbol was replaced with a bulb in the AKP's logo, a modern interpretation of gas lamp – in other words a new perspective of Islamism. The words 'justice' and 'development' were modelled after those

Communicating Religion

Figure 2 Erdoğan's logo.

Figure 3 Former US president Barack Obama's logo.

in the PJD's logo. In 2001's Turkey, it was necessary to build a party on the principles of justice and development, because justice was at stake regarding human rights violations against religious conservative milieu and development was urgently needed to combat the banking crisis of 2000–1.

Figure 4 Morocco's Justice and Development Party's (PJD) logo.

Erdoğan's pragmatist rhetoric

When Erdoğan began his speech in Malatya by commemorating Battal Gazi,[10] Hamido[11] and Turgut Özal,[12] the crowd responded with cheers, because these three important figures were from Malatya. Erdoğan used his speech in Malatya to celebrate these personalities which motivated the people of the city to vote for him. As a member of the Strategy Team noted, in this way, Erdoğan used loyalty to these symbolic figures to win the hearts of supporters, regardless of their ideological background. Significantly, he was also making a reference to the imprint of the Ottoman Empire, drawing on a sense of collective national identity to unite a 'set of beliefs, symbols, and values'.[13] Battal Gazi is a mythical Muslim from the Umayyad whose family ties date to the time of Prophet Muhammad, while Hamido, whose official name was Hamit Fendoğlu, was a Turkish politician and mayor of Malatya.

Figure 5 Turkey's Justice and Development Party's (AKP) logo.

Speaking about Turkey's more recent history, Erdoğan recalls Turgut Özal, who was responsible for employing a liberal economic model and opening up Turkey to the competitive market. By singling out these individuals, Erdoğan positions himself as one of them – a former victim who overcame the elite, on the one hand, and terrorist organizations, such as the PKK and the Gülenists, on the other.

Religious symbols in campaign commercials

Another important example of Erdoğan referencing symbolism was his mention of the AKP's 2014 presidential election commercial. Erdoğan asked the public if they had already seen the new commercial for the AKP. The crowd answered with a decisive 'yes'. This led him to attack the MHP who had filed a petition with the Supreme Electoral Council to ban it. Erdoğan underlined that the reason for this ban was the inclusion of the *azan*,[14] a prayer rug and an Anatolian woman:[15]

> This commercial continues without the azan. However, nobody can prevent the call to prayer in our land.[16]

Upon hearing his words, the crowd booed the MHP. The AKP's presidential candidate went on to link this ban with that of the CHP, the main opposition party, on the call to prayer in Arabic between 1932 and 1950.[17]

> They have banned the call to prayer in Arabic; they have destroyed mosques; they feared to teach the Quran; and they were worried about the headscarf.[18]

Here, Erdoğan listed religious symbols in a portrayal of the 'old Turkey'. The call to prayer, the mosque, the Quran and headscarves are more important to people in Malatya than they are to those in Aydın because of the region's demographic structure.

Yet AKP's relationship with other parties has changed since the first day of its governance. Depending on political circumstances, Erdoğan acts pragmatically. In the post-coup attempt in 2016, he started a new journey with the ultra-nationalist MHP as both ideologies reached a consensus in changing the constitution and introducing a new presidential system. This honeymoon continued in the 2018 presidential elections as well as in the 2019 local elections. According to Faruk Acar, chairman of Andy-Ar research, it could have been difficult for the AKP to win without MHP's support.[19] PO5 underlines that although the support of MHP was decisive in the 2018 and 2019 local elections, this alliance has played a key role in influencing AKP's discourse and political ideology. There is a high possibility that Erdoğan reaches out to the other nationalist party in the parliament, IYI Parti, in the near future to guarantee the majority in the parliament. Erdoğan has adopted a nationalist populist discourse after 2016 coup attempt which had expanded during the 2018 presidential and 2019 local elections. His messages of unity were not only present in his speeches but in the way he greeted the crowds. Erdoğan used *Rabaa* hand gesture, adopted from the MB who used it as a sign of anti-military awareness during the 2014 military crackdown, reinterpreting it to express the sentiment of 'one homeland, one state, one flag and one nation'.

Similarly, during his speech, Erdoğan raised the Palestinian cause in connection with Gülenists' leader Fethullah Gülen. He underlined that Gülen is not empowered to raise his voice against Israel's crime in Gaza, claiming that '[i]f he says something, his lords will be disturbed'.[20] Oppressed Palestinians are a sensitive subject for conservative people such as the inhabitants of Malatya. Therefore, Erdoğan presented the Gülenists as a pro-Israel organization in order to raise awareness that they are not a religious and spiritual movement as they typically portray themselves. Erdoğan draws on religious motifs here to show awareness of how they dominate political and symbolic life. When the Mavi Marmara aid ship flotilla was attacked in 2010, the self-exiled Gülen, who was once a prominent preacher in Izmir, Turkey, gave an interview to the *Wall Street Journal* in June 2010, stating that the organizers of the flotilla should have expressly requested permission from Israel before delivering aid.[21] As the attack happened in international waters, this reaction by Gülen sparked a debate in Turkey. This meant that later, when the Gülenists and AKP became foes, Erdoğan alluded to the events to suggest that Gülen has no religious sensitivity and is following a 'secret agenda'.

The above-mentioned dispute between the AKP and the Gülenists was not the first. Mavi Marmara had been a critical turning point for both organizations as until then they had always had a reasonable relationship. Gülen had mobilized his support base to Erdoğan's advantage, in particular human resources such as the judiciary , the police, and the academia; this had enabled the AKP to change the political landscape in Turkey swiftly. However, during the Gezi Park protests in 2013, the Gülenists' supported the uprising against the government and started openly issuing anti-AKP propaganda via their media channels. They suggested that Erdoğan's political decisions in 2012 and 2013 had sparked the Gezi Park protests, fuelling an anti-AKP reaction. Some of these decisions – including naming Istanbul's third bridge after Ottoman sultan Yavuz Sultan Selim, removing the Atatürk Culture Centre at Taksim Square, restricting alcohol use, banning abortion and building Turkey's largest mosque in Istanbul , and later when turning the Hagia Sophia to a mosque, in other words taking revenge of Atatürk's secularization policies – were cited as threats to symbolic cultural codes of modern secular lifestyle. Undoubtedly, the fact that Gezi was indeed a reaction to these political decisions sharpened Erdoğan's rhetoric on the campaign trail not just in 2014, but also in his speeches when he talked about freedom of speech or protection of environment.

AKP's identity dilemma

As in the city of Malatya, Erdoğan received a rousing welcome at the Ankara rally. He described Ankara as the capital of the oppressed people of the world – the seat of peace, brotherhood, justice and solidarity.

> I greet youths from Afghanistan to Algeria, from Azerbaijan to Sudan, who have come to Ankara for the presidential elections.[22]

Although greeting the youth does not correspond much on the ground, it summarizes the significance of embracing a common political ideology and expresses shared interests with the mentioned lands. After this greeting, Erdoğan listed the following figures: Haji Bektashi Veli,[23] Seyyid Hüseyin Gazi,[24] Abdulhakim Arvasi,[25] Bünyamin Ayasi,[26] Sheikh Ali Semerkandi,[27] and Taceddin-i Veli[28] as well as the founder of modern Turkey, Mustafa Kemal Atatürk. He also spoke of Mehmet Akif Ersoy. These individuals, while unrelated, convey a message of kinship to both Alevis and Sunnis – an approach used for the first time by a Turkish leader, according to my anonymous source from Erdoğan's Communications Team. It is a way of accepting and respecting important personalities from the same soil despite ideological differences – an intention declared in Erdoğan's manifesto. Erdoğan's style, which was apparent at other rallies too, is to emphasize key images that play a significant role in representation. This also is a means to reflect collective identity, which Erdoğan is aiming to create and keep alive.

In Ankara, Erdoğan communicated his message by referring to tradition, identity and ethnicity, and encouraged people coming together to overcome differences. However, this stance highlights an identity dilemma within the ruling party. The AKP's lack of institutionalization was criticized by some interviewees, such as JO1, who mentioned the need for a solid identity to emerge in preparation for a post-Erdoğan AKP. Although it might be suggested that a sense of shared collective identity helps a leader activate a large share of the electorate, according to JO2, combining religious figures with non-religious ones is nothing more than 'vote chasing':

> This type of approach seems positive at first glance. But after a while, meaning in the long-term, it damages many things, not only the identity but also the socio-psychological perspective of future generations.

Yet the electoral behaviour of young people who were born to conservative families summarizes this reality because the majority, according to AKP politician PO5, had no chance to experience other politicians or parties. 'The expectations have changed with the new generation over time, but we are not able to deliver what they want. Also if we were to talk about new job opportunities for young graduates, we will not be able to convince them because their main intention is for Erdoğan and the AKP to leave the office.' Certainly this approach is questionable, but what is more important is for priority to be given to justice, freedom of speech and human rights as these lead to economic growth and political development.

Erdoğan's popularity in the 'Muslim world'

Compared to attendees in Malatya, the participants at the Ankara rally were notably more cosmopolitan. A young man from Bosnia-Herzegovina who attended the rally expressed his pride at being able to see Erdoğan live. When I asked him why he is so pleased to be there, he explained that it was due to Turkey's support for Bosnia during and since the war that took place from 1992 to 1995:

> When someone asked my grandparents which religion they belong to, they used to say 'We are Turks'. In other words, being a Turk was the equivalent of being a Muslim ... Hence our relationship goes back to the Ottoman era. Since Erdoğan's second term, the AKP government has invested in Bosnia in order to develop our country. Hence, I have an emotional relationship to Erdoğan and the AKP.

Indeed, grassroots activism aligned with the concept of a social movement plays an important role in the AKP's appeal to non-Turkish Muslims from other countries. In this manner, common interest translates to common identity within the frame of the 'Muslim world'. Erdoğan's neo-Ottoman side will become more apparent when discussing the Konya rally during which he refers to Alija Izetbegovic's[29] (1925–2003) son Bakir Izetbegovic (1956–), former president of Bosnia and Herzegovina and president of the Party of Democratic Action (SDA) who delivers unity messages. As mentioned by my source above, the emotional relationship between Turkish and Bosnian people dates back to the Bosnian War in 1992 when millions of Bosnians suffered and Turkey offered help. Izetbegovic called to express gratitude to Turkish government for their support during the war:

> As Turkey supported Bosnian people during and after the war, Bosnian people are supporting Turkey and in particular Erdoğan for his efforts.[30]

Here the AKP uses a foreign leader as a propaganda tool to deliver a message of unity among conservative Muslim people and persuade potential voters to join his party. Four years later, Izetbegovic praised Erdoğan during a conference in Sarajevo, which both leaders attended, with following words:

> Today you have a person whom Allah has bestowed upon you. This person is Recep Tayyip Erdoğan. Help him, support him.[31]

In the same year, speaking at his party's event, he pointed out that Erdoğan is not popular in the West because he is 'a long-awaited great leader for the Muslims':

They (West) are not disturbed by primitive and ignorant Muslims. But when it comes to economic development, they are disturbed by a man who opens his doors to three million refugees, builds the world's largest airport, and deals with terrorism and wars at his country's borders.[32]

Izetbegovic's hailing of Erdoğan is another aspect of personalization, but in this case this validation has been provided by someone other than himself or from within his party. This notion of unity is another interpretation of Abdulhamid II's 'Muslim world' presentation as one body under the Ottoman authority, even as the empire started to crumble. Furthermore, it represents the collective identity of similar Muslim ideologies.

Role of women in campaigning

At the Malatya rally, the participation of women was significantly higher than in Aydın. Undoubtedly, the dynamics of the city played a key role in this. The AKP received 68.5 per cent support in the 2011 elections, possibly illustrating the religious stance of the people in Malatya. Interestingly, the role of women as participants in elections in religious conservative cities were higher than in secularly oriented ones. With the establishment of the AKP, conservative women were encouraged to raise their voices in a way never seen before in Turkey, which also had an impact on the election rallies. However, the involvement of women did not start with the AKP but with the RP. In fact, it was during Erdoğan's mayoral campaign as RP's candidate in the 1994 elections that women were involved for the first time in an election campaign, and this had an important impact on the outcome. By visiting conversation circles across Istanbul, RP's Women Branch's direct communication with women supporters was initiated, which enabled them to contribute to the campaigns.

Erdoğan's political life, which has seen struggles, deadlocks and crises, encourages people to believe in a future under his guidance, according to a student who was present at the rally to support Erdoğan. When I asked her the reason for her support, she explained that, in 2000, her sister could not study at the university as she wore a headscarf. However Erdoğan's government removed the 'pejorative ban' allowing women to wear headscarves, as explained earlier, thus enabling her sister to pursue her education. She also notes that previous parties could not find solutions to the problems of the religious conservative people, but the AKP started making life easier by ensuring freedom of education and protecting civil rights. It is not frequently the case that young university students attend AKP rallies, but there is a difference between rallies in eastern and western Turkey. The support of young people in eastern Turkey is considerable higher than in cities like Istanbul, Ankara or Bursa, as evidenced by my personal observations as well as by PO5's explanations based on AKP's internal researches.

Praising oppressed Muslims

Ankara is a politically important city because it is the capital of Turkey; however, Konya, a city in central Turkey, is strategically significant as it is the capital of the Seljuk Empire and home of Sufi mystic Mevlana, or Rumi as he is known in the West. It is also known to be one of the most conservative cities in Turkey. Hence Erdoğan increased his religious tone at the Konya rally accordingly. He started by praising God and the crowd replied 'Amen'. Again, he listed the names of revered people from the region, citing those who had developed a spiritual relationship to Konya during the Seljuk and Ottoman period.[33] He then continued by remembering Atatürk, Adnan Menderes and Necmettin Erbakan. Erbakan was elected for the first time to the National Assembly with the support of the people of Konya in 1969. He was also a crucial figure in Konya, and people supported his party up until the foundation of the AKP. Hence, showing respect for Erbakan is crucial for Erdoğan as it enables him to gain votes from the SP, a continuation of the RP, which also gives him access to the votes of more religiously oriented people. Erdoğan continued with a prayer for other parts of the 'Muslim world':

> Oh Allah! Protect Gaza, protect Syria, protect Iraq, Egypt and Libya. Help people in Somalia and Myanmar.[34]

Later, he also made a mention of Gaza, Baghdad, Damascus, Basra, Mosul, Erbil, Kirkuk, Baku and Skopje, which he had not referred to in his previous rallies. Therefore, it is strikingly apparent that Erdoğan moulds his political message according to the city he is campaigning in. Furthermore, after he finished his speech in Konya, he prayed for several minutes, which was not something he had done previously. As well as using religion and religious figures to get a positive response at rallies, he also tries to carefully balance the demographics, in other words the audience. Nevertheless, for me the Konya rally was climactic when compared to the previous rallies I had attended – not only in terms of the excited atmosphere, but also regarding the extent to which Erdoğan communicated religion. In fact, Erdoğan ended the rally by asking the crowd to recite the first chapter of the Quran, the Surah al-Fatiha, for the deceased:

> You alone do we worship, and You alone do we ask for help. Guide us on the straight path, the path of those who have received your grace; not the path of those who have brought down wrath, nor of those who wander astray.

Erdoğan's traditional 'balcony speech'

It is Erdoğan's tradition to give a victory speech after every election result from the balcony at the AKP headquarters, and this is called the 'balcony speech' (*Balkon konuşması* in Turkish). Although initially it was unclear whether he would win the presidential elections in the first round as a 50 per cent + 1 threshold applies to avoid a run-off, or if he would give the 'balcony speech' from the AKP headquarters because of his new independent post as president. Although in Turkey the president can be nominated from a political party, after the nomination has been approved, the candidate's relationship to the party must be severed.

Regardless of these unknown factors, I chose to observe the reactions of the members of the AKP, and, in particular, those of the Publicity and Media Department team as the results arrived; hence I spent my evening at the AKP headquarters. The Publicity and Media Department was primarily responsible for the PR, media and communications during the 2014 presidential elections and so their reactions were viewed as important. When I arrived at the headquarters it was midday, and Turkish citizens and the diaspora were still voting in polling stations. The majority of the attendees at the headquarters at this time were members of the Youth Branch.

At the AKP headquarters, I spoke with two young party members, one aged 25 and the other, 28. These two Youth Branch members had grown up under the rule of Erdoğan. In particular my interest relates to their approach to politics, their views on Erdoğan's leadership and more importantly freedom of speech in Turkey – one of the important concerns, especially after the coup attempt in 2016, that was regularly raised by young people during my fieldwork.

Electoral behaviour of young party members

First, I asked my sources about what they anticipated the election result would be. Both were convinced by the election campaign and believed that the election would be over in the first round with a victory for Erdoğan. I felt it was important to learn about the engagement of young voters with Erdoğan and his party, because my in-depth interview with research centre chairman TT1 suggested the party most favoured by the younger generation is the HDP and its co-leader Selahattin Demirtaş,[35] while the AKP is the least preferred. The young activist members of the AKP I spoke with confirmed that the party struggles to find common ground with the younger generation, as 'young people do not feel comfortable with the language used by Erdoğan' because of his focus on issues associated with the 'old Turkey'. Speaking of infrastructure, health and economic policies is insufficient to inspire the younger generation, as young man, suited in black, told me:

> The younger generation wants to see themselves in politics. They want to be represented with new projects related to technology, education, culture and innovation.

Whether Turkey's new parties or leaders like IYI Parti's (Good Party) Meral Akşener – a nationalist female politician who resigned from the MHP and started her own party in 2017, and who received a 10 per cent vote share in 2018 elections – will be able to convince generation Z is dependent on their policies, how they can gain trust among the youth and in what sense communication strategies will be successful in a country that is more and more polarized whether from journalism, from academia or from a general societal perspective.

AKP receiving more support from Eastern Anatolia

On the day of the 2014 presidential election results, when members of the Publicity and Media Department arrived at the AKP headquarters, they were very cheerful, as first results started emerging at around 4.30 p.m. The election committee, consisting of representatives from every party at each local polling station, started counting the votes from 5 p.m. However, as party members were present at every single polling station, headquarters could access figures regarding turnout and thus predict the outcome. Actual figures were notably positive as they were released, and the first results were from the eastern part of Turkey where support for Erdoğan was the strongest, according to one of the members of the department:

> We always receive more support from the eastern part of Turkey than the West. It is part of the demographic structure. People in the east are more conservative, in other words, religious. This is a presidential election and the possibility is high that we will get more support from the east than ever before.

My interviewee admitted that religious conservative oriented people in Turkey have only one option to vote for, that is the AKP, despite the fact that the rise of the HDP and its leader Demirtaş, especially in Kurdish majority cities such as Diyarbakır, undermined this to some extent. In particular, Demirtaş's 'soft style and rhetoric'[36] won him 9.76 per cent in the 2014 Turkish presidential election. This support was made more apparent in the June 2015 general elections when the HDP passed the electoral threshold of 10 per cent for the first time in Turkey.

When I asked another member of the same department to compare the campaigns of Erdoğan and Demirtaş from the perspective of their use of media and PR, he deliberately ignored the question, and only mentioned Erdoğan's charismatic leadership style, the projects he has overseen and his politics since 2002 which he noted should be enough to convince people to choose him as their next president. It is unsurprising that people might feel antagonized when a 'foreigner' asks them questions about another party. However, unfortunately, this was not only the case with members of the Publicity and Media Department; whenever I asked party members a question related to another party, most of them looked at me suspiciously, displayed a lack of tolerance and refused to address criticism.

Here, however, I should distinguish between the two kinds of party members: voluntary and professional members. During my observations at the AKP headquarters, I recognized that voluntary members embraced the understanding of *dawah*, that is, Islamic activism, and seemed very enthusiastic. They worked 'for the sake of God', as a 68-year old woman in Istanbul's Üsküdar district pointed out. Furthermore volunteers 'sacrifice' much of their time for party work, including their weekends. In contrast, professionals, who are paid to work on a full-time basis, seemed less enthusiastic. They usually adhered to regular working hours, and gave a general impression that their main concern was their job and not the success of the AKP's politics or ideology. Interestingly, during a tea break, one member of the Publicity and Media Department admitted that she supported the main opposition party, the CHP, until 2014, but switched loyalty to Erdoğan in the presidential elections of 2014 as the candidate for the CHP offered no vision for the future. Economic stability was important for this team member, and she observed that this is heavily reliant on the 'successful agreement between the president and the government'. Within the frame of economic development and new presidential system, PO5 related an anecdote with the justice minister of Denmark.

> When Turkish and Danish delegates met in Copenhagen, the justice minister of Denmark asked his Turkish counterpart why we have decided to move to

a new presidential system. One of our delegate members explained that it was important in order to act faster without bureaucracy being an obstacle in economic development. The Danish minister waited for couple of seconds and replied by saying that their intention is the opposite. 'We try to discuss an important policy first with the support of different institutions in order to take a decision, not short-term but long-term, to fulfil the needs of democracy and state propriety.'

This example delineates how a real checks and balance system works, and why they are needed in a democratic society to protect the rights of the citizens. In fact, Denmark is one of the most happiest countries in the world, which is connected with the democratic standards, health and education system, as well as freedom of speech and human rights in the country.[37]

When the first 10 per cent of official results were announced in the 2014 presidential elections by news agencies' websites on television at 7 p.m., as expected, Erdoğan was leading the race owing to the votes from the cities in eastern Turkey. An hour later, it was clarified that the outcome of the election was a success story for Erdoğan; he went on to become the twelfth president of the Turkish Republic. An advisor to Erdoğan shared a tweet noting that Erdoğan was to leave Istanbul and head to Ankara to give his victory speech. Immediately preparations were underway at the AKP headquarters. This was the first definitive indication that the speech would take place at the AKP headquarters in Ankara. In order to start making the necessary arrangements, one of the members of the Publicity and Media Department called their director and asked for updates. When the confirmation arrived that Erdoğan would be giving a 'balcony speech', the department prepared to display AKP and Erdoğan flags, a portable wall for the balcony and digital billboards. While the Publicity and Media Department started making arrangements for the visual display, the Organization Department and the Youth Branch started mobilizing people to attend the victory speech. A member of the Organization Department called the Ankara province members and requested that they organize around 1,000 people to attend Erdoğan's speech. The Youth Branch used social media to mobilize younger AKP members and sympathizers. By sharing tweets and Facebook posts, the AKP's Youth Branch utilized the technical infrastructure available on social media to mobilize around 1,000 people from the local branches of the AKP's Ankara province. One of the Youth Branch members emphasized in a phone call that 'they need an energetic audience to cheer when Erdoğan enters the stage'. In another call to an AKP Youth Branch in Ankara, the same person asked the branch to organize at least 300 young men and women to attend the 'balcony speech'. 'The Youth Branch is seen as an engine', as noted by a young member.

> We support the party with our young and dynamic members. Because we have the enthusiasm, the energy, and we work passionately. Erdoğan's attaches importance to the Youth Branch.

The emphasis on Erdoğan's appreciation for his youth supporters is important to elaborate on here. Erdoğan joined Erbakan's party when he was just 15 years old. Being involved at such a young age had an enormous ideological impact on him. By reading about Turkey's Islamist intellectual pioneers, he became aware of Kemalism and modernization, and what motivated people to become involved in politics. A Youth Branch member highlights that their 'aim is to create a generation with a specific mission of *dawah*'; this ideal is also shared by other young interviewees volunteering in Istanbul's districts.

To ensure that the hard work and effort put into building an image for the new Turkish president did not go to waste, much effort was taken in order to check technical preparations were in place: 'Erdoğan attaches importance to professionalism', emphasizes the person responsible for the technical part of the Publicity and Media Department. Apart from the billboard and portable wall, it was important to arrange a teleprompter for Erdoğan, as he uses one at every speech. On this important evening, successful image management was the primary objective of the Strategy Team's leader. Olçok gave instructions to the members of the Publicity and Media Department on how to anticipate and handle any issues that could arise during the event and cause potential damage to Erdoğan's image. It is important here to discuss the power dynamics between the Strategy Team and Publicity and Media Department on the day of the election. While the head of the latter emphasized, in an interview, that they have the upper hand concerning issues related to PR, the head of the Strategy Team claimed the opposite. In fact, when observing the relations between both teams, it was apparent that the Strategy Team has the upper hand, although the head of the Publicity and Media Department never admitted this. When the 'Communications Directory' was found, information, knowledge and communication flow could be controlled under Erdoğan's presidency. As a result, since 2018, the whole communications process is managed similarly under the control of the presidency.

Erdoğan's revenge on Kemalist elites

On election night, the Publicity and Media Department was busy preparing for the balcony speech, while the Organization Department and the Youth Branch were working on mobilizing supporters at the headquarters. As the time of Erdoğan's arrival drew close, I relocated my observations to Ankara Esenboğa Airport's VIP lounge, as one of Erdoğan's senior advisors, who was one of my high ranking interviewees, offered me a seat in his car, a black German Volkswagen. During the short drive, I had the opportunity to speak with him about the election results and Turkey's future prospects. As might be expected, elated with the results, he was proud to have played the role of an advisor to an 'exclusive leader who succeeds in every single election'. It was clear to him that this election was a turning point not just for Turkey, but for the wider 'Muslim world':

> We have never had a leader such as Erdoğan since the fall of the Ottoman Empire. His charisma is indisputable. But more important is his way of governing. He wrestles with elites, in other words the Kemalists. He is the right person, who people can trust because he has the same religious orientation as the majority of this country.

Indeed, the oppression of people with conservative orientation by the Kemalist elite has a long history in Turkey. Kemalism was the driving force behind the creation of modern Turkey in 1923, and the postmodern coup in 1997 was an achievement for the 'Kemalist bloc' who successfully 'intervened in the democratic process'. Under the Kemalist elite, religious education at Imam Hatip schools was restricted, headscarves were banned for female university students and Quranic instruction courses in which pupils memorize the Quran were shut down. Thus, for Erdoğan much of his political life has been spent wrestling with the Kemalist elites, which his chief advisor summarizes as 'bringing Kemalist elites to account'.

Established cultural and religious norms help build an important foundation for a healthy relationship between the public and political actors. For Erdoğan it was easier to find a common ground with the religious conservative majority, with whom he could communicate: 'authentic, humble, and uncorrupted Turkish people who were dominated and oppressed by secular and modernist elites'.[38] Yet the comments of the interviewee above reveal how Erdoğan's charisma has been identified as the main impetus behind his success in his struggle with the Kemalist regime. In this manner, the 2014 presidential elections were seen as a 'normalization process', in which the barriers between 'state and society' were removed. But when the political climate in 2014 is compared with that of 2019, it is as clear as crystal that polarization has increased, not only in society, according to PO5, but also within the party itself. This could also be observed in Erdoğan's speeches after his presidency. A far more religious nationalist discourse was embraced within the frame of populism, which was mainly based on polarizing the society in order to garner at least 50 per cent support to consolidate votes against the opposition. The resignations of former prime minister Davutoğlu as well as former economy minister Babacan from the AKP in 2019 were indicative of how consultation mechanisms are limited within the party. Davutoğlu pointed out in his press conference where he announced his resignation that the AKP has served the society in last eighteen years but has moved away from its founding principles, and is not capable of focusing on resolving human rights violations, corruption and poverty anymore.[39] Furthermore he underlined that he will work to establish a 'new democratic order'.[40] But Davutoğlu was minister of foreign affairs during the Gezi Park protests at a time when human rights violations were discussed feverishly, and he has not advocated any other step than the one proposed by Erdoğan.

When I arrived at Ankara Esenboğa Airport's VIP lounge on the night of 10 August 2014 presidential elections, a majority of the ministers, a few parliamentarians and advisors were already there; however, some of them arrived later. In every corner of the hall, conversations were taking place. In one of these, a parliamentarian and former mayor of a large city was discussing the AKP, in particular, the appointment of a new prime minister and AKP chairman. It was certain that the man selected would be Ahmet Davutoğlu, who was at that time the foreign minister. An advisor who joined the discussion later said it mattered little, suggesting that, in reality, Erdoğan would be the de facto prime minister and chairman of the AKP. While these discussions were taking place, Davutoğlu entered the lounge with his advisors. A few eyes in the hall turned towards him while others welcomed him by shaking hands. The attitudes of the people in the hall reflected the expectation that he would be appointed as the new prime minister. However, it was too early to make a prediction at that time, because Abdullah Gül's handover of the presidency to Erdoğan would take place in several days, and the appointment of the prime minister and chairman would follow afterwards. In another group, three party members were discussing a poll conducted at the AKP headquarters and in key districts to ascertain who the party preferred as prime minister. Three names had emerged: Binali Yıldırım, Abdullah Gül and Ahmet Davutoğlu. When I joined the discussion with the advisor I travelled with to the airport, and asked who had emerged as the first choice, one of the MPs responded that it was someone not present in the lounge. This meant it was either Gül or Yıldırım. When I continued this conversation later with Erdoğan's chief advisor, he informed me that the first preference of the party members was Yıldırım. However, although Yıldırım was the frontrunner, Erdoğan chose Davutoğlu. This was a decision he came to regret, and Davutoğlu was replaced thirty-three months later by Yıldırım. Differences between Erdoğan's and Davutoğlu's political styles led to several significant clashes during the latter's term as prime minister.

A long queue of people stood outside the lounge to welcome the new president-elect, and it was curious to observe the ministers lining up this way. Some of the ministers pushed ahead of others to get closer to the head of the line to be among the earliest to congratulate Erdoğan. Based on the order of the queue, one could intuit that Davutoğlu would indeed be appointed as the next prime minister and chairman of the AKP; he was at the head of the line, and he appeared both poised and confident. Erdoğan also greeted and shook hands with high-profile personalities from the capital upon his arrival, and they congratulated him on his victory.

Erdoğan arrived in Ankara with his family members – wife, son, daughter and grandchildren – with the intention of including them on the balcony during his speech. The personal politics surrounding the 2014 presidential elections was far reaching for the political party system in Turkey, as it was the first time the president was elected directly through popular vote. Moreover, Erdoğan had been elected on a campaign that pledged to change the constitution in the new term by replacing the parliamentary system with a new system. Thus, the expectation going forward was that political parties would become less relevant and candidates more so.

When Erdoğan made his way to the AKP headquarters, all the ministers and MPs got into their cars and followed Erdoğan in a convoy. Interestingly, the chauffeurs who drove each of the ministers became agitated, jostling and hooting their horns, as they vied with each other to position their vehicle to be the one that would immediately follow Erdoğan's Mercedes S-Class. This was a continuation of the scene at the welcoming ceremony. Erdoğan's adviser, with whom I returned to the AKP headquarters, explained that this sort of power struggle reveals the true face of all politicians. After a ten-minute drive, Erdoğan's escort stopped on the motorway; Erdoğan got out of his vehicle and boarded one of AKP's official election buses, designed with campaign slogans, Erdoğan's photos and logo, which had been used while campaigning in various cities and districts. Some of the ministers and

Erdoğan's chief advisors joined him on the bus, and so did I by the invitation of my interviewee. When I took my seat on the election bus as a fieldwork researcher, I realized that Erdoğan's family members were already on it. In total there were thirty people on the bus. The bus driver started playing the election song loudly so that it could be heard on the outside and on the streets that we were travelling through. As the bus passed through Ankara's different districts, a corridor of people assembled along the route. This was a 'natural mobilization', according to Erdoğan's senior advisor, meaning that AKP officials had not 'arranged' for local residents to assemble along Erdoğan's route as they done so for the 'balcony speech'. When Erdoğan saw this response from his supporters, he got up and went to the front of the bus to greet them accordingly. The rhythm of Erdoğan's campaign music encouraged people to wave their hands, thus reflecting a tide of emotion. The use of sound in this manner is an aspect of political public relations that can be used effectively to raise awareness and strengthen communication. At some point, Erdoğan asked to stop the bus. He took the megaphone and thanked the people of Ankara for their support, promising that this would be the beginning of a 'New Turkey'. Also, the new first lady could be seen accompanying him, thus intentionally presenting a visual that was important as more than 50 per cent of the people on the streets were women. After this, Erdoğan and the new first lady presented chess sets and T-shirts bearing the Erdoğan logo to young children who were awake despite the late hour. This act was one of 'purposeful communication and action' to 'influence and establish a beneficial relationship'[41] with the public. This not only appealed to the elderly, or even to those old enough to vote, but it created a memorable moment that children will not forget. During the half-hour journey, Erdoğan received calls from his international counterparts, which he answered joyfully. He was in a good mood, and it was clear that he was relieved to have achieved success in the first round of voting. Despite his cheerfulness, he adhered strictly to the arranged schedule and worked on updating the upcoming programme with his chief of staff.

Balcony speech: First step to Erdoğan's 'New Turkey'

When Erdoğan arrived at the AKP headquarters, ministers, MPs and party officials welcomed him. He went straight to his office on the twelfth floor. As his office door was left open, I could observe Erdoğan's preparations. He ran through his victory speech and welcomed special guests from other countries, with whom he had photographs taken. One of the guests was the former president of Kyrgyzstan (2011–17) Almazbek Atambajev. When I asked an advisor about the reason behind this visit, he stated that the personal relationship between the two leaders and countries is wonderful.[42] Meanwhile, ministers and MPs were following news updates and watching political shows on TV and Twitter as well as receiving calls.

Before the victory speech was delivered, Olçok made plans regarding who would join Erdoğan on the balcony. Although quite a few ministers, MPs, deputy chairmen and mayors were present and ready to accompany the president-elect, Olçok decided that only Erdoğan's family should be present with him at the beginning of the speech. He announced this decision in an aggressive tone, emphasizing that it should not be questioned. This was certainly not well received, and some of the ministers and MPs were clearly disappointed. Olçok's decision suggested the use of an Americanized communication strategy, mirroring traditional practices in the US presidential elections. It also revealed the importance of 'individualization', and 'candidate-centred politics', presenting Erdoğan as a 'family figure'. When I spoke to Olçok about this decision, he emphasized that his aim was to personalize the elections, as this was a new period for Turkey. Olçok's decision was a clear sign that he had the last word on Erdoğan's PR. Nevertheless, after Erdoğan's speech, selected high-profile personalities from the party were encouraged to accompany the president-elect and participate in welcoming guests. But before they joined in, Erdoğan, once again, greeted the crowd with the first lady. Olçok also revealed that the AKP was keen to personalize its political communications, and the presidential elections was an ideal opportunity to do so, a decision related to Erdoğan's interest dominating the political landscape.

Before Erdoğan was announced on stage, the election song was played to enthuse the crowd. When Erdoğan appeared, as in other rallies, there were cheers, in particular from the younger party members; some were also shouting slogans. Erdoğan's speech conveyed his message of unity, representing a continuation of his election campaign. Erdoğan's unity approach involves building mutual relationships between his party, himself and the Turkish public, as well as the wider Islamic world. Similar to the election rallies, in his speech, he made references to critical cities in the Islamic world and underlined that this victory is also one for 'Baghdad, Islamabad, Kabul, Beirut, Sarajevo, Skopje, Damascus, Aleppo, Hama, Homs, Ramallah, Nablus, Ariha, Gaza and Jerusalem'.[43]

One of the key advisors to the prime minister explained that this sentence made history, because the 'Muslim world is witnessing this historic moment in Turkey and supporting Erdoğan with their prayers'. When I asked if Erdoğan used the same populist jargon in his 2002 or 2007 balcony speeches, he informed me that previously it was more 'balanced', whereas on this occasion he clearly was taking the

'Muslim world' into consideration. This provides further evidence of how the AKP's message evolved during time. When I interviewed the same advisor in 2019, he pointed out that after the coup attempt in 2016 Erdoğan's speeches became not only more populist Islamist but also nationalist in tone. However, it would be wrong to ignore the reality that the crowd wanted to hear a speech that emphasized 'unity of the Muslim world'. For example, when Erdoğan spoke about the significance of his victory for Muslim societies, the enthusiasm of the audience significantly increased. Accordingly, it can be argued that this shift in Erdoğan's political direction after 2016 influenced his supporters' willingness to embrace a religious rhetoric, as he appeared to turn away from a discourse mollifying the West and reduced efforts towards joining the EU. As highlighted earlier, Turkish public's approach to the EU has changed dramatically, according to TT3, after the coup attempt. The reason behind this anti-EU attitude is because of the lack of support from European countries during and after the coup attempt. In an interview to Euronews in August 2016, during the post-coup period, Erdoğan brought this issue up. Accusing the EU members of not standing with the people of Turkey, he stated that the Turkish people have always shown their support for the EU countries in similar situations, such as during the terror attacks in Brussels and Paris. Moreover, the Turkish president alluded to the fact it is a double standard to refer to this as a clash of ideologies – or in Huntington's (1993) thesis, the clash of civilization – between the Western and Islamic civilization. Nevertheless, EU countries' criticism needs to be taken into account, as they were concerned with the post-coup crackdown on journalists and political figures when the Erdoğan government declared a state of emergency for two years, 'taking advantage of political upheaval'.[44]

Erdoğan's hand gesture: *Rabaa*

Before Erdoğan finished his speech from the AKP headquarters' balcony, he asked the crowd if they were ready for what is to come. When the audience replied with a resounding 'yes', Erdoğan made the four-fingered *Rabaa* gesture, which was the symbol used by the MB in Egypt during their protests against the military crackdown that ended with a coup against the democratically elected Islamist president of Egypt, Muhammad Morsi. In fact, gestures are a form of non-verbal communication. *Rabaa* means 'four' in Arabic, and is associated with Cairo's Rabaa Square where the protests took place. Erdoğan started using this gesture as a symbol after the military coup in Egypt in 2013. Initially, he used the *Rabaa* salute only when he was greeting people before and after his public speeches, remembering the MB in support of Morsi. But eventually he began to associate it with his religious nationalist perspective: one homeland, one state, one flag and one nation. Consequently it is understood in Turkey more as a local symbol than as adopted from another social movement. Castells argues that society is influenced by images and symbols, which can be instrumental in promoting political viewpoints and have a symbolic meaning.[45] Thus, the use of the *Rabaa* gesture by Erdoğan, during the presidential campaign at every single public speech, symbolizes his political stance with respect to Egypt. After Morsi became Egypt's president, there have been two state visits between the two countries. Erdoğan's support of Morsi was well known, and for his part Morsi sought to implement the methods modelled by the AKP to benefit the MB. Since the military coup in Egypt, Erdoğan has not acknowledged the presidency of the current Egyptian president al-Sisi, and has on occasion raised his voice in favour of the MB.

Erbakan used the raised thumbs up as a political gesture, denoting success and progress. When Erdoğan created the AKP in 2001, they had no specific gesture associated with the party. The coup in Egypt was an opportunity for Erdoğan to show solidarity and associate himself with a specific sign. In an informal conversation in London's Russel Square, one of Erdoğan's advisors, who chose to remain anonymous, told me that this 'gesture is not only in support of the MB but is also used by oppressed people worldwide from Palestine to Iraq, from Myanmar to Sudan'. This is known at grassroots level; according to my source, 'AKP supporters are using this as a gesture of respect to the MB in particular'. During my fieldwork, I had observed Erdoğan regularly use this gesture during meetings, rallies and public speeches, especially in Istanbul, to associate it with the AKP, himself, and wider 'Muslim world' and Islamist movements, emphasizing collective effort.

Erdoğan as a central figure in communication

In order to get a clearer impression of how Erdoğan is perceived within the AKP, I spent a lot of time at the AKP headquarters and on the ground. I found that he is typically referenced to as *Reis* ('leader', 'chief' or 'guide'), and that whenever AKP members discuss Erdoğan, they use this particular word. One of the main inspirations for Erdoğan is the work of poet and ideologue Kısakürek, who uses the word *Reis* in some of his poems. Whereas people in higher positions, such as a minister, MP or deputy chairman, are found to use 'Tayyip *bey*', which is the formal way of addressing someone in Turkish (this would be 'Mr Erdoğan' in English). Many others who work with Erdoğan, such as his advisors and chief of staff, employ the word *beyefendi* ('sir', 'lord' or 'gentlemen') as a more polite way to address a statesman. Titles used in political communication can convey a message about the style of political actors, or institutions, to the general public. In this case, the word *Reis* suggests the importance of a populist authoritarian style leadership, as one of Erdoğan's senior advisors explains:

> Turkey is becoming more and more dependent on its leader [Erdoğan]. Every single decision is taken by him. We opened a new airport somewhere in Anatolia. But the problem was that Turkish Airlines had not arranged a flight to that city at that time. When *Beyefendi* [Erdoğan] heard that the airport is still not in use although it is ready, he gave me directions to call the CEO of Turkish Airlines to give him an order to arrange flights from Istanbul. This is a level of micromanagement that would not be possible for any other leader in Turkey. This level of involvement in daily politics contributes to him [Erdoğan] being referred to as *Reis*.

Another example of Erdoğan's micromanagement relates to foreign students studying in Turkey. According to the same source, Erdoğan once called the editor-in-chief of the English language newspaper *Daily Sabah* to ask if they post copies to student dormitories where foreign students, mostly from Africa, the Middle East and Asia, who receive 'Turkey Scholarships' managed by the Presidency for Turks Abroad and Related Communities, are living. When he learnt that they do not, he instructed them to start sending copies of the paper to every single dormitory immediately. This type of management style could be perceived as an attempt to undermine freedom, because, owing to an authoritarian governance, it exerts too much control over every single aspect of politics as well as the media. The above example shows how Erdoğan uses pro-government news outlets to influence non-Turkish people, who he feels act as Turkey's ambassadors when they finish their studies and move back to their home countries, as my informant from London emphasizes.

Erdoğan's authority

Certainly images and symbols play a key role in communicating narratives, themes and messages. Erdoğan's image as *Reis* characterizes Turkish society's need for a strong leader, a tradition inherited from the Ottoman era. Turkey is a patriarchal society, and owing to his Islamist ideology, some of Erdoğan's supporters associate him with Sultan Abdulhamid II. This was mentioned by an AKP-affiliated lawyer with whom I spoke at the party headquarters in Ankara:

Abdulhamid II and *Reis* [Erdoğan] have similarities; first of all their Islamist ideology, which seeks to build a strong *ummah*. Abdulhamid II was keen to govern not only the Ottoman Empire's territory, but also the Islamic world at large. Obviously, *Reis* is imagining this in a democratic framework by mobilizing neighbouring Islamic countries. In terms of development, both leaders were interested in introducing technology to the military in particular. Abdulhamid II was criticized by the *New York Times* during his reign, just as Erdoğan is today.

When I asked my interviewee about how Erdoğan envisions achieving unity with neighbouring Islamic countries, he gives the example of Erbakan, who established an initiative called D-8[46] in 1997, imitating the G-7,[47] by bringing together the eight most developed Islamic countries to cooperate specifically on economic and military issues, with the possibility of a shared currency like the Euro in the future. Another AKP-affiliated interviewee I met at the headquarters suggested that Erdoğan is waiting for the right time to either create a different institution by bringing together countries such as Qatar, Tunisia and Iran or revive the D-8 idea. The Kuala Lumpur Summit, which failed even before it started in 2019, was an attempt towards this vision. Leaders of Malaysia, Turkey, Iran and Qatar met in Malaysia's capital to discuss major issues relating to the Muslim world, such as the Rohingya refugee crisis, Uighur mass detentions in China, Yemen war, gender inequality and economic disparity, and fight against Islamophobia by jointly launching an international news channel. Pakistan's Prime Minister Imran Khan was also invited to the conference; however, under pressure from Saudi Arabia because of diplomatic issues, he had to skip the summit.[48] Pakistan's economic deadlock has left them with no other option but to follow the orders of Saudi Arabia. A similar attitude applies to the AKP government too. China's Rohingya genocide has been an important issue for ideologically motivated human rights foundations and organizations in Turkey. They criticized the AKP government for not taking any action against China. Turkey's unstable economy makes the country dependent on China's authoritarian leader Xi Jinping, according to PO7.

Erdoğan's *Reis* image and the 'Muslim world' belief are closely related to identity politics, which then has an impact on political activity. Moreover, symbols matter in terms of common values, and it is argued that they can play a key role in expressing and developing identity. The latter plays an important role in the case of Erdoğan. When I scrutinized how the *Reis* image developed, it was apparent that this had emerged from Erdoğan's strategy of excluding rivals, which started in particular after 2013, with the Gezi Park protests and corruption scandal. One of my informants, who works for the Ministry of Justice, explains that whenever Erdoğan learns that colleagues or high-ranking party members disagree with him or have a secret agenda, he jettisons them. When I asked for examples, he only pointed to former president Gül and former deputy prime minister Bülent Arınç, but he stressed that others would follow. He attributed these actions to Erdoğan's 'power struggle' within the party:

> Basically Erdoğan does not want to share his power because he thinks that he is on track and any other idea or political approach would damage or limit his movement and all the efforts which he has put in since 2002. Vision 2023 is part of this aim.

The year 2023 is critical for Turkey as it is the 100th anniversary of the modern Turkish republic. Erdoğan's aim is for Turkey to become one of the top ten strongest economies in the world. By eliminating critical voices, starting with Gül and Davutoğlu, Erdoğan eroded the collective identity of his party, thereby strengthening his personal identity and power at the party's expense. This contributed to the shift in the identity of the party to an authoritarian one-man style politics, away from pluralist principles.

When Erdoğan decries any divergence from his message within the party, this creates, within the public mindset, a view that he is an impeccable and untouchable leader. 'In fact, this changes his perception of his role', notes an editor-in-chief for a small semi-AKP critical in-depth news portal in Istanbul. It increases his self-confidence and, as the journalist asserts, Erdoğan's ego is fuelled daily by the people around him, 'such as his advisors and ministers'. He emphasizes that Erdoğan's advisors also frequently fail to share the truth of situations with him, 'which leads Erdoğan to make mistakes, naturally'. He encapsulates the problem with the following Turkish expression: 'the followers of the king are more royalist than the king himself'.

Erdoğan's choice of colour

Another significant factor relating to the image of the president is his use of colour. One can note a substantial change in Erdoğan's style since 1994 by studying what he has chosen to wear throughout this period. His suits have changed in type, his ties have changed in colour and his overall appearance has become more refined. Following the Gezi Park protests in 2013, Erdoğan started wearing green ties more often until the July 2016 coup attempt, when he started using more red tones based on 'unity under the Turkish flag' messages. Choosing green seemed in some way to evoke the protests, and during an interview after the Gezi Park protests when a journalist asked him about the meaning of the colours of his ties, Erdoğan replied that the colour green shows his concern for nature and environment, while blue represents the sea, and red, the colour of the Turkish flag. His green ties were worn as a sign of reassurance, especially to those who raised concerns about the Gezi Park, that his party is environmentally friendly; in other words, this was done to counter any negative illusion created by the protest. According to one of Erdoğan's advisors, when participating in critical meetings, visiting foreign countries or welcoming an important foreign leader, Erdoğan chooses the colour red 'because it is a national symbol'. 'On Sundays or "balcony speeches", he only wears a blue plaid jacket without a tie which symbolises his accessibility'. His garish blue plaid jacket has become a symbol among his loyalists too.[49]

In reference to the choice of the green tie, I was interested in whether the colour was being used as a religious symbol, as it is by the Green Movement in Iran. When I asked one of his advisors about this, he refuted the possibility. But when I had an opportunity to ask this question to a journalist who travels with Erdoğan frequently on foreign trips, he explained that it is related to both religion and environment. He also noted that many other journalists were aware of this connection.

Erdoğan's waistcoat: Is he the new Atatürk?

Another example of media interest in whether Erdoğan's fashion choices are symbolic relates to his wearing of waistcoats since winter 2017. This addition to Erdoğan's wardrobe was evidenced when one journalist asked during a live TV interview, 'if this is his new style', because despite the warmer weather, in spring 2017, he was still wearing a waistcoat. Erdoğan replied laughingly by saying that he recommends that he (the journalist who asked the question) wears one too, because it protects one from the cold. However, it has since become apparent that this is a style statement, because even during the summer months Erdoğan continued to sport waistcoats in a mix of the styles and colours.

I was interested in whether Erdoğan has taken to wearing a waistcoat in imitation of Atatürk's style, as the founding father of the modern republic wore waistcoats regularly. This might then signify his aim to be seen as the 'second father of the Turkish Republic', which he often makes reference to with his actions. Clothing in Turkey is also an important indicator of the nation's modernization. Atatürk imposed the modern Turkish costume as follows:

> Low-cut shoe, pants, waistcoat, shirt, tie, jacket and, of course, as a supplement to these, a European style headdress.[50]

It was after the 2014 presidential elections that Erdoğan became the most powerful statesman of the post-truth era, and so I asked a high-ranked chief advisor of Erdoğan if he was adopting the modern style of Atatürk to give a message to both the Kemalists and the conservatives: to the former, that he is becoming a leader who knows how to dress in a modern fashionable style, and to the latter, that he is a new leader marking the end of the Atatürk era. My source in Ankara agreed that Erdoğan's new mode of dressing was indeed a symbolic act. He stated that Erdoğan sees 'himself as the new Atatürk, in particular after the referendum in 2017'. This was based on information he had received from his sources at Beştepe, where the presidential palace of Turkey is based. In addition, it was underlined that some AKP members in Ankara had also started wearing waistcoats, imitating Erdoğan's style. The contradiction between wearing a green tie reflecting Islam and the environment, and adopting fashionable modern dress is a reflection of the AKP's identity. It is a paradox, which demands, or presents, religiosity alongside modern Western methods and styles.

Moustache: A symbol of virility

Erdoğan's moustache (*badem bıyık* or 'almond moustache') is another symbol to consider as part of the discussion concerning his image. Clean-shaven politicians have been favoured by the AKP in the early days, in order to distinguish the party members' appearance from those of the Milli Görüş, who grew moustaches or beards as a symbol of their stance against Kemalism in Turkey. After the 15 July 2016 coup attempt, Erdoğan started instructing his family members, advisors, ministers, MPs and even security team members to sport moustaches.

This change in etiquette became an important matter of debate. Kemal Öztürk,[51] a journalist and former columnist of the Islamist *Yeni Şafak* newspaper, one of the most popular conservative newspapers in Turkey, wrote about the fact that members of the party had started wearing moustaches; at this time no mention was made of Erdoğan's intention behind encouraging this. However, Professor Mesut Tan, from Istanbul Marmara University, described the move as signifying a 'strong and stern image' during war time, highlighting the ongoing wars being fought by Turkey – domestically against the PKK and Gülenists, and internationally against the ISIS. Perhaps more important than this were Tan's comments linking the wearing of a moustache to the traditions of the Ottoman era. In fact, moustache was a symbol of virility in Ottoman Empire, in other words a 'proper way of looking and behaving like a Turk or Ottoman'.[52]

This leads us to consider a two-fold purpose of wearing a moustache: first as a symbol and second as creating a sense of collective identity. Symbolically, by recalling this practice from the time of the Ottoman era, Erdoğan is acknowledging the significant role of appearance in image building. The notion of 'collective identity is a product of conscious action',[53] which in this case demonstrates Erdoğan's relationship with Ottoman era. The same source in Ankara with whom I discussed Erdoğan's decision to wear a waistcoat explains that ministers, MPs and bureaucrats feel compelled to grow moustaches. The other alternative to show independence, which was recommended to his companions, is to grow a beard – this was also a practice of Prophet Muhammad.[54] It can thus be noted as to how Erdoğan intervenes in private spheres in order to create and preserve a macro image of his 'movement', a self-declared mission

Erdoğan's indulgence

Since Erdoğan became president, two symbolic steps have been taken to reinforce his position of power and authority; in the context of his image, it is important that we mention both here. The first is the building of the presidential palace in 2014, and the second is the purchase of a presidential plane, an Airbus 330, in the same year. When Erdoğan became president, it was unclear whether he would move to the Köşk in Ankara's Çankaya district, the presidential mansion since Atatürk's time, or to a new palace, the 'Ak Saray' (White Palace) as it was originally called before it became known as the 'Presidential Complex'. There was some uncertainty at first regarding whether Erdoğan would live in the new palace, because the building was planned for the prime ministry when Erdoğan was prime minister. However, after it was announced that he would run for the presidency, plans changed, and Erdoğan decided to move in to the new palace, which is described more as 'an Ottoman Versailles or Moscow's Kremlin than the residence of a leader who came of age in Turkey's working-class heartland and who has often marketed himself as a man of the people'.[55] The new palace was built inside Atatürk's forestland in Ankara. Erdoğan has received much criticism from the national and international media, as commentators have variously denounced the cost of development, the palace's location as well as its architecture because it blended modern, Ottoman and Seljuk art with contemporary material. Nevertheless, the new kitsch presidential palace represented a historical and symbolic break from Köşk, which was inherited from Atatürk. The issue of where Erdoğan should live created a heated debate at the AKP headquarters. The coverage by the media was criticized, and one of AKP's Publicity and Media Department members hailed the decision by Erdoğan to take up a new residence as significant, as 'this building will represent Turkey to the global world'. It was seen by the party as an important milestone in the development of 'Turkey's image'. In addition, there is no doubt that most of the AKP's members were happy that Erdoğan would not govern from Çankaya, and would hence leave his imprint distinct from the old Kemalist regime.

A senior government member commented on both decisions positively, emphasizing how important such moves are to show the capacity and strength of a country. One Youth Branch member was proud that the new presidential residence was 'bigger than France's Versailles Palace and Washington's White House'. Thus, status symbols clearly play an important role within AKP circles. A brief note concerning attitudes towards the Americanization of the president's image is relevant here. When it was announced that the name of the new building would be the 'Ak Saray' (White Palace), as the AKP's Turkish abbreviation is 'Ak', it was thought to also be a reference to the White House in the United States. Later its name was changed to Cumhurbaşkanlığı Külliyesi (Presidential Complex). *Külliye*, an Arabic word from the Ottoman era, is used to refer to a complex including a mosque, religious *madrasa* (school), *waqf* (charitable foundation), and *dar al-shifa* (clinic) in particular. In fact, a huge mosque, a library and an opera house was built on the premises. When it is announced that Erdoğan will pray in the Beştepe People's (Millet) Mosque, as it is called, the interest of people, who are keen to meet or even just see him from a distant, increases in a very short period of time. Usually, due to security reasons it is not announced prior the visit. However, some pray the Friday prayer in the mosque with the aim of meeting the president, as PO7 underlines. This allusion to history, in conjunction with the complex's architecture, sparked a debate about Erdoğan's neo-Ottoman policies. This way of referencing the country's history also reinforces Erdoğan's charismatic leadership style. Due to the uniqueness and controversy around the presidential palace, there is no doubt that the building will long be remembered as one of Erdoğan's magnum opus.

6

Politics and p(owe)r: Evolvement of political messaging

Political language is designed to make lies sound truthful and murder respectable, and to give an appearance of solidity to pure wind.

– Orwell

This chapter presents the analysis from the sixty speeches given by President Erdoğan over a period of two decades, and displays how politics and power relations has shaped the AKP's communication and how the party's political messaging has evolved. The first speeches date to 2002, when the AKP, a mere fifteen months after its formation, received 34 per cent of the vote in the first election in which it participated, becoming Turkey's governing party. The study evaluates speeches given each year, up to and including 2019 – the year AKP lost major cities like Istanbul and Ankara in local elections. This period has witnessed many ups and downs for the AKP and Erdoğan.

Indeed, it has been a long journey, in which a party, born out of the ashes of an Islamist movement, promoting EU membership and focusing on justice and pluralism, came to be associated with a coup attempt in 2016, resulting in the deaths of 251 people defending the status quo. Thus, the AKP transitioned from being a party that respects human rights, freedom of speech and diversity to one that now restricts all these rights and is renowned for jailing the highest number of journalists in the world.[1] An indictment of the party's current position can be found in the report by Freedom House, which ranks Turkey 32nd out of 100.[2] Meanwhile, Erdoğan's approach to governance has developed to imitate that of a spiritual leader; his government interferes in the private lives of its people, restricting alcohol use, banning abortion, censoring Netflix over LGBTQ+ content, and introduced new laws to control social media use. Moreover, converting Hagia Sophia museum to a mosque, building new mosques like Çamlıca and Taksim as well as supporting Imam Hatip schools are actions that reflect a new kind of branding of Islam by Erdoğan which represents his Islamist ideology. Yet, though these steps are in broader sense a challenge to Atatürk's secularisation policies, Erdoğan does not condemn Atatürk; rather he frames it as part of Turkey's broader struggle with its past and as representation of an Islamic civilization.[3] AC3 underlined during our interview in his office in Istanbul that Erdoğan believes Muslims across the world should gain their strength as in the Ottoman era. 'Therefore, Palestine is an important issue for him. But on the other hand, it is the reason why he uses Palestine as one of his tools to fight against increasing Islamophobia in the West', AC3 explains. These are the words of Erdoğan at the Necip Fazıl Kısakürek Awards Ceremony in 2017:

> Muslims are never desperate or weak. Where there is faith, there is a way. Those kids, who walk tall among Israeli soldiers, are our source of inspiration. We salute them. Those Palestinian women, mothers, who have never given up their freedom despite this much pressure, violence and state terror, are our biggest source of confidence. We salute them. With the help of our Lord, with the support of our brothers and sisters, and with the prayers of the innocent and the oppressed, we will hopefully become successful in this struggle.[4]

The available evidence drawn from the post-2010 literature as well as the data from the interviews and fieldwork undertaken in Turkey suggest that the AKP has witnessed two distinct periods in terms of its policies and approach. In this chapter, the first period will be examined by analysing the thirty speeches rendered from 2002 to 2009, while the second period will be reviewed by looking at the thirty speeches given between 2010 and 2019. Significant moments will be explained throughout this chapter with reference to historical facts where relevant.

Speeches play a significant role in understanding the ideology and worldview of an institution or individual.[5] Political speeches by political leaders serve an additional purpose, as they are key to motivating electorates, building relationships on the ground and persuading people about the value of political ideologies. They also offer a means of unifying the aims of 'political institutions, citizens and politicians'.[6] Herein, the primary aim of the quantitative content analysis is to focus on the words and language used systematically; this is done by first reading, counting and recording the number of repeated words to identify the message(s) conveyed by Erdoğan's speeches.[7] Linking frequent words and terms establishes a general overview of both textual content and ideological representation.[8] To reveal key themes and shifts in ideology, I have coded the speeches systematically across the two periods according to key recurrent themes.

Table 1 Themes of Erdoğan's speeches

Themes of Speeches
European Union
Cultural Dialogue
Human Rights/Freedom of Speech
Atatürk/Secularization
Religious Discourse
Economic Development
Anti-Israel
Anti-Establishment
Ottoman Empire
Gülenists

In order to perform a comprehensive, fair and rational analysis, I have randomly selected three to four speeches from each year, given on different occasions (i.e. at rallies, party meetings) in response to the need for official statements, at universities, to think tanks and during meetings of the parliamentary group. Speeches given on international platforms were also included to ensure a broad-spectrum approach. I coded every speech according to themes (see Table 1). These topics were initially identified from primary sources of Erdoğan's speeches and secondary sources, books, journals and newspaper articles about the AKP and Erdoğan. Overall, the themes cover issues from domestic to foreign affairs, from general politics to religious messages addressed with a specific ideology behind, thereby allowing a broader perspective.[9] Obviously topics related to the PKK or Syrian civil war are part of Erdoğan's agenda, but they are mainly in the foreground prior to elections or after terror attacks. For this comparison, I chose specific topics that are relevant from 2002 to 2019.

Erdoğan's shifting political message

When studying the speeches, I figured out systematically that the dominant topics varied significantly between the two periods. Initially, as seen in Figure 6, Erdoğan focused principally on discussing EU membership, establishing a cultural dialogue with the West, engaging in human rights and freedom of speech issues in addition to promoting a pro-Kemalist discourse by emphasizing the importance of Atatürk. Themes such as religious discourse as well as anti-Israel

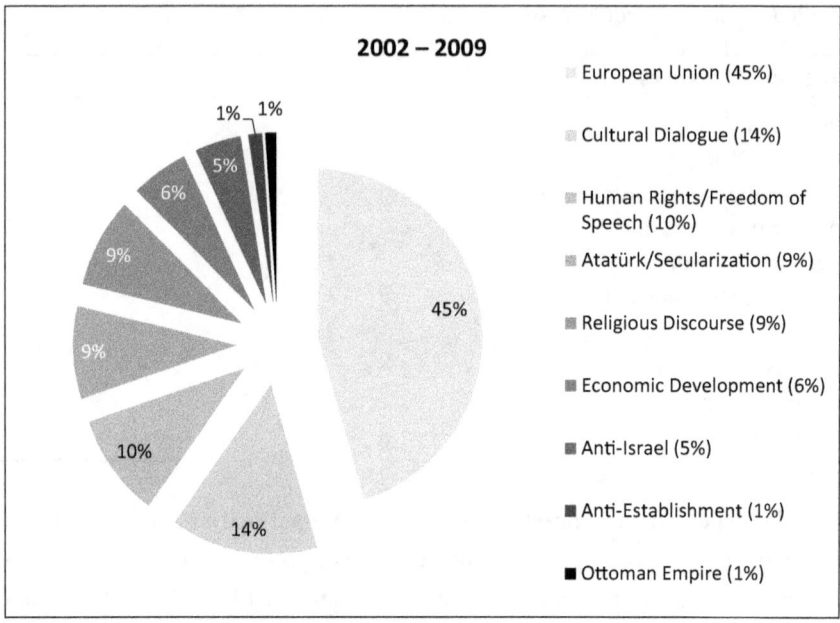

Figure 6 Themes of Erdoğan's speeches from 2002 to 2009.

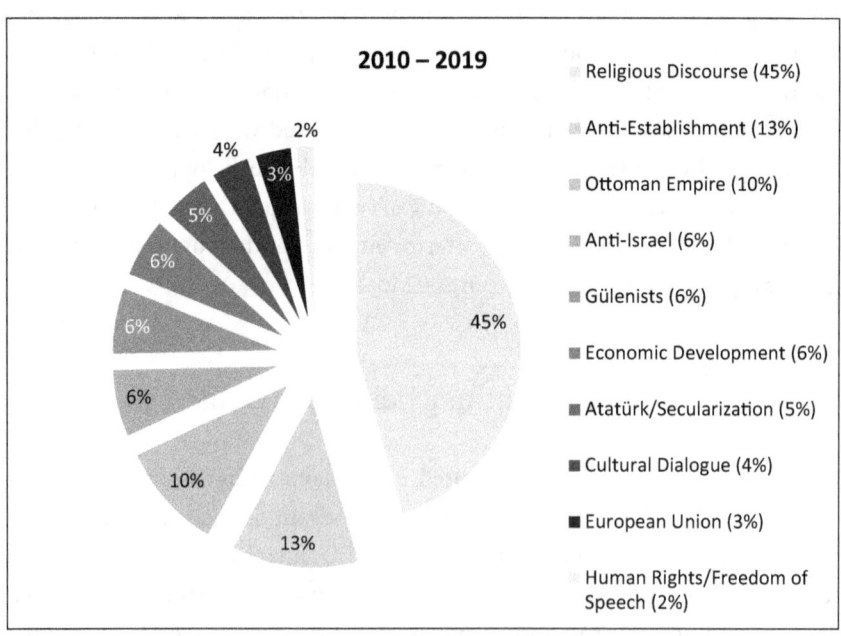

Figure 7 Themes of Erdoğan's speeches from 2010 to 2019.

Table 2 Themes, frequency and percentage of Erdoğan's speeches from 2002 to 2019

Themes	2002–9		2010–19		Change in %
	Frequency	%	Frequency	%	
European Union	169	45.4	22	3.4	-87
Cultural Dialogue	54	14.5	23	3.6	-57.4
Human Rights/Freedom of Speech	37	9.9	11	1.7	-70.2
Atatürk/Secularization	33	8.9	30	4.7	-9.1
Religious Discourse	32	8.6	291	45.5	809
Economic Development	21	5.6	36	5.6	71.4
Anti-Israel	17	4.6	41	6.4	141.2
Anti-Establishment	5	1.3	80	12.5	1500
Ottoman Empire	4	1.1	66	10.3	1550
Gülenists	0	0	40	6.2	4000

or anti-establishment sentiments were also present but did not account for a significant percentage of the whole.

By comparison, in the second period, prominent themes discussed by Erdoğan were religion, anti-establishment sentiment, the Ottoman Empire, anti-Israel discourse and opposition to the Gülenists (see Figure 7). The focus on Atatürk and secularization, cultural dialogue, the EU, human rights and freedom of speech significantly decreased in this era. The differences between both eras and the reasons behind for these changes will be answered comprehensively in the next chapter.

According to the data in Figure 7, religious discourse is the dominating theme in all coded speeches during this period. Moreover, although the EU and cultural dialogues are still discussed, they are far from being significant.

AKP's EU delusion

The rise of the AKP, necessitated a strong and forward-looking approach. This meant that a new agenda, distinct from that of Milli Görüş, emerged. While Erbakan described the EU as a 'Christian club', the AKP presented themselves as a pro-EU party, desirous of swift acceptance into the EU.[10] With this goal in mind, Erdoğan highlighted the issue of Turkey's EU membership 169 times in the speeches assessed from 2002 to 2009. This theme was present in 45.4 per cent of all coded speeches from that period. By contrast, in the period from

2010 to 2019 there was a serious reduction in the frequency of references to the EU. Erdoğan mentions it only 22 times, representing a drop of 87 per cent in frequency. Not only the political landscape but also the overall approach of the Turkish society towards the EU have changed over time. According to research by the TAVAK Foundation in 2011, 60.1 per cent of society were positive about the EU, whereas this had fallen to 48.8 per cent by 2019.[11] According to the TEPAV Foundation,[12] 66 per cent of young people, between 18 and 24 years of age, supported Turkey's EU membership.

The goal of EU membership was a priority for the party at the start of the period, as Turkey had already waited for more than fifty years to become part of the EU. At the close of the Cold War, European countries began to consider Turkey as a future member, but political, economic and cultural issues remained an obstacle. That it would prepare the country for full EU membership was one of the promises made by the AKP in 2002, and the focus on this objective in Erdoğan's speeches peaked in 2005 when the accession negotiations had officially commenced. The AKP's emphasis on this process was supported by the party's pragmatic side, because it had accelerated the reform process in Turkey. The government had to fulfil the EU's 'Copenhagen criteria' for EU membership, and these criteria required stable democratic institutions, a viable market economy, rule of law and civil rights for everyone. This meant targeting economic development, and necessitated the institutionalization of government organizations as well as the military. This process allowed the AKP to look towards the West and EU membership while simultaneously fulfilling Turkey's domestic needs, resulting in a positive impact on the economic development. Turkey's GDP increased as a whole and per capita, which made a significant difference to Turkish people's lives. Macro-economic policies boosted the private sector thereby influencing the economy beneficially in the short term. This also advanced the AKP's image at the domestic and international level. Furthermore, a series of laws passed in parliament to support EU candidacy impressed the Kemalist secularists, who saw them as proof that the AKP was serious about implementing democratic values, culminating in a wider support for Erdoğan.

Erdoğan's Kemalism tool

Alongside the pursuit of EU membership, in order to underline his modern and secular identity, Erdoğan, in his speeches between 2002 and 2009, emphasized the work of Mustafa Kemal Atatürk. In fact, Erdoğan mentioned Atatürk and secularism 33 times in the speeches gathered from this period, representing a total of 8.9 per cent of the coded speeches. These clearly portray that Atatürk and his secularist modernization project were viewed as being important to the AKP at that time. However, mention of secularism fell to 4.7 per cent in the second period.

Despite the views he expressed between 2002 and 2009, Erdoğan had previously given anti-secular speeches when he was part of the Milli Görüş. In one such speech, delivered in 1990, he states that 'one cannot be secular and Muslim at the same time'.[13] He adds that one is 'either Muslim or a secularist',[14] suggesting that secularism is ideologically opposed to Islam. Later, the bitter realities of Erbakan's political existence led Erdoğan to embrace pragmatism as well as to adopt the modern and secular values espoused by Atatürk. Notably, not only Erbakan but also the religious leader and politician Ayatollah Khomeini of Iran was critical of Turkey's modernization under Atatürk.[15] After the abolition of the Ottoman Empire, Atatürk was recognized as an anti-religious symbol, when he replaced the traditional style of governance of the Ottoman era with Western-style democracy in 1923. The similarities between the Iranian leader Reza Shah Pahlavi and Turkey's Atatürk, who ruled during a similar time period – the former from 1925 till 1941 and the latter from 1923 to 1938 – shaped Khomeini's approach significantly. Particularly before the Iranian revolution in 1979, the shah followed in the footsteps of Atatürk regarding the modernization process. Indeed, Atatürk 'replaced Arabic script with Roman', and the shah excluded 'words of Arabic or non-Iranian origin'.[16] These steps in what were both Muslim majority countries led some to develop prejudices against not only the two leaders but also the modernization process.

Significantly, Erdoğan's discourse regarding Atatürk varies between the two eras of AKP leadership. Atatürk, which means 'the father of the Turks', was the adopted surname of Mustafa Kemal in 1934, ten years after the foundation of the Turkish Republic. His original name was Mustafa, and his surname was Kemal. While in the first period Erdoğan uses the titles 'Atatürk' or 'Mustafa Kemal Atatürk' to refer to him, after 2010 he refers to Atatürk as either 'Mustafa Kemal' or 'Gazi', meaning 'Muslim warrior who had engaged in jihad'.[17] According to TT2 this change in Erdoğan's approach to Atatürk marks an improvement in his own self-confidence. TT2 argues that it was necessary for Erdoğan to tread gently regarding secularist issues in general and national perceptions of Atatürk in particular. However, once the AKP-nominated Abdullah Gül became the new president, Erdoğan was able to 'calm down', as the two men were close friends and shared the same ideology. Until this time, the AKP's future had seemed insecure, as apparent from the closure trial in 2008. Despite Erdoğan's positive approach to Kemalist elites up to 2009, the AKP failed to prevent the Kemalists in the judiciary from deciding to 'file a case against the AKP, requesting the closure of the party and the ban of the leadership'.[18] Having passed both trials successfully, Erdoğan started to alter his discourse away from Kemalism and secularism.

Issues of Human rights and freedom of speech

When the AKP came to power, there was a high demand publicly for human rights and freedom of speech. The AKP started the process of the normalization of relations in society, by placing these topics at the top of their agenda. Similarly, as discussed in reference to secularism in the previous section, we see human rights and freedom of speech prioritized by the AKP before 2009. The AKP leader refers 37 times to both issues in the first period, which is a total of 9.9 per cent, later reducing mentions to just 1.7 per cent, a total decrease of 70.2 per cent, making this the greatest shift in position after the one pertaining to the EU. In this regard, Erdoğan's personal struggle with freedom of speech is an important aspect to consider. When he was the mayor of Istanbul, during a speech in the city of Siirt, in 1997, Erdoğan read a poem for which he was imprisoned for four months on the grounds that he was reciting a religiously charged material. This hindered his later selection as an MP in the 2002 elections and he lost an opportunity to hold a political position in the party which he founded. He was therefore the chairman of the AKP but not the prime minister of the country, despite the AKP's victory. It was the AKP government that removed the ban on Erdoğan paving the way for his election as MP and prime minister in March 2003. In a speech at the Friedrich-Ebert-Stiftung in Berlin in 2003, Erdoğan defended freedom of speech, underlining that he was imprisoned merely for citing a poem.[19]

Notwithstanding the above, imposing restrictions against the public in a manner restrictive of human rights has been a relevant issue throughout the period of AKP rule. The political and social landscape prior to their ascendancy was considered hopeless for conservative people in Turkey after the postmodern coup in 1997. Imam Hatip schools were banned and constraints on religious expression in public were imposed, such as the headscarf ban for women attending universities. The emergence of the AKP in this political landscape reflected the dreams of those who had been victims of the past system. Hence, the speeches analysed reveal that the AKP leader takes every opportunity to remind the people about these limitations. Yet, despite pressure from AKP supporters on the ground to remove the embargo on Imam Hatip schools and lift the headscarf ban, the AKP did not act for a long time. This was because they believed it to be essential to convince the secular bloc within society that conservative people and their values are a part of Turkish society, notes AC2. The prevalent concern among the Kemalist elites was that reintroducing Imam Hatip schools would Islamize Turkey. However, after 2012, and the passing of ten vigilant years following the AKP's rise to power, Erdoğan finally removed both prohibitions. Even at this stage some perceived it as risky for the AKP to alter laws that had been implemented in the first place to show Erbakan in a poor light.[20] However, Erdoğan was able to cite the AKP's non-Islamist narrative to suggest the novel idea of an ideological balance of Islam and secularism.

The party's enthusiasm to join the EU and willingness to embrace human rights and freedom of speech, as well as its respect for Atatürk's secularist project as a conservative party, supported a new interpretation of politics in Turkey's landscape that helped create a positive image for the AKP during its early days. As Kalın elaborated, 'AKP founders created a political identity to embrace different segments of Turkish society from the religious and conservatives to the urban and the liberal'.[21] This approach in general proved to be an opportunity for Erdoğan to renegotiate the position of Muslims in politics in Turkey. This process was termed 'normalization', as AC2 highlighted during our interview.

The principal aim of Islamist parties is to transform the societies from which they arise. For this reason, they are keen to overcome any obstacles that come in the way of supporting the development of this fundamental incentive for change. In this respect, the AKP first regulated the circumstances that arose by dealing with sensitive issues, as explained above, before moving on to adopt a transformational process. To this end, the regulations not only effected society; the party itself went through a similar process. Dealing with power brokers, forging diplomatic ties to other governments and states, as well as being a member of the government create new challenges in itself, and these automatically lead to a re-evaluation of the political frame. This enabled the AKP to attract new voters up until 2014 elections with no history of ever voting for a religious conservative party to participate in the election.

Alliance versus clash of civilizations

Policies and new interpretations of the AKP related to religion found common ground in the Alliance of Civilizations project. This initiative, overseen by the UN secretary general, was co-sponsored by the then Turkish prime minister

Erdoğan and Spanish prime minister José Luis Rodríguez Zapatero. It was a new foreign policy vision designed to bring Muslim countries together with the West, and overcome 'historical differences and reject calls for clash and confrontation' as Samuel Huntington[22] emphasized in his well-known theory. It portrays a post-Cold War world order in which the conflicts of the twenty-first century will not be primarily economic. Rather they will represent struggles between different cultures and civilizations, with a far-reaching impact on global politics. Huntington categorizes civilizations into eight different types: 'Western, Confucian, Japanese, Islamic, Hindu, Slavic-Orthodox, Latin American and African civilization', although he suggests that it may be inaccurate to classify the final example as a civilization.[23] However, the main prediction he made was that the next clash would occur between the Western and Islamic civilizations because, according to him, the modernization process increases the similarities across cultures, with the result that religious belief then becomes the main distinction, leading to a clash of this kind.[24]

The Alliance of Civilizations project, on the other hand, as the name suggests, defends the notion that 'mutual respect between cultures can prevent the deterioration of mutual suspicion, fear and polarization between the Muslim countries and Western societies'.[25] This is a counterargument to Huntington's thesis. This project was developed as a UN initiative to create the necessary apparatus for the 'recognition' of Turkey in the global sphere to promote peace; when examining Erdoğan's speeches we can see that he takes this issue very seriously. Between 2002 and 2009, he mentions cultural dialogue between Muslim countries and the West 54 times, accounting for 14.5 per cent of the coded speeches. When he uses Islamic references in this period, he generally focuses on the Alliance of Civilizations, with the intention of conveying the message that Islam is the religion of peace, and that all three Abrahamic religions should come together for an interfaith dialogue to build peace.[26] However, Erdoğan's speeches post-2010 show a decline in references to cultural and religious diversity of 3.6 per cent, a total mention of 23 times and an overall fall of 57.4 per cent.

The Alliance of Civilizations project revealed that the AKP's religious identity has changed dramatically since 2001. The Milli Görüş's leader Erbakan opposed interfaith dialogue by labelling it a facet of 'Moderate Islam', which was 'initiated in 1897 to annihilate Islam'.[27] For Erbakan, it signifies the encroaching project of 'Global Imperialism', in other words 'World Zionism', that intends to either annihilate Islam or alter its core meaning.[28] In addition, he argues that 'Global Imperialism' will make Muslim politicians 'slaves of Zionism'.[29] He underlines that 'Zionism does not care if someone is religious, prays five times a day, or if his wife is wearing hijab, because the main thing is that you do not criticise their system.' These sentences were directed towards Erdoğan and his reformist friends responsible for creating the AKP. However, Erdoğan had been Erbakan's loyal student for thirty-two years, and had engaged in Islamic activities, such as being a member of the MTTB, since he was 15 years old; it is apparent that he shared the ideology of the Milli Görüş.

Nevertheless, despite his roots and connections during his youth, Erdoğan did engage in interfaith dialogue. This resulted in harsh criticism from Erbakan, who even went so far as to suggest that 'Erdoğan became the slave of Zionism to protect the State of Israel in the Middle East'.[30] Every single action by Erdoğan was censured by Erbakan until his death in 2011; he felt it was his right to caution his former students. Erdoğan's participation in the opening ceremony of the 'Garden of Religions' in Istanbul in December 2004 is one example of his support for interfaith dialogue.[31] JO2 explains that Erdoğan believed in his first seven years of leadership that a close relationship with the Western world was necessary to grow the nation. This situation has now changed, as it is apparent not only in the speeches he makes, and from the stories of the people working closely with him, but also because people on the ground have observed it. While Erdoğan formerly strived to eliminate fundamental divisions between different civilizations, cultures and religions, the in-depth interviews I conducted reveal that several successive events reversed his support of the interfaith dialogue project. PO4 argues that owing to the ineffective role of the UN after the Mavi Marmara incident in 2010, Erdoğan started labelling the UN as incompetent and riddled with prejudices. PO4 says that Erdoğan did not openly criticize the UN in the early 2010s but brought it up during internal meetings. He also claims the Mavi Marmara incident and the military coup in Egypt led Erdoğan to lose faith in the Alliance of Civilizations project as 'both incidents were related to the Muslim nations but the UN did not take them seriously'.

Gülenists: Former ally, new enemy

In the first period, until the Mavi Marmara crisis, there was 'the sharpest public split' between the AKP and the Gülenists.[32] As explained earlier, the AKP supported the Gülenists politically, because they were the only organized conservative group in Turkey who had an institutionalized base with human resources. This is noticeable when reviewing Erdoğan's speeches. Between 2002 and 2009 there is no mention of the Gülenists in his speeches, as the Gülen movement was seen as a moderate religious group in Turkey. Interestingly, JO5 asserts that the Gülenists and the AKP were part of a US-led plan to modernize Islam in the Middle East:

> Whereas Gülen adopted the non-governmental organization [NGO] and in particular education part, Erdoğan focused on politics.

In fact, Gülen mobilized people via NGOs, such as 'schools, study centres, student dormitories' and through NGO activities, such as charity work, as he had access to a large database in different fields.[33] The network was not only active in Turkey but also in 150 other countries. Hence, the AKP turned a blind eye to the rise of the Gülenists who were actually benefitting from the AKP's influence. TT1 explains that both Erdoğan and Gülen supported one another, because they had no other choice but to stick together in order to overcome the Kemalist establishment. As a result, Erdoğan 'saved' the judiciary, the military and the police, in particular, from the Kemalist establishment, controlling these institutions through the Gülenists. However, as Ünal notes during our interview, when the Gülenists became arrogant about their power, seeking to appoint their own candidate to Turkey's MIT, and then to the Ministry of the Interior and Justice, Erdoğan recognized that Gülen's intention was to control Turkey through the AKP government. Immediately Erdoğan started to detach the Gülenists from all state institutions.

If we review their jargon, we can observe similarities in the religious issues mentioned by the Gülenists and the AKP, as TT1 highlights. The 'interfaith dialogue' described as part of the Alliance of Civilizations project is one of main initiatives they agreed upon. However, when the split began with the Mavi Marmara incident, huge conflict arose between both groups. Erdoğan's speeches after 2010 show clearly how the attitude of the AKP had changed, expressing anger and disappointment at the Gülen movement and its leader. Discussion of the use of religious symbolism in the struggle between the Gülenists and the AKP is important. In particular, after the rift began, both parties started smear campaigns using religious symbols or tools. For example, when the AKP decided to close down Gülenists' private prep-schools, one of the main financial sources of the movement, Gülenists responded with corruption allegations against ministers and businessmen supporting the AKP. Then in December 2013, the AKP passed a law to shut down all Gülen-affiliated schools and education institutions. In response, Gülen attacked Erdoğan in one of his weekly sermons from Pennsylvania with these words:

Dear God, incinerate their houses! Demolish their homes! Ruin their unity! May their hopes never see the light of day! Obstruct their path ahead! ... O God, defeat them! And make them quake! And break their unity! And split their congregations! And break them into a thousand pieces! And inflict them with evil against one another! And grant us victory over them.[34]

This message, full of religious symbolism, not only addressed the AKP and Erdoğan, but also Gülen's support base, urging them not to back the AKP in the local elections of spring 2014. Such symbols that served as a public relations tool helped convince Gülen to reconsider his relationship with the AKP. Then, for the first time, Gülen attacked the AKP government directly through using a religious tool, the prayer. Erdoğan retaliated by accusing Gülen of wanting to create a parallel state by using his religious support base. It is important to note here that 'power is diffused in images and information' as Castells explains.[35] Gülen's social movement was widespread in Turkey, and acted with a collective will. Erdoğan himself aimed to convince the Gülenists by 'using religious symbols'. To avoid losing ground, Erdoğan accused Gülen of being a 'fraud' and a 'fake Imam', first in the local and presidential elections in 2014, then in later events, especially after the coup attempt in 2016.

Erdoğan's populist Islamist narrative

The data gathered provide strong evidence that an Islamist narrative emerged in the post-2010 period of Erdoğan's leadership. These changes appear to be linked to key events, such as the Davos debate in 2009, the Mavi Marmara aid flotilla in 2010, the Gezi Park protests in 2013, corruption allegations against the government at the end of 2013, PKK's attacks after 2015 and the coup attempt in July 2016. Consequently, domestic and international threats altered Erdoğan's narrative. After 2009, there appears to have been considerable re-evaluation in three important areas.

The first concerns the use of religious – that is, populist Islamist – discourse. In his speeches between 2002 and 2009, Erdoğan uses words such as Allah, Islam, Prophet Muhammad, Hadith,[36] Islamic civilization, martyrdom, death, after life and refers to cities and countries that carry an important meaning for Muslims such as Mecca, Medina and Jerusalem occasionally. While a careful approach was taken in the first period with regard to the use of such words, a rise of 809 per cent is observed after 2010. At the same time, there is a change in the use of anti-establishment language. He criticizes the UN, the UN Security Council, the World Bank and international news agencies, such as the *New York Times* and the BBC, a popular method employed by populist leaders to undermine institutions and media outlets.[37] While in the first period, he makes only few negative statements, the figure rose during the later period to indicate a 1500 per cent difference between both periods. The third area relates to Erdoğan's criticism of Israel – a change of 141.2 per cent when analysing his speeches. An additional development was the more frequent mentions of the Ottoman Empire in the second period, which was significant. In the thirty speeches that were analysed, there were only four mentions of the 'Ottoman Empire' before 2009, whereas after 2010, the AKP leader refers to the term 66 times, a notable rise of 1550 per cent. In fact the latter is not just reflected in Erdoğan's speeches, but in buildings inspired by the Ottoman architecture, or in cultural and art events with a reference to Ottoman sultans.

The findings of the quantitative content analysis illustrated in this part of the research suggest that as Erdoğan's power and dominance increased between 2002 and 2019 while the AKP underwent a transition. What was once a party that stood for respect for human rights, freedom of speech, separation of powers, democracy, tolerance and cultural diversity became a pro-Muslim party that has progressively narrowed its focus towards the Muslim world in post-2010, by developing an anti-establishment and anti-occupation discourse, questioning international organizations for not being functional or supportive of Turkey and censuring mainstream media outlets for covering the AKP as an Islamist party and its leader as an authoritarian leader. The Syrian refugee crisis is a leading story in this regard. Turkey's hosting of more than three million refugees has been a political tool for Erdoğan to pressure the EU and mainly Germany to either accept refugees and grant them a status, or support Turkey financially. However, EU's lack of support has been severely criticized by Turkish people according to PO7, who is in charge of AKP government's EU affairs. According to him, the image of the EU became fundamentally related to ideological differences not necessarily with the Turkish people but with the Turkish government.

7

Erdoğan's communication: Populist Islamism

For the last 15 years, we have been striving to build a Turkey, a strong Turkey, a country which is a source of confidence for its friends, its kin and its Muslim brothers and sisters as well as for the oppressed and the victims ... If we are constantly being subjected to attacks at home and abroad, if we are being slandered, if attempts are being made on our lives which we dedicated to our cause, it is because we do not give up on this struggle. Believe me, if we sat down, remained silent, looked when ordered as we did in the past, we would not face any of these attacks. But we do not care what [world] powers say. We only care what Allah (God) says.

– Erdoğan[1]

This chapter evaluates and synthesizes the evidence provided by quantitative and qualitative dataset. It begins by identifying the political communication strategies implemented by the AKP. In reference to this, the modernization process will be explained briefly, as it is fundamental to understanding the role of Americanization in the party's political communication. The focus will then shift to Americanization, bringing together local symbols and interpretations. The role of Erdoğan's charisma will be explained in conjunction with the changes in the party's political message over time. The central finding of this chapter, and indeed this entire research, is that Erdoğan is at the epicentre of the AKP's communication. Similarly, the evolution of the AKP's political message from 2002 to 2019 can be directly correlated with Erdoğan's discourse. In addition to highlighting the significance of Erdoğan's personality, the results indicate that the AKP's political message has evolved to become increasingly populist Islamist since 2010. Further, the HDP's increasing role after 2015, the PKK's attacks, the coup attempt in 2016 and the deepening refugee problem in 2019 were events that led to the rise of populist nationalist ideology in the AKP's political discourse.

Undoubtedly the time frame covered in this research encompassed many significant historical events, both domestically and internationally, all of which unsurprisingly have shaped the focus of the AKP and its leader. The transformation of Erdoğan – from one of the most liberal thinking leaders in the Middle East to one now renowned for showing less tolerance for freedom of speech and his authoritarian stance – is dramatic, and so is of great interest. By referencing key moments marking this transition, and the course of that change, as evidenced by fieldwork, interviews, and in the speeches analysed, it can be suggested that the AKP is best defined as a populist Islamist party.

AKP's communication brand: Erdoğan

The research findings revealed that the AKP's communication strategy is centred on Erdoğan, and not on an independent institutionalized political communication framework. In mapping the Americanization of political communication within the framework of Turkey's AKP, modernization emerges as key to understanding the process. The extensive acceptance of modernization in Turkey also explains why the AKP is willing to apply the Americanization theory to its political communications, according to JO1. Certainly, economic development during the AKP era increased the standard of living in the country; in particular, the religious, conservative working middle class adapted its lifestyle, turning its eyes towards the West, as many were suddenly in a position to send their children abroad to study, to wear expensive brands from the fashion capitals of Europe or to spend their honeymoons in the Maldives. Lerner explains that the change in terms of society starts with the individual and continues until it reaches complete 'economic and political participation'.[2] Although these changes were a result of the improvement in the economic status of individuals, they were a direct consequence of the AKP's economic success in the early days and until 2013, in particular.

AKP's success was an essential first step preceding investment in political communication, because when they were first elected they had to deal with 'corruption, unemployment, the unequal distribution of wealth, and decay in moral values'.[3] However, once the AKP was able to 'take a breath' after securing economic and political success, during the 2002 and 2007 general elections, it started exploring new communication strategies. The initial changes it made reflected a growing emphasis on institutionalization within the party. In fact, Americanization was recognized as a key strategy in the Western world, because the American style of political communication has become the modern and professional mode of campaigning in Western democratic countries; in other words, AKP's pragmatic approach helped learn from – or rather imitate – the Western world.

It is useful to compare events at the end of the Ottoman Empire in the eighteenth century with the modernization process today, because in both eras emphasis was placed on forging strong relationships with other European countries and politicians and on renewing the military, bureaucracy and education. The Ottoman Empire framed the period internally as one of reform, but it also marked the start of the process of Westernization in the Ottoman lands.[4] However, while the Ottoman Empire modernized by looking to the European countries, in particular France, today, the AKP is seeking inspiration, especially for its political communication tools, from the United States. This is elaborated in the following section which explains key aspects of the Americanization model as applied by Erdoğan administration.

Americanization supports AKP's leader-based communication

The transformation of the AKP's political communication along the lines of Americanization began with the professionalization of its political communication mechanisms. This research clarifies that the AKP's communication strategy is dependent on its leader. Specifically, Erdoğan's dominating one-man leadership style correlates with the Americanization model in terms of its nature of communication. To understand this more fully, I asked my informants about 'How it started?', 'What dynamics are behind it?' and 'What are the local aspects?'; answers to these questions will also help present a clearer picture of the current situation and how it developed.

Olçok, who helped answer the first question, was a valuable resource for this study as he has studied Americanization theory and was involved in applying it. Undeniably creative, he shared many of his perspectives during our interviews. Olçok commented that as societies' historical and sociological frameworks differ, and as America's and Turkey's problems and expectations are dissimilar, Americanization did not mean simply copying political communication strategies directly from that of the United States. For him, the strategies applied by the AKP were necessarily unique. Thus, because of their uniqueness in the Eastern, or rather sociocultural context, they have been imitated by other Islamist parties in the region as well. He adds that Erdoğan's leadership style, discourse and the AKP's political style have also been copied by their opponents. Although the United States is the principal source of effective political communication strategies, Olçok notes that the Communications Team follows global news and examines campaigns in the West carefully before implementing them so as to ensure an effective, targeted, unique, innovative and, more importantly, local campaign. Erdoğan's Communications Directory also supports Olçok's viewpoint and bases its strategies on the legacy of Olçok.

Erdoğan's new weapon: Communications Directory

It is necessary to describe the AKP's political communication model as observed during my study. It comprises three main structures: the Communications Directory, the Strategy Team and the AKP's Publicity and Media Department. The chairman of the latter is also vice chairman of the AKP. According to PO5, it was only after the 2018 presidential elections that the Communications Directory was added to the list while, the PR agency has changed with every election. The Communications Directory then took charge, leading to another form of authoritarian style governance, highlights PO5, who opines that Communications Chief Fahrettin Altun controls everything related to communication in Turkey while Serhat Albayrak, Erdoğan's son-in-law Berat Albayrak's brother, who is the head of Turkuaz media, is in the background. Berat Albayrak is the name behind Turkey's economic recession, as markets and investors react sceptically amid nepotism allegations. His brother, who heads Turkuaz or SETA, according to high-ranked AKP official PO5, considers himself to be media mogul like Rupert Murdoch and aims to take over all media outlets in Turkey. According to Smith, Altun, who is known to be 'Turkey's second most powerful man' and who had a close relationship with Serhat Albayrak, became influential in a short period of time.[5] Altun was the director of SETA's Istanbul branch who wrote columns for *Sabah* and *Daily Sabah* newspapers and participated in programmes on TV channels, such as AHaber; he travelled frequently with Erdoğan, which increased his credibility and loyalty in the eyes of Erdoğan's family. According to AC3, Altun not only controls the Turkish state's communication but also the Erdoğan family's communication. Some of his responsibilities include advising the family 'what to share online on social media accounts', 'how to approach to public issues' and 'how to react in crisis periods'. Altun's objective is to model the US administrative communication, according to JO6, by 'personalizing the communication and restructuring hierarchies'. In an interview, Altun[6] emphasized that his mission is to build a collective communication system across all state institutions, which basically reflects

Erdoğan's need to have control over all 'ideological state apparatus' in Turkey, as Althusser[7] emphasizes. Altun notes that coordination has improved since the Communications Directory has been created and that collective cooperative identity has been introduced, starting with the initiative of standardizing logos of the all ministries. Restoring Turkey's image abroad is another important focus of the directory. *Turkey Talks* and *Today Turkey* are two programmes – in which pro-government academics, journalists and bureaucrats participate – that are aired abroad such as the United States, the UK, Germany and Russia, where Turkey has interest. However, PO8 admits that these activities of the directory are more a part of the propaganda tool for Ankara and not devised as a means to address non-Turkish or biased policymakers in the West and elsewhere, 'because mainly Turkish people who support the AKP attend these talks'. Moreover, Altun underlines that Erdoğan's diplomacy and communication with world leaders demonstrate the strength of his office.

The Publicity and Media Department, on the other hand, is in charge of publishing an official monthly review of the AKP, *Türkiye Bülteni* (Turkey Bulletin), maintaining the party's website, issuing press releases and organizing internal media. Interestingly when MPs or board members from the AKP are invited to attend TV talk shows as commentators or spokespersons, they need to get an approval from the Publicity and Media Department. After the creation of the Communications Directory, they now have to get the permission of this department. PO1, who was previously the chairman of the Publicity and Media Department, explains that this rule was implemented after the Gezi Park protests, and prior to that incident 'there was freedom within the party and politicians could act easily in such matters'. The Publicity and Media Department functions more in the capacity of an internal communication channel since the Communications Director at the presidential palace has the upper hand in Erdoğan's communication. Overseeing all structures related to communication, according to PO8, my source from the communications office, 1,500 people work under the leadership of Altun to manage communication across the country and abroad. Besides the Communications Team, during every election period, a selected team of Erdoğan's chief advisors, ministers, MPs, representatives from research centres, think tanks and journalists skilled in strategic-thinking is formed to manage the election campaign.

The role of Erdoğan's longest serving chief advisor Ibrahim Kalın is also critical in this circle. As a key resource, Kalın advices Erdoğan on foreign policy, attends critical meetings with world leaders, translates secret bilateral meetings with leaders like Trump and, more importantly, acts as presidential spokesperson as he addresses journalists at every press conference. Kalın's intellectual knowledge, analytical thinking and policymaking skills are respected within AKP circles which makes him a credible voice.

Professionalization of a campaign

The interview data reveal how the AKP became professionalized in its political communications after 2007. Negrine's three-step model for the professionalization of political communication appears to have been followed by the AKP.[8] First, the AKP 'changed organisational structures' by creating a dynamic team of people from multiple backgrounds.[9] This has been the case with the Strategy Team and Communications Directory. Second, the AKP reconsidered the 'use of technologies in communication'.[10] From campaign music to billboards to the use of social media, every possible modernization technique has been considered. And third, the AKP continues to utilize conventional media channels, such as Erdoğan's TV appearances on political news shows. Undeniably, the TV is a useful way to address middle-aged and older adults.

This all leads to personalization, another important aspect of Americanization. During every election, including the local ones, Erdoğan can be found campaigning on the streets in nearly every single city. Using such candidate-centred politics diminishes the 'traditional affective ties between voters and parties'.[11] The relationship between Erdoğan and his supporters – and their loved ones – is critical. Middle-aged and older adults from conservative backgrounds love Erdoğan because they see him as one of them, unlike previous politicians who were more elitist in nature. Equally important, as Erdoğan's former speechwriter Ünal explains, is the fact that in the past Erdoğan has brought together teams of people from across society – mostly youngsters who do not support the AKP – to understand what the public desires:

> Our creative speechwriter team members consisted of people who had a relationship on the ground. They used public transport when they came to the prime ministry (later presidency). Hence a conversation between two old women about health care or an anti-government discussion between two university students would be on our table the next morning. That is the reason why Erdoğan is an 'up to date leader' who knows exactly what those on the ground need. We wrote his speeches keeping these dynamics in mind.

According to Ünal, this creation of roles for individuals who feel negatively about the government is a novel way of approaching secular Kemalist people or even Kurds and other minorities. By communicating with the public, the AKP can develop politics that respond to contemporary concerns, and Erdoğan can introduce new essential policies on the ground; as a result, mutually beneficial communication is established. Ünal's work can be viewed as a component of public relations, and, as Bernays notes regarding PR, it is a means of managing the 'communication between an organization and its public',[12] wherein the main objective is the persuasion of people. However, as PO5 highlights, things like being the voice of the voiceless, listening to the public and considering poll data have disappeared especially after the introduction of the new presidential system.

Nevertheless, Erdoğan still has credibility on the ground, which brings success to the party despite a decline in their popularity since 2019. Highlighting the benefits of attending to the needs and lived experiences of the people, a 52-year-old taxi driver in the Fatih district of Istanbul recalls the time Erdoğan visited the cab centre where he works, sat with the drivers, drank a glass of tea and enquired about their needs, their families and their opinions regarding the general politics of the AKP.[13] Despite not supporting the AKP in the 2011 elections, Erdoğan, whom he framed as 'modest', through his actions made him reconsider his choice in the 2014 presidential elections.[14]

In Turkey, cultural norms and values play a central role. Thus, Erdoğan's relationship with the public draws on his awareness of the expectations associated with cultural norms, such as making visits to people who are in need, removing his footwear before entering their homes, sitting on the floor when meeting poor families who have little or no furniture, as well as kissing the hands of elderly family members present. Erdoğan's humility and 'common-man' image are hence associated with that of a man who, being close to 'the people', who understands them very well because of his demographic background. Being from Istanbul's Kasımpaşa district, which is known for working-class community housings, Eroğan uses this reality regularly when discussing issues related 'the elite' in the country. There are many other stories depicting the relationship between Erdoğan and his people. He enjoys interacting directly with the voters and always emphasizes that nobody can come between him and his people; this is another reason he does not use social media personally because it ruins what he believes to be natural in his relationships. This relationship with the electorate has generated positive responses in elections according to TT1, who conducts polls in his research centre regularly to follow updates on the ground. He claims that no other leader has such a relationship with their support base.

Opinion polls play an important role in the AKP's political communication strategies, and are a recognizable component of the professionalization of electioneering in the United States, as Butler and Ranney explain.[15] The willingness to conduct and listen to the findings of polls is 'one of the main reasons behind the AKP's sustainable success', according to JO3. Polls not only evaluate the current opinions of the electorate, but also provide information concerning their future expectations, which is useful in shaping the political agenda. The results of polls conducted for the AKP are discussed and analysed by the Communications Directory, which take them into consideration while developing political communication strategies. As an instrument of political communication, opinion polls have also been central to the PJD's success in Morocco.[16] Bouyahya explains that it was the Americanization of electioneering that led to the use of 'opinion polls' and 'political consultants' for the first time by an Islamist party (found in 1967) in Morocco,.[17]

Rather than indoctrinating the public with a specific ideology, opinion polls provide Islamist parties with the opportunity to engage in a dialogue and to respond to people's demands. Thus JO4 explains that dialogue and openness with the public have made Erdoğan stronger than his opponents. He observes, 'When he criticizes something that he does not like, he says this openly, although some people do not agree, they at least appreciate his frankness and honesty'. While it seems positive on the surface, this approach also reflects Erdoğan's growing intolerance. Another important aspect here is the difference in the attitudes between generations. Middle-aged and older religious conservatives, whose education level is not higher than the high school, prefer this type of leadership. But when the education level increases, the acceptance of intolerant leadership decreases. Obviously this is an important aspect regarding the generation Z and Y in particular.

Yet despite the lack of interest among the younger generation, outdoor rallies held by the AKP, which demonstrate Erdoğan's willingness to communicate directly with the people from religious conservative background, have been hugely successful. But the impact of outdoor rallies has decreased in 2019 local elections. Despite the huge number of people attending these gatherings in particular in Istanbul and Ankara, it was a setback for the ruling government, a sign how the AKP is losing ground.

AC2 goes on to explain that 'interest in indoor meetings is increasing' due to Turkey's socio-economic transformation. Meetings with fewer people are associated with Americanized campaigns, and this may inform the AKP's future election campaigns. Smaller gatherings are also a consequence of the modernization process: when a country begins applying neoliberal economic policies, the likely result is greater individualization and individual practices 'as a means of finding jobs, money, respect and self-esteem'.[18] This self-centric approach to life, and also to politics, is a shift away from collectiveness. According to AC2 this individualization of the public is a concern to Erdoğan, because, while a social movement is composed of individual members, 'ideas, identities and ideals' can be realized only when a group of people come together to take 'collective action'.[19] As Kısakürek describes in his poems, it is also the essence of an Islamic community to act collectively, which is Erdoğan's main intention, as he is interested in promoting Islamic consciousness.[20]

Furthermore, JO2 notes that the society is becoming younger, and young people have a different worldview that will transform the dynamic of politics as well as the direction of political communications. JO2's principal argument here is that the younger generation is more educated and therefore less interested in attending mass rallies. Moreover, young people prefer smaller gatherings so that they can benefit from networking, which can have a positive long-term impact on their future. In fact, high-profile AKP members who were interviewed for this study agreed that number of young people participating in the AKP's outdoor rallies has gone down when compared to ten years ago. In other words, young electorates are in search of new political solutions.

Reportedly, Erdoğan dreams of a young generation which holds the Quran on the one hand and a computer on the other. The reality on the ground is somewhat different, and this has upset the outcome of the 2019 local elections as noted earlier. This explains why the AKP is organizing mass rallies at present, appealing to the religious conservative working middle-class people in particular, who are socio-economically dependent upon one another. It has however been predicted that factors such as socio-economic changes and the modernization of society will have an impact on the communication style of the AKP in long term. As a consequence, one can expect people to show higher preference for American-style meetings – a campaign style which was used by Babacan when he established his party. He organized a gathering with young university students in which he discussed their needs, expectations and dreams. In addition, the use of digital media to reach educated youths will be increasingly relevant; this approach has proved successful in the 2008 and 2012 as well as in the 2016 presidential elections in the United States.[21]

Family portrayal as a cultural symbol

'Family, personal appearance, lifestyle and religion'[22] are important aspects of personalization and are considered in the portrayal of Erdoğan as the leader of the AKP.

As AC2 explains, the electorate is arguably more interested in the personal character and lives of politicians than ever before, because they are able to identify with someone who shares their values and lifestyle. By appearing with his wife, Erdoğan is conveying to the public that family is important to him. Symbolically, he is placing a value on marriage and family life. This is clearly important to him because when Erdoğan attends wedding ceremonies he encourages couples to have at least three children. Procreation is believed to be related to Prophet Muhammad's advice of having as many children as possible because, as PO7 explains, the community's (*ummah*) size on the day of judgement is said to make the Prophet proud. PO4 also emphasized the benefits of having more children, stating that it is the 'essence of his Islamist ideology to have a healthy society'. This is implied when Erdoğan describes abortion as an 'airstrike on civilians' and indicated by the fact that the AKP government supports couples with children.[23] However, during the AKP governance the number of suspicious female deaths has increased enormously. It is the same government that does not publish data on female deaths, and introduce laws to protect women and children. When a discussion broke out in 2020 about a possibility of withdrawing from Istanbul Convention which prevents violence against women, AKP was harshly criticized by women and human rights activists. The reason behind the possible withdrawal was the believe of the AKP leadership that the Istanbul Convention is damaging traditional conservative family mentality and challenging Islamists' understanding of gender equality. As a result, Erdoğan believes that marriage and family based on religious and cultural codes are the ideal result that should be protected.

Erdoğan reviving the image of Ottoman sultans

Erdoğan's approach is akin to that of past leaders of the Ottoman era, who also placed great importance on image building. An examination of his speeches reveals a significant increase in references to the Ottoman era, highlighting Erdoğan's depth of feeling for the past. Comparisons between Abdulhamid II and Erdoğan have been widespread among conservatives in Turkey, because, according to JO4, both set 'Islamizing society and leading the Muslim world' as their objectives. Significant here is that Erdoğan sees himself as equivalent to an Ottoman sultan, and that he is desirous of developing a similarly legendary image. This impression is supported by the fact that the AKP government built new bridges, tunnels and highways and name after Ottoman Sultan's, and by Erdoğan's instruction to build Turkey's largest mosque on Istanbul's Çamlıca

Hill, a symbolic act of Ottoman Sultans who also bequeathed to be buried next to the mosque they built, as historically such projects have symbolized the strength and vanity of the Ottoman sultans. Through the Turkish Cooperation and Coordination Agency (TIKA), financial support was lent by the AKP government to restore historical mosques, palaces, buildings and bridges built hundreds of years ago. Though TIKA's main responsibility is to assist developing countries, its primary focus is on Turkic countries.[24] Although TIKA was created in 1992, it was Erdoğan who revived this institution when he came to power. Apart from Turkic countries, TIKA is an important propaganda tool for Erdoğan to show presence in the Middle East, Balkans, Africa, in particular Somalia, and Latin America. Undoubtedly, these initiatives are seen as part of Erdoğan's Islamic mission to leave an imprint behind – something he also admits in his speeches.[25]

Religious nationalist symbols from the days of the Ottoman Empire play an important role in the AKP's political communications, reflecting Erdoğan's reactionary political stance. From using the *Rabaa* gesture after the military coup in Egypt; to giving directions to his staff, ministers, MPs and security service personnel to grow moustaches after the coup attempt in 2016; to representing a 'strong and stern image';[26] to creating a personal logo using the name of Prophet Muhammad; to developing a campaign advert including the *azan*; building new mosques'; to emphasizing that 'the world is bigger than five'; to building a new presidential palace based on Ottoman and Seljuki mélange architecture with a modern touch; to using key palaces and premises in Istanbul found in Ottoman era as presidential offices; in the same way, converting Hagia Sophia to a mosque after 86 years, Erdoğan is engaged in a reactionary style of political communication that prioritizes constructing a new identity.

Ünal explains the above further, claiming that 'Erdoğan creates an image based on symbols that are conducive to the creation of an Islamic identity in young people in particular'. Although at present the reactions of the younger Turkish generation to Erdoğan's charismatic leadership style is relatively muted, his image building is principally religiously motivated. It is designed to position him as the leader of the Muslims in the twenty-first century, inspiring the vast majority of the religious conservative community, with a unique style of leadership. This approach fits with Erdoğan's aim to transform society through cultural domination, framed by his Islamist ideology. Consequently, Erdoğan is described as a 'conservative revolutionist' by some of his communication officers. In addition, as discussed earlier, Erdoğan's *Reis* image strengthens the impression that he prefers one-man leadership over collective mind. Certainly, his purging of possible opponents, whom he had himself appointed, is a clear signal that he does not want to share power, and that he is not open to other political discourses.

Religious nationalist populism

Erdoğan's image not only relates to key symbols integrated into his political communications, but also informs the message of the AKP. During the past two decades, Turkey has faced diverse, domestic and geopolitical challenges. The AKP's reputation in Western mainstream media was once positive. Nevertheless, even then, domestically, the party was struggling with the Kemalist bloc in the country; that is, in the judiciary, and, more specifically, in the military.

Initially, perceptions of the AKP were based on its parting of ways with Erbakan in 2001 – repression forced the moderation of Islamist parties. This moderation resulted in the democratization of internal organizations, cooperative relationships and restrained policies. The AKP's early years, from 2002 to 2009, can be categorized within this framework. Consequently, the 'conservative democrats' were advocating development, democracy, human rights, pluralism, freedom and the rule of law, which was a positive sign after the challenging years of ideology politics that ended with the postmodern coup in 1997. On the other hand, there were some fears over the religious backgrounds of the founding members of the party, even as they strived to convince the elites they had changed and were willing to uphold the secular constitution.

The data collected for this research show how the party message evolved in six key ways between 2002 and 2019. The first and foremost change was in post-2010 when the AKP adopted a pro-Muslim stance, as reflected in Erdoğan's increasingly religious discourse. Second, the leader's relationship with Israel changed the party's rhetoric at the international level, marking the adoption of a pro-Palestinian discourse. This change began in an era in which the influence of Erdoğan's charismatic leadership style was felt more widely throughout the Middle East. Third, the Gezi Park protests in 2013 simultaneously increased Erdoğan's willingness to act in an authoritarian manner and led him to embrace a more heavily religious discourse, which on the other hand, had an enormous impact on society's polarization. Fourth, the military coup against Egypt's Islamists and Erdoğan's support for this organization triggered the inclusion of a more anti-establishment rhetoric. Fifth, the coup attempt in 2016 motivated Erdoğan to more frequently espouse religious and anti-Gülenist messages, and marked the beginning of an alliance with the nationalist MHP. Finally, the Syrian civil war, and the growing flow of immigrants from there, as well as the increasing dominance of the PYD, the PKK's offshoot in Syria, in the region have led to the development of a strong nationalist discourse, which strengthened the alliance with the MHP. And yet, when AKP lost its majority in the parliament, the political dynamics made the AKP dependent to the MHP.

Islamists' identity crisis

The interviews, fieldwork and content analysis of the speeches demonstrate that there are two types of party representation. One is the official representation, which is based on the term 'conservative democracy', respecting 'fundamental human rights and freedoms', and this coincides with the period from 2002 to 2009. This has been part of the official party programme since 2001, according to PO1. Also, these years represent AKP's moderate face. Far from extravagancy, vanity and arrogance – and from establishing new institutions or favouring only those who support the same ideology – the party's main aim was to serve the people, as PO8 summarizes.

After 2010, references to 'Atatürk and his principles' such as 'secularism', 'laïcité', and 'modernization' in Erdoğan's speeches, were far fewer in number. In this respect, the tendency increased tremendously towards a religious, nationalist and anti-establishment discourse in the second term. Apparently the AKP is now seen as a party with an 'Islamic mission', in other words serving to protect society by retaining the 'core identity and character of Islam', actively defending the rights of oppressed Muslims globally.[27] Although this is not the official position, the research evidence suggests that at least in the mind of the AKP's leader and some of the party members who are loyal to Erdoğan, this has been a policy objective since the presidential election in 2014. This approach suggests the importance of collective identity as a key driver for mobilizing the party and its members towards change. Yet both AC3 and AC4 underline that AKP's religiosity is only a case of rhetoric which is used to gain the votes of conservative people. AC4 notes,

> AKP uses religion as a populist discourse. It is a reflection of Erdoğan's personal attitude and character. If someone else were to be the leader of the AKP, I am not sure the party would stick to religion like it does today. However, it is not

possible to say that this discourse led to the increase of religiosity or spirituality in the country. On the contrary, the use of religion does have a negative impact on people in the country. This is the reason behind the rise of deism in high schools. Young people do not want to be connected with religion , consequently with the AKP.

Rather, it is a result of pragmatic policies of Erdoğan whose main concern is to survive. AC3, in this regard, believes that the AKP has created a new identity. He emphasizes that religion is an important tool for Erdoğan which he uses in relation to his power. In other words, to 'use political and economic dominance to build new mosques, Imam Hatip schools, dormitories and institutions where an Islamic identity is propagated; increase the budget of the Presidency of Religious Affairs (Diyanet), because Erdoğan's aim is to be remembered as the person who did many things for Islam in order to leave an imprint behind. This is his main objective as a Muslim.' What Erdoğan wants is to create an image of himself which is similar to that of Egypt's Gamal Abdel Nasser or Palestine's Yasser Arafat, who continue to be hailed as heroes of their nations.

Erdoğan's Palestinian cause

A key factor observed in this research is that a political shift occurred in the AKP and Erdoğan's political communication after encounters with Israel. Content analysis of the speeches showed clearly that a change took hold after 2010, following the Mavi Marmara incident. However, most interviewees mentioned both incidents together when explaining the change. Thus, examining the content of the speeches proved important for assessing this. From 2002 to 2009, only 4.8 per cent of the overall texts refer to anti-Israel sentiment.[28] However, when reviewing the second period, from 2010 to 2019, the number increases to 141.2 per cent. Nevertheless, we need to consider that taking only the anti-Israel discourse into account is not sufficient to demonstrate the authenticity of a shift. Thus, perhaps more significantly is the massive increase of anti-establishment discourse after 2010.[29] This is critical, because informal conversations with eighty-one people ideologically close to the AKP aligned Erdoğan's anti-establishment discourse with anti-Zionism.[30] This was confirmed by research centre director TT1, who explained that, as each day passes, progressively more Turkish people believe that 'there is a secret power in the world which is controlling the money, and thereby mainstream media and politics' and that this is based on Zionism. Aviv[31] elucidates this, noting that 'international organizations such as the UN,

IMF, World Bank, and big international firms' are part of this West versus East imaginary.

Erdoğan and the effect of Turkish dramas in the Middle East

Social and political realities affect how a leader's image is perceived – a phenomenon related to the 'art of presence'.[32] It is important to highlight this facet of charismatic leadership as it helps answer questions concerning the impact of Erdoğan's leadership style on the AKP's political communication. In fact, when Erdoğan returned home to Turkey from Davos, he was given a hero's welcome. Moreover, subsequently, Erdoğan's popularity peaked in the Arab world after the Mavi Marmara incident.[33] Both events had an associative impact on Erdoğan's and his party's image among Muslims worldwide. Yet, his charisma arises from 'inner determination', as Weber explains. It is related to his belief and ideology, which can be related to the incidents with Israel.

As PO8 explains, both events reflected a distinct transformation in Erdoğan's image, who had, prior to 2010, placed only limited emphasis on the Palestinian struggle and followed a liberal line. This 'courage' on the part of Erdoğan was viewed as 'a new stand against injustice' in the region.

Not only the personalities that I interviewed but also people on the ground agreed that Erdoğan started focusing on Muslim values after the crisis with Israel, by declaring that an ideological division remains and, as Erbakan emphasized, there exists a 'fundamental conflict between the Western and Islamic civilization'.[34] Erdoğan founded the new political party in 2001 because his ideologies and worldview conflicted with those of Erbakan; however results of this study clearly indicate that after nearly two decades of governance, Erdoğan reached the same conclusion as his former mentor regarding the global political struggle between the West and Islam. Erdoğan is in part also motivated by his personal religious belief, and the desire to bring back the glorious days of the Ottoman era as the founder of the 'New Turkey'. In fact, this change after 2009 was highlighted by Babacan in an interview in May 2020.

> We got spoiled when we reached a certain level of economic prosperity after 2009.[35]

Here, it is interesting to consider the role of Turkish drama and soap opera as a tool of cultural diplomacy. Historical dramas such as *Resurrection Ertuğrul* and *Payitaht Abdulhamid* became popular not only in Turkey but also in the Latin America, Balkans, the Middle East and even Eastern Europe. 'Along with the rise of Erdoğan's image in the Middle East, the role of Turkish production series glorified the image of Turkey, particularly regarding its Islamic identity', notes to AC6, whose field of research is Turkish soft power. This was nation branding through 'culture, rhetoric and broadcasting' in the Middle East where soft power was used.[36] Despite political disagreements between both countries, Israelis show high interest in Turkish programmes.[37] The rise of Turkish dramas and soap operas have a significant impact on the country's tourism.

Yet, it is vital to observe that the AKP not only pulled back from its relationship with Israel, but perhaps, more importantly, furthered its engagement with the Middle East, Africa and other Muslim-majority and -minority countries such as Myanmar. Engaging with Somalia – with Turkey contributing to eliminate famine there – and forging a strong bond with the Palestinian Hamas – whose leadership Erdoğan welcomed dozens of times in Ankara and Istanbul, and whose legitimacy and international recognition he openly advocated – were only some of the steps taken after the shift in political orientation occurred. Therefore, undoubtedly, as Erdoğan's message shifted, the AKP's political standpoint and actions followed suit.

Turkey-Qatar alliance

With regard to Erdoğan's association with the Muslim world, his close relationship with the Qatari ruling family Al-Thani is another dynamic in the region to consider when analysing the shift in political discourse. The Qatar blockade has brought Ankara and Doha closer to each other. But it has resulted in the development of two blocs in the region: Turkey and Qatar, one the one hand, and the strong alliance of Saudi Arabia, UAE, Bahrain and Egypt, on the other. Trump's visit to Saudi Arabia a month before the Qatar blockade in 2017 encouraged the latter to take economic actions against Qatar with the argument that Qatar is supporting terrorists like Hamas and the MB. Erdoğan has not hesitated to show his support of the Qatari Emir as national sovereignty was at stake. In fact, according to PO8, Erdoğan was pretty sure that the next target will be Turkey, as it is supporting Islamist movements in the region, and, as discussed earlier, is keen to develop a unity among Muslim nations in the world. However, one year later, on 2 October 2018, when *Washington Post* journalist Jamal Khashoggi, a Saudi citizen, was murdered inside Istanbul's Saudi consulate, the rift between these two blocs grew wider because Turkey used its intelligence service to effectively investigate the murder which was in fact ordered directly by the Saudi Arabia's Crown Prince Mohammed bin Salman (MBS), according to US Central Intelligence Agency's report.[38] Turkey's Communications Directory, which was established around two and a half month before this incident, followed a 'drip-by-drip' strategy in leaking footages from the embassy to international and national media. Communications Chief Altun underlined that Saudi tried to blame Turkey for the murder, but Turkey adopted a justice-based communication policy.[39] This was no doubt an opportunity for Erdoğan to restore his image in international media. In fact it was a case of suppression of freedom of speech and expression that Erdoğan was accused of, and hence he dealt with this issue very carefully and was in the spotlight for couple of months. Furthermore, according to JO7, Qatar took advantage of this opportunity by putting pressure on Saudi Arabia through its Al Jazeera network.

The close partnership between the Saudi crown prince and his mastermind Abu Dhabi's Mohammed bin Zayed (MBZ) is comparable with that between Erdoğan and Al-Thani, Emir of Qatar. While MBZ and MBS follow a 'secular Islam' agenda in the Middle East, Erdoğan and Al-Thani prefer having a pro-MB agenda. In this regard, Trump's 'Deal of the Century' projects 'a two-state solution but favours Israel's further occupation of Palestinian territory', according to political scientist AC7. This plan was supported by Saudi Arabia and the UAE.[40] Moreover, in August 2020, UAE normalized its relations with Israel, which was announced by Trump, who brokered the peace agreement.[41] By showing four different maps of Israel and Palestinian territory from 1947 to 2019 at the 74th General Assembly of the UN in 2019, Erdoğan once again raised his voice against Israel, the US plan of backing a new deal in the Middle East and the international institutions for not being capable of peace-building in the region:

[*Erdoğan shows a map*] Look at this map. Where was Israel in 1947 and where is Israel now? Especially between the years 1949 and 1967 where was Israel and where is Israel now. [*Erdoğan shows another map*] Look this is 1947 the land of Palestine. There's seemingly almost no Israeli presence on these lands. The entire territory belongs to the Palestinians so the map suggests. But [in] the year 1947 the distribution plan gets ratified[,] Palestinian lands starts shrinking and Israel starts expanding ...[*Erdoğan shows another map*] And today, [in] the current situation, there is seemingly no Palestinian presence[;] the entire land belongs to Israel. But would it suffice Israel? No. Israel is still willing to take over the remaining of the land. But what about the UN Security Council? What about the UN? What about the resolutions therein? Are those resolutions being activated?

Are they being implemented and enforced? No. So we have to ask ourselves. What does the UN serve?[42]

In 1969, when a 'Christian Zionist zealot set fire to the pulpit of the al-Aqsa Mosque in Jerusalem', Saudi King Faisal invited all Muslim-majority countries to a summit held in Morocco's capital Rabat; this was attended by Iran's Shah and many other representatives from Turkey, Pakistan and other Muslim-majority countries.[43] The main agenda was the future of Palestinian territory – as it is even to this day. However, the difference between today's Muslim world and what it was half a decade ago is that there is a lack of cooperation and unity among leaders resulting in a failure to collaborate or come to a consensus. Changes in the MENA region caused by the Iranian revolution in 1979, the 9/11 incident and the Arab Spring has shifted politics; this has resulted in each country pursuing an agenda based on their own political interests.

Post-Gezi Park Turkey

While the tension in the relationship between Israel and Turkey escalated the pace of change internationally, it was the Gezi Park protests of 2013 at Istanbul's famous Taksim Square that resulted in policy transformation domestically. TT1 is of the opinion that the protests prompted the beginning of a new era in Turkey: one in which the divergence between the supporters of the AKP and its opponents is increasingly apparent. This demonstration against Erdoğan's government, which received serious coverage in the national and international media, encouraged Erdoğan to increase his authoritarian approach to governance. Commentators have claimed that this represents his stubbornness and refusal to tolerate those with alternative views. Undoubtedly, he increased his religious discourse after the protests in 2013, and referred more often to the Ottoman era, as apparent from the content analysis conducted for this study. Meanwhile, there was a parallel decline in his focus on human rights and freedom of speech as he became distinctly less tolerant. The transformation that occurred affected more than Erdoğan's political stance; it also altered the amount of emphasis placed on collective identity and effort within the AKP, according to JO2. Erdoğan was even unwilling to listen to former president Gül, who favoured some measure of reform and reconsideration of the politics of the AKP after the Gezi Park protests.

Post-Arab Spring Egypt

Another, significant factor contributing to the AKP's policy developments after 2010 was the military coup in post-Arab Spring Egypt, which occurred immediately after the Gezi Park protests in 2013. When the Egyptian military ousted Erdoğan's close ally Mohammed Morsi in 2013, he saw this as a threat to Turkey. Consequently, the silence on the part of international organizations and Western countries increased Erdoğan's criticism of the so-called establishment. Indeed, it is critical to remember that Erdoğan employed the slogan 'the World is bigger than five' in the post-2013 period for the first time, in order to criticize not only the Western countries' attitude towards Egypt, but also the deadlock in the ongoing war in Syria. The permanent five members of the UN Security Council – China, France, Russia, the UK and the United States – had found no solution to end the crisis. JO1 argues that Erdoğan's slogan questioned the functionality not only of the UN but also of other international organizations. He also notes that after Erdoğan's use of the slogan at the 69th UN General Assembly, it became popular throughout the Muslim world.

Furthermore, according to TT2, Erdoğan's discourse became religiously motivated after the military coup. His emphasis not only on Islamic values but, more importantly, on the unity of Muslims peaked after this incident. At the rallies I attended, I observed Erdoğan giving importance to Egypt; he would include Egypt while welcoming his supporters by stating that greets 'the people of Egypt'. More important is his use of the *Rabaa* gesture in every single election campaign and event; this clearly shows his support for raising awareness of an image and symbol that could come to dominate politics, as Castells interprets.[44] Here it is important to underline that this support of Morsi was connected with the notion of a collective Muslim identity. In fact, despite differences in terms of style, organizational model and party programme, the AKP is viewed as sharing key similarities with the MB in Egypt and the Ennahda in Tunisia. Moreover, Erdoğan's Communications Team revealed that they worked with the Ennahda and the MB after the Arab uprising in the Middle East 'because of an ideological affinity', demonstrating clearly that there is also a commonality in terms of political communication.

The so-called 15 July coup attempt in 2016 was a major hurdle for Erdoğan, and it resulted in a noticeable increase in his nationalist populism in terms of domestic messages. The orchestration of the coup attempt by the Gülenists followed an earlier corruption scandal implicating businessmen and politicians close to the AKP in 2013. Led by Gülen's supporters in the military, the coup enabled Erdoğan to declare war against a religious movement for the first time in Turkey's history. After the coup attempt, Erdoğan's punitive actions against the coup plotters, as well as journalists, academics, and civil servants who criticized the AKP's post-coup actions, were relentless. Many were jailed or suspended from their posts, and Erdoğan's nationalistic discourse became hugely amplified.[45]

Populist Islamist party

The findings presented above lend support to the claim that since its political message has changed, the AKP can now be categorized as a populist Islamist party. The principal aim of Islamism, in political terms, is to establish 'a political order centred on the name of Islam', locating religion at the heart of the political realm.[46] In the context of Turkey, Islamism is a response to Kemalism and Westernization, as PO4 explains. However, Roy[47] and Mandaville[48] argue that the AKP can better be described as an organization representing post-Islamism. Here, I am inclined to use the word 'Islamism', as defined by Kara,[49] along with 'populism' because when comparing both Erbakan and Erdoğan, it is apparent that there are no material differences today in terms of political approach as both advocated similar politics. But Erdoğan's use of Islamism is a discursive one compared to Erbakan's. Nevertheless, primarily with a pragmatic focus on winning elections and surviving politically, Erdoğan aims to spearhead a societal change in the direction of religious conservative.

I would contend that the first period of the AKP, from 2002 to 2009, could be termed post-Islamism, as this wave marries Islam and democracy, modernity and liberty, acknowledging the values of tolerance, freedom of speech and human rights.[50] Today's AKP does not promote the latter three values, instead preferring to implement its own agenda in pursuit of a religious society – an agenda that is less tolerant of human rights and freedom of speech. Therefore, this research accepts the definition proffered by Sayyid[51] who states that an 'Islamist' is 'someone who places her or his Muslim identity at the centre of her or his political practice'.

Another important fact to consider is that 'Islamists are people who use the language of Islamic metaphors'.[52] The speeches given by Erdoğan, especially after 2010, broadly concentrate on conveying a religious discourse. By contrast, when Erdoğan demands to foster a generation that has an Islamic consciousness, he does so in opposition to 'Muslim societies' integration into the world capitalist system', which he suggests is responsible for the 'weakening of Muslim identities'.[53] For him, as PO4 mentions, Muslim nations should operate independently, or with one another, united under one umbrella, and not regulated by Western countries.

Erdoğan's religious discourse reflects an enthusiasm to imbue the AKP with a specific ideology, similar to that of the Milli Görüş. Certainly, Turkish people in the country generally believe the AKP has a religious and cultural vision based on its neo-Ottoman idea. There is an engraved understanding that Erdoğan's politics is *dawah*, in other words, an 'Islamic mission'. However, whereas Erbakan manifested his political ideology through projects such as Adil Düzen or D-8, the evolution of Erdoğan's message after each event discussed in this research reveals him to be a pragmatic man, suggesting that while he remains leader it is unreasonable to make assumptions about the party's direction based on its past.

Further, it is interesting to note that Erdoğan's Islamist discourse is not based on a fundamental project, politics or diplomatic relationship; rather, it is a rhetorical approach, adopted as Turkey's earlier conciliatory foreign policy posturing 'lost credibility' domestically.[54] Erdoğan was able to become 'the Muslim and Arab world's champion' because of his rhetorical reinterpretation of regional politics. As PO4 explained, this has no doubt led Erdoğan to compare himself to Sultan Abdulhamid II, who had pursued an Islamist agenda and sought to unite the Muslim world.

Additional support was lent to the above argument in December 2017. When US President Donald Trump declared Jerusalem the capital of Israel, Turkey's president did not shirk from voicing his opinion. He intensified his hostile rhetoric against Israel. In one of his speeches, he stressed on the importance of *Al Quds* ('Jerusalem' in Arabic) with the following words:

> If Al Quds is gone, we cannot protect Medina, if Medina is gone, we cannot protect Mecca, if Mecca is gone, we would lose Kaaba. Brothers and sisters, the world has a twisted order. One day, this twisted order manifests itself in the body of an innocent Syrian washed ashore. One day, this twisted order manifests itself in a Palestinian whose house is razed to the ground and whose rights are all seized. One day, this twisted order manifests itself in Rohingya Muslims gasping their lives out in swamps and rivers as they are being banished from their own lands. But we do not remain silent.[55]

In the statement above, Erdoğan cites examples from different Muslim nations to emphasize the oppression of Muslims globally and the skewed representations of Muslims by the media. He delineates between each incident by mapping out a broad canvas, conveying the message that he cares about the events in all the countries where Muslims live, and, according to JO4, that he is willing to act as their patron. When I asked Professor Kara if Erdoğan would accept the term 'Islamist' if applied to himself, he agreed that he would indeed, but only off-the-record, and not in front of cameras as it would be too risky in terms of the potential loss of support from his non-religious base.

The consequence is that, today, the secular versus religious conservative division in Turkey is polarizing the country in a way that has never been seen before. The AKP's centralization of Islam within its political message since 2010 in particular is not necessarily a rejection of the West. The question that arises from the research conducted here concerns whether or not the AKP is isolating itself with the populist Islamist and nationalist agenda.

During our interview, AC4 clarifies that there is a new kind of Kemalism among conservative people in Turkey. The AKP's soft approach to Kemalism, that is, 'their attempts to protect Mustafa Kemal Atatürk's legacy, as they cannot deny the past, changed the perception of Kemalism in the eyes of the religious conservative majority', says AC4. 'We can see this reality on 29 October Republic Day celebrations; every year more and more people from conservative backgrounds are celebrating this day.' It is an unusual situation in Turkey because conservative people were silently opposed to celebrating this day for many years as they were against Atatürk's secularization policies. But now, according to AC4, religious conservative people are celebrating in particular with social media messages. The AKP has changed this reality in public sphere, but 'Erdoğan personally is still in a competition with Mustafa Kemal Atatürk', underlines AC3.

Erdoğan first real challenge: Imamoğlu

Indeed Erdoğan's first real challenge in his nearly two-decade-long journey was Istanbul's new mayor Ekrem Imamoğlu. Imamoğlu took advantage of the polarized atmosphere by concentrating not on conflict, dispute and further polarization, but rather on positive messaging. Imamoğlu's campaign director explains this strategy as a 'new generation style politics'.[56] In fact Imamoğlu was an unknown figure until the local elections in 2019. He was the mayor of Istanbul's western district Beylikdüzü and hence was rarely known beyond the borders of this district. But his journey is remarkable because he has beaten Erdoğan who ruled Istanbul for twenty-five years, and Turkey for seventeen years, and who has power over all political institutions. 'Everything will be fine', which was one of Imamoğlu slogans, delivered the message that the situation in Istanbul and across the country is gloomy, and his victory will be a turning point. His basic communication strategy was 'word of mouth' because from public-funded to privately owned media outlets, all state apparatus were controlled by Erdoğan. A few media outlets such as Fox Haber, *Sözcü* newspaper and a handful of digital media platforms sided with the National Alliance candidate, that is, the CHP and IYI party. 'We have got social media, which have been left alone for the time being. Right now my biggest weapon on the ground is a 1,000-year-old communication strategy of word of mouth.'[57] İmamoğlu described his disadvantaged PR situation with these words.

When the campaign started, the people on the ground – from secular neighbourhood of Cihangir to the religious conservative Üsküdar – was that Binali Yıldırım, the candidate of the People's Alliance (i.e. the AKP and MHP) will become the next mayor of Istanbul. 'A comparison between İmamoğlu and Yıldırım was out of the question', says PO7, 'because Yıldırım was a sympathetic political figure who used a moderate tone compared to Erdoğan, and he was respected by people outside of AKP's circle.' Yıldırım served as a prime minister during the period between post-Davutoğlu and the new presidential system, which has since then abolished the prime ministry. Yet economic instability in the country since 2018 was more at the epicentre than Yıldırım's image itself. In this regard, İmamoğlu focused on the AKP's squandering and ideological distribution of Istanbul's public funds. But Erdoğan believed that his polarization discourse during election rallies, TV appearances and local meetings would be enough to succeed again. Erdoğan himself was more on the billboards in Istanbul than was Yıldırım or other candidates. Although it was the local election, where the campaign is focused on each candidate in every city and district and not based on party leaders, Erdoğan believed that his presence in rallies will have an impact on Yıldırım to win Istanbul. Hence Erdoğan campaigned on the ground as he was keen to keep Istanbul and all its economic assets from which the AKP and its supporters, particularly some foundations and companies, benefits for years. Once again, Erdoğan tried to turn it into an issue of national survival. He accused the opposition of collaborating with terrorists by referring to the HDP and PKK, 'who are not even able to read the national anthem'.[58] The national anthem is a critical symbol used in this context by Erdoğan to raise awareness that İmamoğlu, who was supported by the Kurdish HDP, would not respect core values when he is elected. In this way Erdoğan believed that he could persuade those who attend the campaign rallies as well as those who watch the happenings on TV or on social media. But despite becoming the first party to win fourteen elections in a row from 2002 to 2019, this discourse has lost him some critical cities like Istanbul, Ankara and Antalya. Although İmamoğlu and National Alliance's Ankara candidate Mansur Yavaş have not responded to AKP's accusations – but rather ignored Erdoğan totally – they are yet to concentrate on new projects either. Instead their only focus was harmony, peace and equal allocation of financial sources. Above all, what worked for Imamoğlu was that he has not portrayed himself as an elite as a CHP politician normally would. He cited the Quran, visited mosques and prayed with the community; he was also humble, young and charismatic, and respected the sensitive feelings of the middle-class religious conservatives. This enabled him to reach out to AKP supporters and win their votes. In essence, the changing dynamic of electorate as well as Kemalist party behaviour reveals details about the current situation in Turkey. Although Erdoğan's populist agenda is questionable, how sustainable and effective will it be in the near future and, more importantly, in the long term is something to ponder upon. The AKP changed the sociological sphere in the country and enabled religious conservatives rebuild their self-confidence after the postmodern coup in 1997. The perception of this social class will hence be a crucial dynamic to be considered even if the AKP do not continue to be in power in the coming decades. In a similar context, this has changed the way the CHP develops new communication strategies to reach out to conservatives. Imamoğlu and Yavaş's campaign were the first concrete results of this process. Imamoğlu's strategy of focusing on rebuilding Ottoman water fountains as part of urban culture, acquiring Sultan Fatih's portrait of Italian painter Gentile Bellini at a Christie's auction in London for £770K or tweeting Erdoğan's favourite poet Karakoç are some of the concrete steps taken towards seeking for the support of the conservatives.

Furthermore, the CHP has supported Erdoğan's Hagia Sophia move to convert to a mosque. In fact, it was Atatürk and his CHP who converted Hagia Sophia to a museum in 1934.[59] And yet, the CHP's acquiesce in converting the historical building to a mosque has stopped Erdoğan from turning this issue into another debate and using Hagia Sophia as a political tool in domestic politics.

8

Post-Erdoğan Turkey

Suddenly, there is a curve in the road, a turning point. Somewhere, the real scene has been lost, the scene where you had rules for the game and some solid stakes that everybody could rely on.

– Baudrillard

This research has revealed how Erdoğan used political communication in favour of his populist Islamist ideology to change the image of religious conservatives in Turkey and Muslims abroad, and build a legacy that serves as the foundation for 'New Turkey'. Yet despite coming to power after having witnessed the postmodern coup in 1997 with the promise of expanding human rights and freedom of expression, the AKP has 'respectively consolidated the military tutelage, bureaucratic tutelage and dissident academia'.[1] Freedom is granted selectively only to those religious conservatives who support the same ideology as the governing elite and glorify strong leadership. Kırmızı argues that if sultan-centred historical teachings is part of the official syllabus at schools, it will be inevitable that one-man leadership is internalized.[2] In fact, celebrating the Ottoman sultans, their governing styles, their identity and Weltanschauung legitimizes Erdoğan's political ideology and leadership. Although young citizens prefer a more diverse political atmosphere, where they have more freedom and rights, middle-aged and older adults are easier to manipulate with romanticism and emotionality, both characteristics of populist leaders. Consolidating power with the aim of unity first within the borders of Turkey, and then in the wider Muslim world, is part of Erdoğan's main political agenda based on his Islamist ideology.

Erdoğan mainly suppressed, in post-Gezi protests, opposition voices that supported the upheaval against his government. However after 2016, in a post-coup attempt, he targeted religious conservatives like clerics, academics, Islamic institutions, foundations and, more alarmingly, universities that could pose as a threat to the AKP's continuity. 'National survival' is one of the slogans that Erdoğan employs in his speeches. Kara underlines that during Abdulhamid II's era, the *ulama* were very diverse and mainly opposed Abdulhamid's regime.³ In this regard, similarities between both Abdulhamid and Erdoğan are incontrovertible when it comes to Islamist approach. Both leaders used a populist tone to consolidate power and maintain their political struggle.

In this regard, 2010 is a turning point for Erdoğan, when he adopted a cynical attitude towards international institutions and started expressing his resentment at the negative portrayal of Muslims across the world in his speeches. But 2013 is a critical year as this is when he realized that not only Western powers and opposition parties in Turkey are a threat to his survival, but also internal voices, such as the Gülenists and founding members of the AKP like Gül, were equally a cause for concern. Erdoğan's success in the presidential elections that was held after the Gezi Park protests proved that his dominance had increased tremendously, while indicating that his populist Islamist agenda had emerged.

The result of Erdoğan's unity messages led to polarization. In fact, he uses the classical populist jargon of 'we and them'. He not only tries to unite his base around a collective identity, and effort but also frames the opposition as collective one; by doing this, he is able to entrap his followers in a 'good guys versus bad guys' dichotomy. He simplifies his message but more importantly, develops a religious framework to strengthen his base as well as enable Turkish citizens to interpret his caliphate-like political leadership and ideology as part of their religious duty, as seen in post-eighteenth-century Ottoman era.⁴

Erdoğan is not only the head of the government, judiciary, military and police, but also the religious authority. He intervenes in *fatwas* of the Diyanet, the Presidency of Religious Affairs, and imposes rules and regulations. Historian Anscombe[5] points out that Atatürk generally followed the European model in his modernization process by 'embracing the religious establishment so tightly that it could not oppose regime's interests', which is similar to Erdoğan's strategy. This is one of the reasons why the former head of Diyanet, a respected figure within religious conservative elites, was replaced by a low-profile academic who follows the directions of Erdoğan without questioning them. Certainly Erdoğan is keen to give Diyanet its respected position back in lieu of the office of the Şeyhulislam[6] and the Ministry of Religious Affairs and Pious Foundations that were abolished in 1924.⁷ Yet, by doing this, Erdoğan aims to control the entire society through Diyanet, not allowing any other religious group, leader or *cemaat* to fill the slightest of gaps in religious authority. Certainly this is part of his agenda of creating a society around a religious collective identity by eliminating any kind of opposition.

Paradoxically, when the Ottoman Empire became more secular with the *Tanzimat* reforms, its Muslim image and the perception of the caliphate – both within the Muslim world and beyond – became more prominent.[8] Today, under the religious conservative government, Turkey is facing a similar experience. While Erdoğan's image as a leader of the oppressed Muslims and the perception of Turkey as a country that embraces more and more religious ideology become more prevalent, his populist agenda has also led to secularization on the ground, particularly among the generation Z, whose parents are supporters of the AKP. Professor Kara emphasizes that younger people from conservative families are questioning the AKP's focus on religion; the reason for this behaviour is a direct consequence of an economically progressive yet religiously conservative governance whose political discourse juggles both a modernization and a religious piety stance.[9] For Kara, this is caused by the increasing role of digital communication. In fact the impact of this reality and the role of digitalization of culture is the reason why Erdoğan decided to introduce new laws to control social media, as it became a threat to the ruling party, because unlike the mainstream media, the AKP could not control digital media platforms, and, consequently, the online public sphere of generation Z.

As the majority of middle-class conservatives move from the periphery to the centre of the political sphere, it is necessary for parties to adapt their communication styles and strategies accordingly. The AKP employs strategies that can be classified as American in origin to frame their message. Erdoğan combines these with religious, cultural and historic symbols and features that are locally driven. The use of the Americanized model of political communication was found to interact with two other significant aspects, both of which are crucial. First is personalization of communication, which upholds Erdoğan's authority by emphasizing one-man leadership. Second, modernization plays a key role in Americanization. The neoliberal economic policies of the party led to an increase in the GDP per capita, despite the Turkey's fluctuating economy since 2018; this resulted in an improvement in the socio-economic conditions of the working middle-class, thereby leading them to embrace a secular lifestyle focused on individualization, rather collectiveness. This individualization unbinds the traditional affective ties between voters and parties causing individual candidates' importance to expand. However, in the context of Turkey, there is a contradiction, in that the latter does not align with the former. To explain, while individualization suggests personal freedom, freedom of choice, tolerance and liberalism, Erdoğan's leadership style seeks to limit these characteristics in favour of a collective identity corresponding to an Islamist ideology by changing Kemalism's laïcité perception. This reminds us of the Pan-Islamism understanding during Abdulhamid's era which Aydın[10] summarizes as 'secular spiritual caliphate perception'.

The clash between collective identity and self-identity as, Giddens[11] suggests, is likely to pose a significant problem for the AKP in the near future. The individualization of society, which enables social mobility and improves quality of life, is expected to heighten the use of Americanization in political communication, potentially eroding the effectiveness of regional strategies, that is, mass rallies, and use of religious symbols and cultural codes. However, increasingly the desire is likely to be for a leader who does not selfishly put himself first, stands for cooperation rather than confrontation, is willing to welcome liberal values and promote freedom of speech and pluralism, and champions the rights of minorities and LGTBQ+. Thus, arguably, the Americanization of political communication in Turkey contributes a further paradox to the research context. There is a clash between the global, national and local, which produces 'heterogeneous disjunctures'[12] rather than a 'homogenised culture'.[13]

There is an apparent struggle between the current populist Islamist objectives of Erdoğan and the AKP's stance as a once moderate post-Islamist party. From both periods that were examined in this study, it can be observed that there is a swing from moderation towards isolation, which generates a reactionary attitude. Notably the quantitative content analysis of Erdoğan's speeches indicates how the AKP engages in both processes. The lack of a unified and consistent party message is a consequence of the de-institutionalization of the party, the dominance of its leader and its history. Although moderate in tone, the first period was nevertheless also reactionary, as the newly formed AKP was intent on creating an identity for itself which was different from that of Erbakan's party. This resulted in the integration of a pro-EU policy, adoption of liberal economics and widely conciliatory foreign policies. In the second period, the discourse was more of a reaction against the Kemalist bloc domestically, and against Western countries and institutions internationally. Erdoğan's aim is to declare Turkey's independence and its preparedness to be among the top ten strongest economies in the world. This would lend the country a powerful voice in geopolitics by winning them a seat at all regional and global tables, and Turkey would thus become a beacon of hope among the Muslim nations. That is the reason why investments in defense industry are increased, drones and warships are built and the country is involved in Syria and in the eastern Mediterranean with the *Blue Homeland* doctrine.

Erdoğan's Palestinian cause and reconversion of Hagia Sophia into a mosque fuelled perceptions of his charismatic leadership style among religious conservative people in Turkey and in the wider Sunni Muslim world. The swiftness with which Erdoğan took on this role appears to have been a direct consequence of the AKP's electoral successes as well as its growing power and influence at home. Economic success, and greater control of the judiciary, with the support of Gülenists until 2013, had strengthened Erdoğan's hand nationally, affording him greater freedom over his actions internationally. The AKP's hold on power palpably increased after their second general election victory in 2007, when the AKP gained the presidency from the secular bloc.

The principal change highlighted in the data is that Erdoğan's discourse became religious-nationalism motivated with a stronger political authority. Simultaneously, rhetoric concerning human rights and freedom of speech as well as sustainable dialogues with the West fell out dramatically. Particularly, the transformation of Erdoğan's political message suggests not only a lack of institutionalization or consistency in the AKP's political message, but also the president's keenness to introduce religious discourse in order to create a pious society with a strong Islamic identity. Building new mosques, de-museumizing Hagia Sophia and Chora Museum, pouring millions of dollars to religious schools and banning evolution from curriculum at schools are only some of his concrete Islamist policies that are aimed at serving his goal of leaving an imprint behind.

Inevitably, as a conclusion, it can be emphasized that the AKP is currently facing an identity crisis, one that reflects the above-mentioned paradoxes regarding secularism versus conservatism, and individualism versus collectivism. The different characteristics of the party that surfaced in the fieldwork data show a dispute over the party's identity. Conversely, Erdoğan's message has never been clearer. He dreams of a Turkey that serves as a model of Islamic collective identity; this is evidenced by his populist Islamist messages, symbolic transformations and political communication. Erdoğan's stated aim is to build a strong nation, to safeguard Muslims globally, fight against Islamophobia and make history as a leader of the Muslim world. Meanwhile, domestically it is and has always been important for Erdoğan to maintain his relationship with tradition, culture and the Ottoman past in order to consolidate his position as the leader of the 'New Turkey' to replace Atatürk and his legacy. Yet, when examining the post-Erdoğan era, future generations will not only remember Erdoğan's populist discourse; Erdoğan's reflections on the various crises and turning points in Turkey's near history are sure to have a significant impact on their Weltanschauung.

Notes

1 Introduction

1 'The French term 'laïcité' 'refers to the control of the clergy by the nonreligious or nonclerical people (through government action)' (Sevinc, Wood and Coleman 2017: 155).
2 Imam Hatip schools are religious schools established first in 1950s to educate qualified religious personnel. It is a combination of liberal arts, science and religious courses.
3 Milli Görüş literally translates as 'National Outlook'. However, although the name 'Milli' literally means 'national', in this context it is better understood in terms of Islamic values (Hale and Özbudun 2010: 5). In order to clarify Erdoğan's previous affiliations, this research will mostly use the term 'Milli Görüş' rather than any other name given to Erbakan's parties. Because the founder of this movement, Necmettin Erbakan, termed his ideology Milli Görüş. He founded five parties in total, under different names, as each of them were shut down for engaging in 'anti-secular activities' (ibid.: 4). Erbakan's Milli Görüş parties were named the following: Milli Nizam Party (National Order Party, 1970–71), Milli Selamet Party (National Salvation Party, 1972–80), Refah Party (Welfare Party, 1983–98), Fazilet Party (Virtue Party, 1997–2001) and the Saadet Party (Felicity Party, 2001–)
4 A major urban waterway.
5 The panel discussion at the 2009 World Economic Forum in Davos turned into a diplomatic crisis between former Israeli president Shimon Peres (1923–2016) and Erdoğan when Turkey's then prime minister criticized the Israeli President over Gaza.
6 Mavi Marmara flotilla, also known as Gaza flotilla aid, happened sixteen months after the Davos spat in 2010. The flotilla was on its way to take aid to Palestinian people in Gaza on 30 May 2010 when it was attacked by Israeli soldiers. Nine activists, including one US citizen, were killed during this offensive.
7 Aydın (2017: 3) prefers to use the term 'Muslim world' rather than the concept of the 'ummah' when he talks about Muslim religious community today. In fact, 'the idea of the Muslim world began to develop in the nineteenth century and achieved full flower in the 1870s' in Abdulhamid II's era (ibid.). The idea of the 'Muslim world' in Erdoğan's mind is similar to that of Abdulhamid II, which will be clarified in Chapter 2.

8   TCCB (2019b).
9   KONDA (2020).
10 Middle East Eye (2019b).
11 Bayat (2013).
12 Kara (2014: 17).
13 Mudde (2004: 542).
14 NZZ Standpunkte (2015).
15 Erbakan brought the 'eight most developed Islamic countries' together to cooperate specifically on economic and military issues, and to consider sharing a currency in the future. These countries are Bangladesh, Egypt, Indonesia, Iran, Malaysia, Nigeria, Pakistan and Turkey.
16 While the movement's leader Fethullah Gülen has been living in self-imposed exile in the United States since 1999, the movement was running a huge business network comprising private schools, factories, think-tanks and media outlets, reaching millions of people worldwide. After the coup attempt in 2016, they are recognized as a terrorist organization in Turkey. However, up until 2013, there was a 'honeymoon period' between the AKP and Gülenists, during which the Gülenists proved an influential supporter of the AKP, particularly helping them gain control of the judiciary, military and police by developing 'a more tolerant and normative framework in terms of their Islamist ideas' (Yilmaz 2013: 67).
17 Both cities were first governed by Milli Görüş parties and then by the AKP.
18 This number is based on AKP's Publicity and Media Department's report (T24 2020).
19 TCCB (2020).

2 The concept of political communication

1   Castells (1996).
2   Bernays (1952).
3   Wilcox, Ault and Agee (1992: 7).
4   Ibid.: 6.
5   Cagaptay (2017: 3).
6   Sen (2011: 57).
7   Hale and Özbudun (2010: 21).
8   Strömbäck and Kiousis (2011).
9   Ibid.
10 Ibid.: 8.
11 Grunig and Hunt (1984: 6).

12 Name of the department can differ from one party to another. The AKP uses 'Publicity and Media' Department.
13 Hürriyet (2018)
14 Strömbäck and Kiousis (2011: 7).
15 McNair (2003).
16 McNair (2017: 4).
17 Cizre (2016: 2).
18 Sen (2011: 57).
19 The term 'Gülenists' is used in this research to refer to Fethullah Gülen's movement.
20 Amsterdam & Amsterdam LLP (2017: 26).
21 Waldman and Caliskan (2016).
22 Lerner (1958: 46).
23 Negrine (2008).
24 Scammell (2007).
25 Scammell (1997: 1).
26 Thussu (2009).
27 Baudrillard (1986: 76).
28 Bell and Bell (1993).
29 Thussu (2009: 68).
30 Thussu (2006: 43).
31 Blumler and Gurevitch (2001: 380).
32 Negrine (2008).
33 Lerner (1958).
34 Ibid.
35 Berkes (1998: 5).
36 Ibid.: 46.
37 Negrine (2008: 152).
38 Negrine and Papathanassopoulus (1996).
39 Negrine and Stanyer (2007: 106).
40 Swanson and Mancini (1996: 106).
41 Ibid.
42 Butler and Ranney (1992: 7–8).
43 Denton, Trend and Friedenberg (2016).
44 McNair (2018).
45 Wring et al. (2007: 17).
46 Ibid.: 48.
47 Ibid.: 49.
48 Although Olçok was shot dead during the attempted military coup on 15 July 2016, he had previously answered my questions concerning how far the AKP had

adopted American campaigning techniques, citing different examples from the presidential elections in 2014 in particular.
49 Dalton, McAllister and Wattenberg (2000: 60).
50 Aelst, Shaefer and Stanyer (2012).
51 Ibid.: 205.
52 Rahat and Schaefer (2007: 68).
53 Ibid.
54 Langer (2010: 61).
55 Langer (2007: 381).
56 Aelst, Shaefer and Stanyer (2012).
57 Negrine (2008: 6).
58 McNair (2003: 8).
59 Weber (1968).
60 Ibid.: 20.
61 Ibid.
62 Weber (1968: 22).
63 Castells (2010: 424–5).
64 Toch (1965: 5).
65 Touraine (1981: 29).
66 Cohen and Rai (2000: 2).
67 Ibid.
68 Ibid.
69 Ibid.: 3.
70 Ibid.
71 Zirakzadeh (1997: 4–5).
72 Wilson (1973a).
73 Zirakzadeh (1997: 4–5).
74 Cameron (1966: 7).
75 Ibid.: 22
76 Blumer (2008: 64).
77 Moghadam (2009: 4).
78 Ibid.: 37–8.
79 Ibid.: 38.
80 Bayat (2005: 904).
81 Diyanet Haber (2020).
82 Pakulski (1991: xiv).
83 Wilson (1973a: 16).
84 Gellner (1995: 40).
85 Povey (2015: 15).
86 Mardin (2006).

87 Sayyid (2003).
88 Ibid.: 52.
89 Johnston and Klandermans (1995: 44).
90 Melucci (1996: 70).
91 Larana, Johnston and Gusfield (1994: 17).
92 Tilly (1978: 7).
93 Ibid.: 7.
94 Tilly (1978).
95 Hale and Özbudun (2010: 5).
96 References to 'conservatives' indicate those 'faithful to Islamic religious and moral traditions' (Ramadan 2012: 101).
97 Crane (1994: 395–6).
98 Eyerman and Jamison (1991: 4).
99 Lindberg and Sverrisson (1997: 2).
100 Ibid.
101 Lindberg and Sverrisson (1997).
102 Garretton (1997: 67).

3 Modernization in the Ottoman era, Islamism in Turkey and AKP's rise

1 Kara (2014: 17).
2 Bobin (2016).
3 Başer and Öztürk (2017: 107).
4 New York Times (2003).
5 Sayyid (2014: 9).
6 Denoeux (2011: 60).
7 Bokhari and Senzai (2013: 6).
8 Bayat (2007: 6).
9 Bayat (2013: x).
10 Ibid.: 85.
11 Kara (2014).
12 Kara (2017).
13 Zürcher (1993: 18).
14 Hanioğlu (1995: 8).
15 Berkes (1998).
16 Zürcher (1993).
17 Hourani, Khoury and Wilson (1993).
18 Ibid.: 53.

19 Abdulhamid (1974: 157).
20 Karpat (2001: 160).
21 'The rule or reign of a caliph or chief Muslim ruler' (*Oxford Dictionary* 2017).
22 Karpat (2001: 160).
23 Aydın (2019: 38).
24 'The chief Muslim civil and religious ruler, regarded as the successor of Muhammad' (*Oxford Dictionary* 2017).
25 Mandaville (2004: 2).
26 'The world community of Muslims' (Mandaville 2004: 2).
27 Aydın (2017: 3).
28 Landau (1990).
29 Ibid.: 1.
30 Aydın (2019: 39).
31 Landau (1990).
32 Ibid.: 3.
33 By considering Kara's (2014) definition of Islamism, I will use Islamism instead of *Ittihad-ı Islam* during the discussion of Abdulhamid II's Islamist policies.
34 Taftazani (1917: 447) in Ardıç (2012: 167).
35 Yasamee (1996: 25).
36 Ibid.
37 Ibid.: 25–6.
38 Ibrahim Temo, Abdullah Cevdet, Ishak Sükuti and Ali Hüseyinzade (Zürcher 2010: 97).
39 Zürcher (2010: 97–8).
40 Hanioğlu (1995: 7).
41 Huntington (1993: 42).
42 When the Turkish Republic was found, Mustafa Kemal, first president of Turkey, introduced the one-party rule in 1923 which lasted until 1946 (Özbudun 1976).
43 *Nakşibendi* is a Sufi order created in fourteenth century to spread the word of Islam, first in Asia, then in the Middle East (Mardin 1993).
44 Yavuz (2009: 138).
45 Star (2014).
46 Cited in Karataş (2005: 984).
47 BBC Türkçe (2017).
48 Hale and Özbudun (2010).
49 Uçar (2000: 77).
50 Hale and Özbudun (2010: 8).
51 Ibid: 6.
52 According to Oxford Professor Avi Shlaim (2000: 2), Zionism is a national liberation movement seeking to end the Jewish dispersion and 'return to Zion', holy

land. However, Shlaim (2005) argues that the occupation of Palestine by the Zionist movement transformed them 'from a legitimate national liberation movement for the Jews into a colonial power and an oppressor of the Palestinians'.
53 Ibid.
54 Yavuz (2003: 207).
55 Hale and Özbudun (2010: 3).
56 White (2002: 3).
57 Yavuz (2003: 215).
58 In 1997, when Erdoğan was the mayor of Istanbul, he read a poem by Ziya Gökalp, a political activist and poet from the city of Siirt, Turkey:

> The mosques are our barracks,
> The domes our helmets,
> The minarets our bayonets,
> And the believers our soldiers.

59 Aydın and Dalmış (2008: 201–2).
60 Ibid.
61 Bayat (2013: 12).
62 According to Freedom House's 2020 report, Turkey is now ranked 32 out of 100 in the World Freedom index, with figures being collated after the July 2016 coup attempt.
63 Hale and Özbudun (2010: 9).
64 Dagi (2013: 74).
65 Ismael and Perry (2014: 203).
66 Kalın (2013: 425)
67 Ibid.: 424.
68 Hale and Özbudun (2010: 21).
69 Kalın (2013: 427).
70 Ibid.: 428.
71 Ibid: 429.
72 Marcou (2014: 66).
73 Eligür (2010: 249).
74 Boubekeur and Roy (2014: 66).
75 Eligür (2010: 249).
76 Ibid.
77 Ibid.: 254.
78 Yavuz (2006: 4).
79 Kalın (2013: 433).
80 Aviv (2017: 78).
81 Ibid.

82 Ibid.: 77.
83 Akyol (2015).

4 The AKP's code of identity

1. Weber (1968: 18–19).
2. Kalın (2013: 425).
3. Waldman and Caliskan (2016).
4. Kalın (2013: 425).
5. Anatolianism refers to the middle- and working-class families in Turkish.
6. Bokhari and Senzai (2013: 173).
7. Landau (1990).
8. Piscatori (2006).
9. Stein (2014: 20).
10. In June 2016, Ankara and Tel Aviv signed a deal to normalize the relations between both countries after six years of 'strained relations' (Hürriyet Daily News, 2016).
11. Hürriyet Daily News (2016).
12. Milli Gazete (2016).
13. Erdoğan refers to the permanent five members of the UN Security Council (China, France, Russia, the UK, and the United States). He frames the rights of these five member states as a 'global injustice' (TCCB 2018).
14. The Gezi Park protests started on 28 May 2013 when the AKP announced that it was going to rebuild Taksim Square and remove the trees and green areas. In a very short period of time, massive nationwide protests erupted challenging the AKP and its policies.
15. Akyol (2015).
16. Istanbul special-authority prosecutor issued summons for MIT Chief Hakan Fidan to question him in a probe regarding Kurdistan Communities Union (KCK), the alleged PKK urban wing. Later it emerged that it was an allegation organized by the Gülenists (Soyler 2015: 181).
17. Anadolu Agency (2014).
18. T24 (2014).
19. Kalın (2013: 429).
20. Daragahi (2019).
21. Hürriyet Daily News (2019).
22. Anadolu Agency (2019).
23. T24 (2016).
24. Evrensel Daily (2019).
25. DW (2019).

26 See entry on Battle-of-Manzikert in Encyclopedia Britannica (https://www.britannica.com/event/Battle-of-Manzikert).
27 Hürriyet Daily News (2019a).
28 Recep Tayyip Erdoğan (2020).
29 TGRT Haber (2020).
30 Arsu (2020).
31 DW (2020).
32 MUSIAD was found in 1990 with the support of former prime minister Erbakan in order to mobilize the 'conservative oriented businessmen' against the secular TUSIAD (Turkish Industry and Business Association), found in 1971 (Atasoy 2009: 114).
33 *Azan* is the Arabic word for the call to prayer.
34 YouTube (2017).
35 Kemalism emerged after the 'overthrow of the Ottoman regime' and is named after Mustafa Kemal who is the founding father of the Turkish Republic (Sayyid 2003: 52). Basically Kemalism is a top-down imposed modernization programme (Sayyid 2003).
36 Gülenists are accused of organizing a coup attempt against Erdoğan and his party. Guns, tanks, helicopters and F16 fighter jets were used against civilians, resulting in the loss of 251 lives with dozens injured. After this event, the government detained tens of thousands of people with alleged links to the Gülenists, which sparked serious concerns in the media.
37 Berktay (2017).
38 'A group of anti-Ottoman officers and students' (Pappe 2004: 56).
39 Hanioğlu (1995: 3).
40 'The rule or reign of a caliph or chief Muslim ruler' (*Oxford Dictionary* 2017).
41 Hawkins (2009).
42 De la Torre (2017).
43 Moffit (2016).
44 Strömbäck (2008: 233).
45 McMannus (1994).
46 Bos, van der Brug and de Vresse (2011: 185).
47 Sabato, Stencel and Linchter (2000).
48 Bucy and Grabe (2009).
49 Waisbord (2012).
50 Weise (2018).
51 Ibid.
52 Middle East Eye (2019b).
53 Dogan (2019).
54 Weber (1968: 18).
55 Langer (2010: 61).

56 Freedom House (2020).
57 Yeneroglu (2020).
58 Stigmatizing Davutoğlu as associated to the 'German school of thought' is possible because he studied at Istanbul High School, which is based on the German education system, *Abitur*.
59 Bruce (1992: 95).
60 Bernays (1952: 12).
61 Negrine (2008: 6).
62 Melucci (1996: 70).
63 Moghadam (2009).
64 Tilly (1978: 7).
65 GlobeScan (2017).
66 Kadir Has Üniversitesi (2019).
67 Davis (2019: 171).
68 Negrine (2008: 6).
69 Bos, van der Brug and de Vresse (2011: 185).
70 McNair (2003: 6).
71 Bouyahya (2015: 77).
72 Larana, Johnston and Gusfield (1994: 17).
73 Castells (1996: 359).
74 Duvar English (2020).
75 TCCB (2020b).
76 'Taqiyyah, in Islam, is the practice of concealing one's belief and foregoing ordinary religious duties when under threat of death or injury' (Encyclopaedia Britannica).
77 Gerges (2013: 199).

5 Communicating religion

1 Castells (2009: 10).
2 D'Urbano (2011).
3 Bayat (2010: 11).
4 Esposito and Voll (1996: 131).
5 Yavuz (2003: 207).
6 Erbakan was termed *hoca* by his friends at the university, because of his Islamist ideology, and he retained this label when he entered politics in 1969. It stands for 'master', 'teacher' 'preacher', 'tutor', and 'wise person' in English.
7 Yerlikaya (2020).
8 Anatolia is another name for Turkey.
9 New York Times (2003)

10 Saintly figure and warrior.
11 Politician who was assassinated in 1978. Hamido was killed by Ergenekon, an alleged clandestine secularist ultra-nationalist organization.
12 Eighth president of Turkey. Özal died in 1993 but due to an earlier assassination attempt in 1989, there remains serious question about whether he might have been poisoned.
13 Yavuz (2003: 23).
14 'The Muslim call to ritual prayer made by a muezzin from the minaret of a mosque' (*Oxford Dictionary* 2010).
15 Culturally traditional woman in Turkey.
16 Erdoğan, 2014 presidential election rally, Malatya, 7 August 2014.
17 In 1932, CHP government banned the call to prayer. During that time, the call to prayer was delivered in the Turkish language. In 1950, when the Democrat Party (DP) came to government, they lifted the ban on call to prayer in Arabic.
18 Erdoğan, 2014 presidential election rally, Malatya, 7 August 2014.
19 Habertürk (2018).
20 Erdoğan, 2014 presidential election rally, Malatya, 7 August 2014.
21 Lauria (2010).
22 Erdoğan, 2014 presidential election rally, Malatya, 7 August 2014.
23 Alevi mystic who taught in Anatolia in the thirteenth century.
24 Warrior and saintly figure.
25 Scholar lived in the times of the late Ottoman Empire and the early Republic of Turkey.
26 Saint lived in Ankara.
27 Scholar who lived in the fourteenth century.
28 Saintly figure.
29 Alija was the leader of Mladi Muslimani in Bosnia and former president of Bosnia and Herzegovina.
30 Ulpe Uplink (2014)
31 Anadolu Agency (2018a).
32 Anadolu Agency (2018b).
33 Erdoğan listed the following names: Kilij Arslan I, Seljuq Sultan of Rum from 1092 until 1107, Alp Arslan, second sultan of Seljuk Empire, Saladin, the first sultan of Egypt and Syria and the founder of the Ayyubid Dynasty, Kayqubad I, Seljuk Sultan of Rum from 1220 to 1237, Rumi, poet and Sufi mystic, and Konevi, Islamic scholar who lived there in the thirteenth century.
34 Ulpe Uplink (2014).
35 On 4 November 2016, Demirtaş was jailed along with co-leader Figen Yüksekdag for 'spreading propaganda for militants fighting the Turkish state' (BBC 2016).
36 Cizre (2016: 14).

37 CNN (2019).
38 Sen (2011: 57).
39 Independent Turkey (2019).
40 Middle East Eye (2019a).
41 Strömbäck and Kiousis (2011: 8).
42 Beyond this individual relationship, there is a political relationship: the Cooperation Council of Turkic-Speaking States includes Azerbaijan, Kazakhstan, Kyrgyzstan and Turkey. This council was founded in 2009 and reflects Ankara's interest in fostering a good relationship with its eastern neighbours.
43 Sabah (2014b).
44 Genç (2019: 6).
45 Castells (2009: 442).
46 Bangladesh, Egypt, Indonesia, Iran, Malaysia, Nigeria, Pakistan and Turkey (Hafez 2000).
47 Comprising the world's most powerful industrial nations namely Canada, France, Germany, Italy, Japan, the UK and the United States.
48 Al Jazeera (2019).
49 Atlantic (2017).
50 Arığ (2007: 38).
51 Yeni Şafak (2019).
52 Yanıkdağ (2013: 66).
53 Larana, Johnston and Gusfield (1994: 17).
54 'The stated reason for growing a beard is to be different from the Jews and Christians' (Al Qaradawi 2013: 99).
55 Hamid (2016: 148).

6 Politics and p(owe)r: Evolvement of political messaging

1 Economist (2019).
2 Freedom House (2020).
3 TCCB (2020b).
4 TCCB (2017a).
5 Finlayson and Martin (2008).
6 Ibid.: 452.
7 Krippendorff (2013); Holsti (1969).
8 Neuendorf (2002).
9 The speeches were taken from four sources. Except for the speeches provided on the website for the Turkish presidency, all the speeches were in Turkish. The

counting for the content analysis was done in the original language; however, the terms and segments referred to in this research have been translated into English.
10 Ismael and Perry (2014).
11 Habertürk (2017).
12 TEPAV (2020).
13 Yavuz (2009: 4).
14 Ibid.
15 Charteris-Black (2007: 140).
16 Axworthy (2013: 39).
17 Feroz (1993: 63).
18 Grigoriadis (2009: 182).
19 Spiegel Online (2003).
20 Ibid.
21 Kalın (2013: 426).
22 Huntington (1993).
23 Ibid.: 25.
24 Huntington (1996).
25 The Alliance of Civilizations Initiative (http://www.mfa.gov.tr/the-alliance-of-civilizations-initiative.en.mfa).
26 Esposito and Shahin (2013).
27 TV5 Haber (2014).
28 Ibid.
29 Ibid.
30 Milli Haber (2013).
31 European Commission (2005).
32 Shively (2016).
33 Ibid.: 186.
34 TRT Kurdi (2016).
35 Castells (1996: 359).
36 'A collection of traditions containing sayings of the Prophet Muhammad which, with accounts of his daily practice (the Sunna), constitute the major source of guidance for Muslims apart from the Quran' (*Oxford Dictionary* 2017).
37 Moffit (2016).

7 Erdoğan's communication: Populist Islamism

1 TCCB (2017b).
2 Lerner (1958: 46).
3 Eligür (2010: 254).

4   Hourani, Khoury and Wilson (1993).
5   Smith (2019).
6   Açık Medeniyet (2019).
7   Althusser (2014).
8   Negrine (2008).
9   Ibid.: 6.
10 Negrine (2008: 6).
11 Dalton, McAllister and Wattenberg (2000: 60).
12 Grunig and Hunt (1984: 6).
13 Ethnographic Interview, 25 August 2014.
14 Ibid.
15 Butler and Ranney (1992).
16 Bouyahya (2015).
17 Ibid.: 77.
18 Mandaville (2017: 288).
19 Garreton (1997: 67).
20 Özdenören (2005).
21 Baumgartner and Towner (2017).
22 Langer (2007: 381).
23 Independent (2012).
24 Azerbaijan, Kazakhstan, Kyrgyzstan, Turkmenistan, Turkey, Uzbekistan.
25 NTV (2017).
26 ABC News (2017).
27 Yavuz (2003: 207).
28 See Table 4.
29 See Table 4.
30 According to Avi Shlaim (2000: 2), Zionism was a national liberation movement seeking to end the Jewish dispersion and 'return to Zion', holy land. However Shlaim (2005) argues that the occupation of Palestine by the Zionist movement transformed them 'from a legitimate national liberation movement for the Jews into a colonial power and an oppressor of the Palestinians'.
31 Aviv (2017: 84).
32 Bayat (2010: 11).
33 Pew Research (2017).
34 Hale and Özbudun (2010: 6).
35 140 Journos (2020)
36 Ibid.
37 Hürriyet Daily News (2017c).
38 New York Times (2019).

39 Açık Medeniyet (2019).
40 Middle East Eye (2019c); Khaleej Times (2020).
41 White House (2020).
42 UN (2019).
43 Aydın (2017: 173).
44 Castells (2009: 442).
45 See Figure 8.
46 Sayyid (2014: 9).
47 Roy (2004).
48 Mandaville (2007).
49 Kara (2014).
50 Bayat (2010).
51 Sayyid (2003: 17).
52 Ibid.
53 Sayyid (2003: 22).
54 Kirişci (2017: 10).
55 TCCB (2017).
56 Özkan (2019).
57 France 24 (2019).
58 TCCB (2019a).
59 Ogur (2020).

8 Post-Erdoğan Turkey

1 Kırmızı (2019: 109).
2 Ibid.
3 Kara (2005).
4 Aydın (2019).
5 Anscombe (2010: 163).
6 Person who has the highest level of authority in religious matters.
7 Mardin (1983).
8 Ibid.: 35.
9 Medyascope (2020).
10 Aydın (2019: 39).
11 Giddens (1991: 14).
12 Appadurai (1996).
13 Thussu (2007: 20).

Bibliography

Abdulhamid, S. (1974), *Siyasi Hatıram* (My Political Memories), Istanbul: Hareket Yayınları.

Aelst, P. V., T. Shaefer and J. Stanyer (2012), 'The Personalization of Mediated Political Communication: A Review of Concepts, Operationalizations and Key Findings', *Journalism*, 13 (2) (1 February): 203–20.

Ahmed, A. S. (1992), *Postmodernism and Islam: Predicament and Promise*, Abingdon: Routledge.

Akbar, A. (1992), *Islam, Globalisation, and Postmodernity*, Abingdon: Routledge.

Akdoğan, Y. (2005), 'Adalet ve Kalkınma Partisi' (Justice and Development Party), in B. Tanıl and M. Gültekingil (eds), *Modern Türkiye'de Siyasi Düşünce: İslamcılık* (Political Thinking in Modern Turkey: Islamism), Istanbul: İletişim.

Al-Anani, K. (2016), *Inside the Muslim Brotherhood: Religion, Identity, and Politics*, Oxford: Oxford University Press.

Al-Azmeh, A. (1993), *Islams and Modernities*, London: Verso.

Alba-Juez, L. (2009), *Perspectives on Discourse Analysis: Theory and Practice*, Newcastle upon Tyne: Cambridge Scholars Publishing.

Al-Ghazzi, O. and M. M. Kraidy (2013), 'Neo-Ottoman Cool 2: Turkish National Branding and Arabic-Language Transnational Broadcasting', *International Journal of Communication*, 7: 2341–60.

Alshaer, A. (2014), 'The Poetry of Hizbullah', in L. Khatib, D. Matar and A. Alshaer (eds), *The Hizbullah Phenomenon: Politics and Communication*, London: Hurst.

Altheide, D. L. and J. M. Johnson (1980), *Bureaucratic Propaganda*, Boston: Allyn and Bacon.

Althusser, L. (2014), *On the Reproduction of Capitalism: Ideology and Ideological State Apparatus*, London: Verso.

Al-Qaradawi, Y. (2013), *The Lawful and the Prohibited in Islam*, Kuala Lumpur: Islamic Book Trust.

Amsterdam & Amsterdam LLP (2017), *Empire of Deceit: An Investigation of the Gülen Charter School Network Book 1*, London: Amsterdam & Amsterdam LLP.

Anscombe, F. F. (2010), 'Islam and the Age of Ottoman Reform', *Past and Present*, 208 (1) (August): 159–89.

Appadurai, A. (1996), *Modernity at Large*, Minneapolis: University of Minnesota Press.

Ardıç, N. (2012), *Islam and the Politics of Secularism*, Abingdon: Routledge.

Arığ, Sezer A. (2007), *Atatürk Türkiyesinde kılık kıyafette çağdaşlaşma* (Modernization in Dressing in Atatürk's Turkey), Ankara: Siyasal Kitabevi.

Armajani, J. (2012), *Modern Islamist Movements*, Sussex: Blackwell.
Ashour, O. (2009), *The De-Radicalization of Jihadist: Transforming Armed Islamist Movements*, Abingdon: Routledge.
Atabaki, T. and E. J. Zürcher, eds (2004), *Men of Order: Authoritarian Modernization Under Atatürk and Reza Shah*, London: I.B. Tauris.
Atasoy, Y. (2009) *Islam's Marriage with Neoliberalism: State Transformation in Turkey*, Hampshire: Palgrave Macmillan.
Atkinson, P. and M. Hammersley (1994), 'Ethnography and Participant Observation', in N. K. Denzin and Y. S. Lincoln (eds), *Handbook of Qualitative Research*, London: Sage.
Atkinson, P. and M. Hammersley (1995), *Ethnography*, Abingdon: Routledge.
Atkinson, P., A. Coffey, S. Delamont, J. Lofland and L. Lofland (2001), *Handbook of Ethnography*, London: Sage.
Axiarlis, E. (2014), *Political Islam and the Secular State in Turkey: Democracy, Reform and the Justice and Development Party*, London: I.B. Tauris.
Aviv, E. (2017), *Antisemitism and Anti-Zionism in Turkey: From Ottoman Rule to AKP*, Abingdon: Routledge.
Axworthy, M. (2013), *Revolutionary Iran: A History of the Islamic Republic*, London: Penguin.
Aydın, C. (2007), *The Politics of Anti-Westernism in Asia: Visions of World order in Pan-Islamic and Pan-Asian Thought*, New York: Columbia University Press.
Aydın, C. (2017), *The Idea of the Muslim World: A Global Intellectual History*, Cambridge, MA: Harvard University Press.
Aydın, C. (2019), 'Osmanlı Hilafetinin Uluslararası Siyasetinde Kutsal ve Sekülerin Müphemliği' (The Ambiguity of the Sacred and Secular in the International Politics of the Ottoman Caliphate), *Cogito*, 94 (Summer): 31–57.
Aydın, E. and I. Dalmış (2008), 'The Social Bases of the Justice and Development Party', in Ü. Cizre (ed.), *Secular and Islamic Politics in Turkey: The Making of the Justice and Development Party*, Abingdon: Routledge.
Ayoob, M. (2004), 'Image and Reality', *World Policy Journal*, 21 (3) (Fall): 1–14.
Ayoob, M. (2008), *The Many Faces of Political Islam*, Michigan: Michigan University Press.
Bali, R. N. (2006), 'The Politics of Turkification during the Single Party Period', in H. L. Kieser and K. Öktem (eds), *Turkey Beyond Nationalism: Towards Post-Nationalist Identities*, London: I.B. Tauris.
Başer, B. and A. E. Öztürk, eds (2017), *Authoritarian Politics in Turkey: Elections, Resistance and the AKP*, London: I.B. Tauris.
Basit, T. N. (2000), *Aesthetics, Politics, and Educational Inquiry: Essays and Examples*, New York: Peter Lang.
Baudrillard, J. (1986), *Amérique*, Paris: Grasset.
Baudrillard, J. (1987), *Forget Foucault:* New York: Semitext(e).
Bauman, Z. (2007), *Liquid Times: Living in an Age of Uncertainty*, Cambridge: Polity.

Baumgartner, J. C. and T. L. Towner (2017), *The Internet and the 2016 Presidential Campaign*, Maryland: Lexington Books.
Bayat, A. (2005), 'Islamism and Social Movement Theory', *Third World Quarterly*, 26 (6): 891–908.
Bayat, A. (2007), *Making Islam Democratic: Social Movements and the Post-Islamist Turn*, California: Stanford University Press.
Bayat, A. (2010), *Life as Politics: How Ordinary People Change the Middle East*, California: Stanford University Press.
Bayat, A. (2013), *Post-Islamism: The Changing Faces of Political Islam*, Oxford: Oxford University Press.
Becker, H. S. (1958), 'Problems of Inference and Proof in Participant Observation', *American Sociological Review*, 12 (6): 652–60.
Beinin, J. and J. Stork, eds (1997), *Political Islam*, London: I.B. Tauris.
Beinin, J. and F. Vairel, eds (2011), *Social Movements, Mobilization, and Contestation in the Middle East and North Africa*, California: Stanford University Press.
Bell, P. and R. Bell (1993), 'Americanization and Australia', *Australasian Journal of American Studies*, 18 (2) (December): 87–9.
Bennett, W. L. (2012), 'The Personalization of Politics: Political Identity, Social Media, and Changing Patterns of Participation', *Annals*, 644 (1) (November): 20–39.
Berelson, B. (1952), *Content Analysis in Communication Research*, New York: Free Press.
Berg, B. L. (2007), *Qualitative Research Methods for the Social Sciences*, Pearson: Boston.
Bergmann, K. and W. Wickert (1999), 'Selected Aspects of Communication in German Election Campaigns', in B. I. Newman (ed.), *Handbook of Political Marketing*, 455–84, London: Sage.
Berkes, N. (1998), *The Development of Secularism in Turkey*, London: Hurst.
Berktay, H., ed. (2017), *History and Memory: TRT World in the Face of the July 15 Coup*, Istanbul: TRT World Research Centre.
Bernays, E. L. (1923), *Crystallizing Public Opinion*, New York: Boni & Liveright.
Bernays, E. L. (1952), *Public Relations*, Norman: University of Oklahoma Press.
Besli, H. and Ö. Özbay (2010), *Bir Liderin Doğuşu: Recep Tayyip Erdoğan* (The Birth of a leader: Recep Tayyip Erdoğan), Istanbul: Meydan Yayıncılık.
Best, S. and D. Kellner (1997), *The Postmodern Turn*, New York: Guilford Press.
Bhaba, H. (1990), *Nation and Narration*, London: Routledge.
Bhaba, H. (1994), *The Location of Culture*, Abingdon: Routledge.
Bilgin, P. (2017), *The International in Security, Security in the International*, Abingdon: Routledge.
Bischof, G. and A. Pelinka, eds (2017), *The Americanization/Westernization of Austria*, Abingdon: Routledge.
Blackledge, A. (2005), *Discourse and Power in a Multilingual World*, Amsterdam: John Benjamins Publishing.
Blommaert, J. and D. Jie (2010), *Ethnographic Fieldwork: A Beginner's Guide*, Bristol: Multilingual Matters.

Blumer, H. (2008), 'Social Movements', in V. Ruggiero and N. Montagna (eds), *Social Movements: A Reader*, Abingdon: Routledge.

Blumler, J., D. Kavanagh and T. Nossiter (1996), 'Modern Communications versus Traditional Politics in Britain: Unstable Marriage of Convenience', in D. Swanson and P. Mancini (eds), *Politics, Media and Modern Democracy*, London: HarperCollins.

Blumler, J. G. and M. Gurevitch (2001), in 'Mediated Politics: An Introduction', in W. L. Bennett and R. M. Entman (eds), *Mediated Politics: Communication in the Future of Democracy*, Cambridge: Cambridge University Press.

Boellstorff, T., B. Nardi, C. Pearce and T. L. Taylor (2012), *Ethnography and Virtual Worlds: A Handbook of Method*, New Jersey: Princeton University Press.

Bogdan, R. and S. J. Taylor (1975), *Introduction to Qualitative Research Methods*, New York: Wiley.

Boggs, C. (1995), 'Rethinking the Sixties Legacy: From New Left to New Social Movements', in M. L. Stanford (ed.), *Social Movements: Critiques, Concepts, Case-Studies*, London: Macmillan.

Bogner, A., B. Littig and W. Menz, eds (2009), *Interviewing Experts*, Hampshire: Palgrave.

Bokhari, K. and F. Senzai (2013), *Political Islam in the Age of Democratization*, New York: Palgrave Macmillan.

Bora, T. and M. Gültenkingil, eds (2005), *Modern Türkiye'de Siyasi Düşünce: İslamcılık* (Political Thought in Modern Turkey: Islamism), Istanbul: İletişim.

Bordieu, P. (1997), *Der Tote packt den Lebenden: Schriften zu Politik and Kultur 2* (The Dead Grabs the Alive: Writings on Politics and Culture), Hamburg: VSA.

Bos, L., W. Van der Brug and C. de Vresse (2011), 'How the Media Shape Perceptions of Right-Wing Populist Leaders', *Political Communication* 28 (2): 182–206.

Boubekeur, A. and O. Roy, eds (2014), *Whatever Happened to the Islamists: Salafis, Heavy Metal Muslims and the Lure of Consumerist Islam*, London: Hurst.

Börzel, T. A., A. Dandashly and T. Risse (2016), *Responses to the 'Arabellions': The EU in comparative perspective*, Abingdon: Routledge.

Bouyahya, D. (2015), *Islam-Oriented Parties' Ideologies and Political Communication in the Quest for Power in Morocco: The PJD as a Case Study*, Newcastle upon Tyne: Cambridge Scholars Publishing.

Brande (1867), *Dictionary of Science, Literature and Art*, London: Longmans, Green.

Brennan, S. and M. Herzog (2014), *Turkey and the Politics of National Identity: Social, Economic and Cultural Transformation*, London: I.B. Tauris.

Brewer, J. (2000), *Ethnography*, Buckingham: Open University Press.

Brown, J. B. and A. Hamzawy, eds (2010), *Between Religion and Politics*, Washington: Carnegie Endowment.

Brown, N. J. (2012), *When Victory Is Not an Option: Islamist Movements in Arab Politics*, Ithaca, NY: Cornell University.

Bruce, B. (1992), *Images of Power*, London: Kogan Page.

Brumber, D. (1997), 'Rhetoric and Strategy: Islamic Movements in the Middle East', in M. Kramer (ed.), *The Islamism Debate*, New York: Syracuse University Press.
Bryman, A. (2011), *Social Research Methods*, Oxford: Oxford University Press.
Bryman, A. (2001), *Ethnography*, London: Sage.
Bucy, E. P. and M. E. Grabe (2009), *Image Bite Politics: News and the Visual Framing of Elections*, Oxford: Oxford University Press.
Buechler, S. M. and F. K. Cylke (1997), *Social Movements: Perspectives and Issues*, California: Mayfield Publishing.
Bulaç, A. (2005), 'İslam'ın Üç Siyaset Tarzı veya İslamcıların Üç Nesli' (Islam's Three Politics Art or Islamist's Three Generation) in B. Tanıl and M. Gültekingil (eds), *Modern Türkiye'de Siyasi Düşünce: İslamcılık* (Political Thinking in Modern Turkey: Islamism), Istanbul: İletişim.
Burgess, R. G. (1982), 'Elements of Sampling in Field Research', in R. G. Burgess (ed.), *Field Research: A Source Book and Field Manual*, London: Allen and Unwin.
Burgess, R. G. (1984), *In the Field: An Introduction to Field Research*, London: Allen and Unwin.
Butler, D. and A. Ranney, eds (1992), *Electioneering: A Comparative Study of Continuity and Change*, Oxford: Oxford University Press.
Byron, M. (1993), 'Using Audio-Visual Aids in Geography Research: Questions of Access and Responsibility', *Area*, 25: 279–85.
Cagaptay, S. (2017), *The New Sultan: Erdogan and the Crisis of Modern Turkey*, London: I.B. Tauris.
Cagaptay, S. (2019), *Erdogan's Empire: Turkey and the Politics of the Middle East*, London: I.B. Tauris.
Çakır, R. (1994), *Ne Demokrasi Ne Şeriat* (Neither Democracy Nor Sharia), Istanbul: Metis Yayınları.
Çakır, R. (2005), 'Milli Görüş Hareketi' (*Milli* Görüş Movement), in B. Tanıl and M. Gültekingil (eds), *Modern Türkiye'de Siyasi Düşünce: İslamcılık* (Political Thinking in Modern Turkey: Islamism), Istanbul: İletişim.
Çakır, R. and F. Calmuk (2001), *Recep Tayyip Erdoğan, Bir Dönüşümün Öyküsü* (Recep Tayyip Erdoğan: The Story of a Transformation), Istanbul: Metis Yayınları.
Çarkoğlu, A. (2006), 'Political Preferences of the Turkish Electorate: Reflections of an Alevi-Sunni Cleavage', in A. Çarkoğlu and B. Rubin (eds), *Religion and Politics in Turkey*, Abingdon: Routledge.
Calhoun, C. (1993), 'New Social Movements of the Early Nineteenth Century', *Social Science History*, 17 (3) (Autumn): 385–427.
Calvert, J. (2010), *Sayyid Qutb and the Origins of Radical Islamism*, London: Hurst.
Cameron, W. B. (1966), *Modern Social Movements*, New York: Random House.
Cannell, C. F. and R. L. Kahn (1968), 'Interviewing', in G. Lindzey and E. Aronson (eds), *The Handbook of Social Psychology*, Vol. 2, 2nd ed., 526–95, Reading, MA: Addison-Wesley.

Carmichael, C. (2015), *A Concise History of Bosnia*, Cambridge: Cambridge University Press.
Castells, M. (1983), *The City and the Grassroots: A Cross-Cultural Theory of Urban Social Movements*, Berkley: University of California Press.
Castells, M. (1996), *The Rise of the Network Society*, Oxford: Blackwell.
Castells, M. (2009), *Communication Power*, Oxford: Oxford University Press.
Castells, M. (2010), *The Power of Identity*, Sussex: Blackwell.
Çetinsaya, G. (2005), 'İslamcılıktaki Milliyetçilik' (Nationalism in Islamism), in B. Tanıl and M. Gültekingil (eds), *Modern Türkiye'de Siyasi Düşünce: İslamcılık* (Political Thinking in Modern Turkey: Islamism), Istanbul: İletişim.
Cevik, B. S. and P. Seib, eds (2015), *Turkey's Public Diplomacy*, New York: Palgrave Macmillan.
Charteris-Black, J. (2007), *The Communication of Leadership: The Design of Leadership Style*, Abingdon: Routledge.
Chomsky, N. (1991), *Media Control: The Spectacular Achievements of Propaganda*, New York: Seven Stories Press.
Cicourel, A. V. (1964), *Method and Measurement in Sociology*, New York: Free Press.
Cicourel, A. V. (1981), 'Notes on the Integration of Micro- and Macrolevels of Analysis', in K. Knorr-Cetina and A. V. Cicourel (eds), *Advances in Social Theory and Methodology: Towards an Integration of Micro- and Macro Sociologies*, 51–80, Abingdon: Routledge & Kegan Paul.
Ciddi, S. (2009), *Kemalism in Turkish Politics: The Republican People's Party, Secularism and Nationalism*, Abingdon: Routledge.
Ciddi, S. (2016), 'Kemalist Advocacy in a Post-Kemalist Era', in Ü. Cizre (ed.), *The Turkish Ak Party and Its Leader: Criticism, Opposition and Dissent*, Abingdon: Routledge.
Cizre, Ü., ed. (2008), *Secular and Islamic Politics in Turkey: The Making of the Justice and Development Party*, Abingdon: Routledge.
Cizre, Ü., ed. (2016), *The Turkish Ak Party and Its Leader: Criticism, Opposition and Dissent*, Abingdon: Routledge.
Cleveland, W. L. (2000), *History of the Modern Middle East*, Colorado: Westview Press.
Cloke, P., ed. (2004), *Practicing Human Geography*, London: Sage.
Coffey, A. (1999), *The Ethnographic Self: Fieldwork and the Representation of Identity*, London: Sage.
Cohen, R. and S. M. Rai (2000), *Global Social Movements*, London: Athlone Press.
Combs, J. E. and D. Nimmo (1993), *The New Propaganda: The Dictatorship of Palaver in Contemporary Politics*, New York: Longmans.
Coombs, W. T. and S. J. Holladay (2007), *It's Not Just PR: Public Relations in Society*, Malden, MA: Blackwell.
Cottle, S. (2003), *News, Public Relations and Power*, London: Sage.
Crane, G. T. (1994), 'Collective Identity, Symbolic Mobilization, and Student Protest in Nanjing, China, 1988–1989', *Comparative Politics*, 26 (4) (July): 395–413.

Crang, M. and I. Cook (2007), *Doing Ethnographies*, London: Sage.
Cutlip, S. M., A. H. Center and G. M. Broom (2000), *Effective Public Relations*, 8th ed., New Jersey: Prentice Hall.
D'Urbano, P. (2011), 'Ikhwan Web: Digital Activism and the Egyptian Muslim Brotherhood', PhD Thesis, SOAS, University of London, London.
Dabbs, J. M. Jr. (1982), 'Making Things Visible', in J. Van Maanen (ed.), *Varieties of Qualitative Research*, Beverly Hills, CA: Sage.
Dagi, I. (2013), 'Post-Islamism à la Turca', in A. Bayat (ed.), *Post-Islamism: The Changing Faces of Political Islam*, Oxford: Oxford University Press.
Dalton R. J., I. McAllister and M. P. Wattenberg (2000), 'The Consequences of Partisan Dealignment', in R. J. Dalton and M. P. Wattenberg (eds), *Parties without Partisans. Political Change in Advanced Industrial Democracies*, 37–63, Oxford: Oxford University Press.
Danahar, P. (2013), *The New Middle East: The World after the Arab Spring*, London: Bloomsbury.
Davies, C. A. (1999), *Reflexive Ethnography: A Guide to Researching Selves and Others*, Abingdon: Routledge.
Davis, A. (2019), *Political Communication: A New Introduction for Crisis Times*, Cambridge: Polity.
Day, Barry (1980) 'The Politics of Communications, or the Communication of Politics', in R. Worcester and D. Harrup (eds), *Political Communications*, London: Allen and Unwin.
Delamont, S. (2004), 'Ethnography and Participant Observation', in S. Seale, G. Gobo, J. Gubrium and D. Silverman (eds), *Qualitative Research Practice*, 217–29, London: Sage.
De La Torre, C. (2017), 'Populism and Nationalism in Latin America', *Javnost – The Public*, DOI: 10.1080/13183222.2017.1330731.
Della Porta, ed. (2009), *Democracy in Social Movements*, Hampshire: Palgrave Macmillan.
Del Valle, J. (2013), *A Political History of Spanish: The Making of a Language*, Cambridge: Cambridge University Press.
Demant, P. R. (2006), *Islam vs. Islamism: The Dilemma of the Muslim World*, Westport, CT: Praeger.
Denoeux, G. (2002), 'The Forgotten Swamp: Navigating Political Islam', *Middle East Policy*, 9 (2) (June): 203–20.
Denoeux, G. (2011), 'The Forgotten Swamp: Navigating Political Islam', in F. Volpi (ed.), *Political Islam: A Critical Reader*, Abingdon: Routledge.
Denton, R. E. and G. C. Woodward (1990), *Political Communication in America*, New York: Praeger.
Denton, R. E., J. S. Trent and R. V. Friedenberg (2016), *Political Campaign Communication: Principles and Practices*, Lanham, MD: Rowman & Littlefield.
Denzin, N. (1970), *The Research Act*, Chicago: Aldine.

Denzin, N. K. (2012), 'Triangulation 2.0', *Journal of Mixed Methods Research*, 6 (2): 80–8.
Denzin, N. K. and Y. S. Lincoln, eds (1998), *Collecting and Interpreting Qualitative Materials*, Thousand Oaks, CA: Sage.
Denzin, N. K. and Y. S. Lincoln, eds (2000), *Handbook of Qualitative Research*, 2nd ed., Thousand Oaks, CA: Sage.
Denzin, N. K. and Y. S. Lincoln, eds (2005), *The Sage Handbook of Qualitative Research*, 3rd ed., Thousand Oaks, CA: Sage.
Devji, F. and Z. Kazmi, eds (2017), *Islam after Liberalism*, London: Hurst.
DeWalt, K. M. and B. R. DeWalt (2002), *Participant Observation: A Guide for Fieldworkers*, Walnut Creek, CA: Altamira Press.
Donatella, D. P. and M. Diani (2006), *Social Movements: An Introduction*, Oxford: Blackwell.
Eickelmann, D. F. (2000), 'Islam and the Language of Modernity', *Daedalus*, 129 (1): 119–35.
Elebash, C. (1984), 'The Americanization of British Political Communications', *Journal of Advertising*, 13 (3) (1 October): 50–8.
Eligür, B. (2010), *The Mobilization of Political Islam in Turkey*, Cambridge: Cambridge University Press.
Ellul, J. (1965), *The Technological Society*, New York: Knopf.
Ellul, J. (1973), *Propaganda: The Formation of Men's Attitudes*, New York: Vintage Books.
Emerson, R. M., R. I. Fretz and L. L. Shaw (1995), *Writing Ethnographic Fieldnotes*, Chicago, IL: Chicago University Press.
Esposito, J. L. (1992), *The Islamic Threat: Myth or Reality*, Oxford: Oxford University Press.
Esposito, J. L., ed. (1997), *Political Islam: Revolution, Radicalism, or Reform?*, Colorado: Lynne Rienner.
Esposito, J. L. (1998), *Islam and Politics*, New York: Syracuse University Press.
Esposito, J. L. and E. El-Din Shahin, eds (2013), *The Oxford Handbook of Islam and Politics*, Oxford: Oxford University Press.
Esposito, J. L. and J. O. Voll (1996), *Islam and Democracy*, Oxford: Oxford University Press.
Esser, F. and B. Pfetsch, eds (2004), *Comparing Political Communication: Theories, Cases, and Challenges*, Cambridge: Cambridge University Press.
Euben, R. L. and M. Q. Zaman, eds (2009), *Princeton Readings in Islamist Thought*, New Jersey: Princeton University Press.
Eyerman, R. and A. Jamison (1991), *Social Movements: A Cognitive Approach*, Cambridge: Polity.
Fairclough, N. (1989), *Language and Power*, London: Longmans, Green.
Fairclough, N. (2003), *Analysing Discourse: Textual Analysis for Social Research*, Abingdon: Routledge.

Farell, D. (1996), 'Campaign Strategies and Tactics', in L. LeDuc, R. G. Niemi and P. Norris (eds), *Comparing Democracies: Elections and Voting in Global Perspective*, Thousand Oaks, CA: Sage.

Farouki, S. T. and B. M. Nafi (2004), *Islamic Thought in the Twentieth Century*, London: I.B. Tauris.

Feroz, A. (1993), *The Making of Modern Turkey*, Abingdon: Routledge.

Fetterman, D. M. (1998), *Ethnography: Step by Step*, Thousand Oaks, CA: Sage.

Fife, W. (2005), *Doing Fieldwork: Ethnographic Methods for Research in Developing Countries and Beyond*, New York: Palgrave Macmillan.

Finlayson, A. and J. Martin (2008), '"It Ain't What you Say…": British Political Studies and the Analysis of Speech and Rhetoric', *British Politics*, 3 (December): 445–64.

Flick, U. (2009), *An Introduction to Qualitative Research*, London: Sage.

Foster, J. and C. Muste (1992), 'The United States', in D. Butler and A. Ranney (eds), *Electioneering: A Comparative Study of Continuity and Change*, Oxford: Oxford University Press.

Foucault, M. (1978), *The History of Sexuality: An Introduction*, Vol. I, New York: Random House.

Foweraker, J. (1995), *Theorizing Social Movements*, London: Pluto Press.

Fraser, L. (1957), *Propaganda*, Oxford: Oxford University Press.

Freedman, J., Z. Kivilcim and N. O. Baklacıoğlu (2017), *A Gendered Approach to the Syrian Refugee Crisis*, Abingdon: Routledge.

Freely, J. (2009), *The Grand Turk: Sultan Mehmet II – Conqueror of Constantinople and Master of an Empire*, New York: Overlook Press.

Garretton, M. A. (1997), 'Social Movements and Democratization', in S. Lindberg and A. Sverrisson (eds), *Social Movements in Development: The Challenge of Globalization and Democratization*, London: Macmillan.

Gee, J. P. (2005), *An Introduction to Discourse Analysis: Theory and Method*, Abingdon: Routledge.

Gellner, E. (1995), 'The Importance of Being Modular', in John A. Hall (ed.), *Civil Society: Theory, History, Comparison*, Cambridge: Polity.

Genç, K. (2019), *The Lion and the Nightingale: A Journey through Modern Turkey*, London: I.B. Tauris/Bloomsbury.

Gencer, B. (2008), *İslam'da Modernleşme* (Modernization in Islam), Ankara: Doğu Batı Yayınları.

Gerges, F. A. (2013), *Obama and the Middle East: The End of America's Moment?*, New York: Palgrave Macmillan.

Giddens, A. (1991), *Modernity and Self-Identity: Self and Society in the Late Modern Age*, Cambridge: Polity.

Giddens, A. (2007), 'Living in a Post-Traditional Society', in U. Beck, A. Giddens and S. Lash (eds), *Reflexive Modernization: Politics, Tradition and Aesthetics in the Modern Social Order*, Cambridge: Polity.

Gobo, G. (2008), *Doing Ethnography*, London: Sage.

Göle, N. (1997), 'Secularism and Islamism in Turkey: The Making of Elites and Counter-Elites', *Middle East Journal*, 51 (1): 46–57.
Goodwin, J. and J. M. Jasper (2003), *The Social Movements Reader: Cases and Concepts*, Oxford: Blackwell.
Gordon, C., ed. (1980), *Power/Knowledge: Selected Interviews and Other Writings 1972-1977: Michel Foucault*, Harlow: Pearson Education.
Gray, J. and I. L. Densten (1998), 'Integrating Quantitative and Qualitative Analysis Using Latent and Manifest Variables', *Quality & Quality*, 32: 419–31.
Greenberg, B. S. (1980), *Life on Television: A Content Analysis of US TV Drama*, Norwood, NJ: Ablex.
Grigoriadis, I. N. (2009), *Trials of Europeanization: Turkish Political Culture and the European Union*, New York: Palgrave Macmillan.
Gülalp, H. (1995), 'Islam and Postmodernism', *Contention: Debates in Society, Culture and Science*, 4 (2): 59–70.
Habermas, J. (1991), *The Structural Transformation of the Public Sphere: An Inquiry into a Category of Bourgeois Society*, Massachusetts: MIT Press.
Hafez, K., ed. (2000), *The Islamic World and the West: An Introduction to Political Cultures and International Relations*, Leiden: Koninklijke.
Hale, W. (2006), 'Christian Democracy and the JDP: Parallels and Contrasts', in M. H. Yavuz (ed.), *The Emergence of a New Turkey: Islam, Democracy, and the Ak Parti*, Utah: University of Utah Press.
Hale, W. (2013), *Turkish Foreign Policy since 1774*, Abingdon: Routledge.
Hale, W. and E. Özbudun, eds (2010), *Islamism, Democracy and Liberalism in Turkey*, New York: Routledge.
Hall, S., ed. (1997), *Representation: Cultural Representations and Signifying Practices*, London: Sage.
Hallin, D. C. and P. Mancini (2004), 'Americanization, Globalization, Secularization: Understanding the Convergence of Media Systems and Political Communication', in F. Esserm and B. Pfetsch (eds), *Comparing Political Communication: Theories, Cases, and Challenges*, Cambridge: Cambridge University Press.
Hamid, S. (2016), *Islamic Exceptionalism: How the Struggle over Islam Is Reshaping the World*, New York: St. Martin's Press.
Hamid, S. and W. McCants (2017), *Rethinking Political Islam*, Oxford: Oxford University Press.
Hammersley, M. and P. Atkinson (1983), *Ethnography: Principles in Practice*, London: Tavistock.
Han, B-C. (2013), *Im Schwarm: Ansichten des Digitalen* (In the Swarm: Digital Prospects), Berlin: Matthes & Seitz.
Hanioğlu, M. S. (1995), *The Young Turks in Opposition*, Oxford: Oxford University Press.

Hansen, S. J., A. Mesoy and T. Kardas, eds (2009), *The Borders of Islam: Exploring Samuel Huntington's Faultlines, from Al-Andalus to the Virtual Ummah*, New York: Columbia University Press.

Harb, Z. (2011), *Channels of Resistance in Lebanon: Liberation of Propaganda, Hezbollah and the Media*, London: I.B. Tauris.

Harlow, R. F. (1976), 'Building a Public Relations Definition', *Public Relations Review*, 2 (4): 34–42.

Hart, R. P. (1987), *The Sound of Leadership: Presidential Communication in the Modern Age*, Chicago, IL: Chicago University Press.

Harvey, W. S. (2011), *Strategies for Conducting Elite Interviews*, London: Sage.

Hawkins, K. A. (2009), 'Is Chavez Populist?: Measuring Populist Discourse in Comparative Perspective', *Comparative Political Studies*, 42 (8): 1040–67.

Heberle, R. (1951), *Social Movements: In Introduction to Political Sociology*, New York: Appleton-Century-Crofts.

Hillhorst, D. (2003), *The Real World of NGOs: Discourses, Diversity and Development*, London: Zed Books.

Holsti, O. R. (1969), *Content Analysis for the Social Sciences and Humanities*, Reading, MA: Addison-Wesley.

Holt, P. M., A. K. S. Lambton and B. Lewis (1970), *The Cambridge History of Islam*, Cambridge: Cambridge University Press.

Hourani, A., P. S. Khoury and M. C. Wilson (1993), *The Modern Middle East*, London: I.B. Tauris.

Howard, D. (2000), *Discourse*, Buckingham: Open University Press.

Hunt, S. M. (1984), 'The Role of Leadership in the Construction of Reality', in B. Kellerman (ed.), *Leadership: Multidisciplinary Perspectives*, New Jersey: Prentice-Hall.

Huntington, P. S. (1993), 'The Clash of Civilizations', *Foreign Affairs*, 72 (3): 3–27.

Huntington, S. P. (1996), *The Clash of Civilisations and the Remaking of World Order*, New York: Simon & Schuster.

Hwang, J. C. and Q. Mecham, eds (2014), *Islamist Parties and Political Normalization in the Muslim World*, Philadelphia: University of Pennsylvania Press.

Hymes, D. (1972), 'On Communicative Competence', in J. B. Prinde and J. Holmes (eds), *Sociolinguistics: Selected Readings*, 269–93, Harmondsworth: Penguin.

Ismael, T. Y. and G. E. Perry, eds (2014), *The International Relations of the Contemporary Middle East*, Abingdon: Routledge.

Jackall, R. (1995), *Propaganda*, Hampshire: Macmillan.

Jameson, F. (1991), *Postmodernism, or, the Cultural Logic of Late Capitalism*, London: Verso.

Jankowski, J. (1991), 'Egypt and Early Arab Nationalism', in R. Khalidi, L. Anderson, M. Muslih and R. S. Simon (eds), *The Origins of Arab Nationalism*, New York: Columbia University Press.

Jensen, K. B., ed. (2012), *A Handbook of Media and Communication Research: Qualitative and Quantitative Methodologies*, Abingdon: Routledge.

Johnson, J. M. (2002), 'In-depth Interviewing', in J. Gubrium and J. Holstein (eds), *Handbook of Interview Research: Context and Method*, 103–19, Thousand Oaks, CA: Sage.

Johnson-Carteem K. S. and G. A. Copeland (2004), *Strategic Political Communication: Rethinking Social Influence, Persuasion, and Propaganda*, Lanham, MD: Rowman & Littlefield.

Johnston, H. and B. Klandermans, eds (1995), *Social Movements and Culture*, Minneapolis: University of Minnesota Press.

Johnstone, B. (2009), *Discourse Analysis*, Malden, MA: Blackwell.

Johny, S. (2009), *The Coding Manual for Qualitative Researchers*, London: Sage.

Jowett, G. S. and V. O'Donnell (2012), *Propaganda and Persuasion*, Thousand Oaks, CA: Sage.

Kaiser, K. (2009), 'Protecting Respondent Confidentiality in Qualitative Research', *Qualitative Health Research*, 19 (11) (November): 1632–41.

Kalın, I. (2013), 'The Ak Party in Turkey', in J. L. Esposito and E. El-Din Shahin (eds), *The Oxford Handbook of Islam and Politics*, 423–39, Oxford: Oxford University Press.

Kaplan, A. and J. M. Goldsen (1965), 'The Reliability of Content Analysis Categories', in H. D. Lasswell, N. Leites et al. (eds), *Language of Politics: Studies in Quantitative Semantics*, 83–112, Cambridge: MIT Press.

Kara, I (2005), 'Turban and Fez: Ulema as Opposition', in Elisabeth Özdalga (ed.), *Late Ottoman Society: The Intellectual Legacy*, London: Routledge.

Kara, I. (2011), *İslamcıların Siyasi Görüşleri I: Hilafet ve Meşrutiyet* (Political Views of Islamists I: Caliphate and Constitutionalism), Istanbul: Dergah Yayınları.

Kara, I. (2014), *Türkiye'de İslamcılık Düşüncesi 1* (Islamism Though in Turkey, Vol. 1), Istanbul: Dergah Yayınları.

Karataş, T. (2005), 'Sezai Karakoç: Bir Medeniyet Tasarımcısı' (Sezai Karakoç: A Civilization Architect), in B. Tanıl and M. Gültekingil (eds), *Modern Türkiye'de Siyasi Düşünce: İslamcılık* (Political Thinking in Modern Turkey: Islamism), Istanbul: İletişim.

Karpat, K. (1959), *Turkey's Politics: The Transition to a Multi-Party System*, New Jersey: Princeton University Press.

Karpat, K. (2001), *The Politicization of Islam*, Oxford: Oxford University Press.

Kedouri, E. (1966), *Afghani and 'Abduh: An Essay on Religious Unbelief and Political Activism in Modern Islam*, London: Frank Cass.

Kentel, F. (2016), 'The Right to the City during the AK Party's Thermidor', in Ü. Cizre (ed.), *The Turkish Ak Party and Its Leader: Criticism, Opposition and Dissent*, Abingdon: Routledge.

Kepel, G. (1985), *Muslim Extremism in Egypt: The Prophet and Pharaoh*, London: Al Saqi Books.

Kepel, G. (2002), *Jihad: The Trail of Political Islam*, London: I.B. Tauris.

Kepel, G. and J-P. Milelli, eds (2010), *Al Qaeda in Its Own Words*, Cambridge, MA: Harvard University Press.
Kerlinger, F. N. (1973), *Foundations of Behavioural Research*, 2nd ed., New York: Hold, Rinehart & Winston.
Keyman, E. F. and A. İçduygu (2005), *Citizenship in a Global World: European Questions and Turkish Experiences*, Abingdon: Routledge.
Khalidi, R., L. Anderson, M. Muslih and R. S. Simon, eds (1991), *The Origins of Arab Nationalism*, New York: Columbia University Press.
Khatib, L. (2012), *Hizbullah's Image Management Strategy*, Los Angles: Figueroa Press.
Khatib, L. (2013), *Image Politics in the Middle East: The Role of the Visual in Political Struggle*, London: I.B. Tauris.
Khatib, L., D. Matar and A. Alshaer (2014), *The Hizbullah Phenomenon: Politics and Communication*, London: Hurst.
Khoury, N. A. (1976), *Islam and Modernization in the Middle East: Muhammad Abduh, an Ideology of Development*, Michigan: University Microfilms International.
Kieser, H. L. and K. Öktem (2006), *Turkey Beyond Nationalism: Towards Post-Nationalist Identities*, London: I.B. Tauris.
Kirişci, K. (2017), *Turkey and the West: Fault lines in a Troubled Alliance*, Washington, DC: The Brookings Institute.
Kirk, J. and M. Miller (1986), *Reliability and Validity in Qualitative Research*, London: Sage.
Kırmızı, A. (2019), '19.Yüzyılı Laiksizleştirmek: Osmanlı-Türk Laikleşme Anlatısının Sorunları' (Secularizing the 19th Century: A Critique of Ottoman-Turkish Secularization Narrative), *Cogito*, 94 (Summer): 93–109.
Kitchen, P., ed. (1997), *Public Relations, Principles and Practice*, London: International Thomson Business Press.
Knut, B. and W. Wickert (1999), 'Selected Aspects of Communication in German Election Campaigns', in B. I. Newman (ed.), *Handbook of Political Marketing*, 455–84, London: Sage.
Kolt, J. (1996), 'Relationship Initiation Strategies: Interpersonal Communication in Personal Advertisements', Unpublished master's thesis, Cleveland State University, Cleveland, Ohio.
Kraus, S. and D. Davis (1981), 'Political Debates', in Dan D. Nimmo and Keith Saunders (eds), *Handbook of Political Communication*, New York: Sage.
Krippendorf, K. (2013), *Content Analysis: An Introduction to Its Methodology*, Thousand Oaks, CA: Sage.
Krippendorf, K. and M. A. Bock, eds (2009), *The Content Analysis Reader*, Thousand Oaks, CA: Sage.
Kubicek, P. (2017), *European Politics*, Abingdon: Routledge.
Kurzman, C., ed. (1998), *Liberal Islam*, Oxford: Oxford University Press.
Kvale, S. (1996), *Interviews: An Introduction to Qualitative Research Interviewing*, Thousand Oaks, CA: Sage.

Landau, J. M. (1990), *The Politics of Pan-Islam; Ideology and Organization*, Oxford: Oxford University Press.

Landau, J. M., ed. (1997), *Ataturk and the Modernization of Turkey*, Leiden: Brill.

Langan, M. (2018), *Neo-Colonialism and the Poverty of 'Development' of Africa*, Cham: Palgrave Macmillan.

Langer, A. I. (2007), 'A Historical Exploration of the Personalisation of Politics in the Print Media: The British Prime Ministers 1945–1999', *Parliamentary Affairs*, 60 (3): 371–87.

Langer, A. I. (2010), 'The Politicization of Private Persona: Exceptional Leaders or the New Rule? The Case of the United Kingdom and the Blair Effect', *International Journal of Press Politics*, 15 (1): 60–76.

Lapidus, I. M. (1988), *A History of Islamic Societies*, Cambridge: Cambridge University Press.

E. Larana, H. Johnston and J. R. Gusfield, eds (1994), *New Social Movements: From Ideology to Identity*, Philadelphia: Temple University Press.

Laswell, H. D. (1927), 'The Theory of Political Propaganda', *American Political Science Review*, 21(3) (August): 627–37.

Lerner, D. (1958), *The Passing of Traditional Society: Modernizing the Middle East*, New York: Free Press.

Lewis, B. (1963), *The Middle East and the West*, London: Weidenfeld and Nicolson.

Lilleker, D. G. (2014), *Political Communication and Cognition*, Hampshire: Palgrave Macmillan.

Lindberg. S and A. Sverrisson, eds (1997), *Social Movements in Development: The Challenge of Globalization and Democratization*, London: Macmillan.

Linebarger, P. M. A. (1948), *Psychological Warfare*, Washington, DC: Infantry, Journal Press.

Lockman, Z. (1994), *Workers and Working Class in the Middle East: Struggles, Histories, Historiographies*, New York: SUNY Press.

Lofland, J. and L. H. Lofland (1995), *Analyzing Social Settings*, 3rd ed., Belmont, CA: Wadsworth.

Luke, S. H. (1955), *The Old Turkey and the New: From Byzantium to Ankara*, London: Geoffret Bles.

Lunn, J., ed. (2014), *Fieldwork in Global South: Ethical Challenges and Dilemmas*, London: Routledge.

Mandaville, P. (2004), *Transnational Muslim Politics: Reimagining the Umma*, London: Routledge.

Mandaville, P. (2007), *Global Political Islam*, Abingdon: Routledge.

Mandaville, P. (2014), *Islam and Politics*, Abingdon: Routledge.

Mandaville, P. (2017), 'Post-Islamism as Neoliberalisation: New Social Movements in the Muslim World', in F. Devji and Z. Kazmi (eds), *Islam after Liberalism*, London: Hurst.

Mango, A. (1999), *Atatürk: The Biography of the Founder of Modern Turkey*, New York: Overlook Press.
Mansel, P. (1995), *Constantinople: City of the World's Desire, 1453–1924*, London: John Murray.
Marcou, J. (2014), 'Turkey: Between Post-Islamism and Post-Kemalism', in A. Boubekeur and O. Roy (eds), *Whatever Happened to the Islamists: Salafis, Heavy Metal Muslims and the Lure of Consumerist Islam*, London: Hurst.
Mardin, Ş. (1962), *The Genesis of Young Ottoman Thought: A Study in the Modernization of Turkish Political Ideas*, New Jersey: Princeton University Press.
Mardin, Ş. (1964), *Jön Türklerin Siyasi Fikirleri 1895–1908* (Young Turks Political Thoughts 1895–1908), Istanbul: İletişim Yayınları.
Mardin, Ş. (1983), 'Religion and Politics in Modern Turkey', in J. Piscatori (ed.), *Islam in the Political Process*, Cambridge: Cambridge University Press.
Mardin, Ş., ed. (1993), *Cultural Transition in the Middle East*, New York: Brill.
Mardin, Ş. (2006), *Religion, Society, and Modernity in Turkey*, New York: Syracuse University Press.
Markel, N. (1998), *Semiotic Psychology: Speech as an Index of Emotions and Attitudes*, New York: Peter Lang.
Marshall, C. and Rossman (1989), *Designing Qualitative Research*, Newbury Park, CA: Sage.
Martin, L. J. (1958), *International Propaganda*, Minneapolis: University of Minnesota Press.
Matar, D. (2008), 'The Power of Conviction: Nasrallah's Rhetoric and Mediated Charisma in the Context of the 2006 July War', *Middle East Journal of Culture and Communication*, 1 (2): 122–37.
Mays, N. and C. Pope (1995), 'Qualitative Research: Reaching the Parts Other Methods Cannot Reach: An Introduction to Qualitative Methods in Health and Health Services Research', *BJM*, 311 (6997): 42–5.
McAdam, D. and D. A. Snow (2000), *Readings on Social Movements: Origins, Dynamics and Outcomes*, Oxford: Oxford University Press.
McDowall, D. (2007), *A Modern History of the Kurds*, London: I.B. Tauris.
McLeod, J. M., G. M. Kosicki and McLeod (1994), 'The Expanding Boundaries of Political Communication Effects', in J. Bryant and D. Zillman (eds), *Media Effects: Advances in Theory and Research*, 123–62, Hillsdale, NJ: Erlbaum.
McMannus, J. H. (1994), *Market-Driven Journalism: Let the Citizen Beware?* Thousand Oaks, CA: Sage.
McNair, B. (2003), *An Introduction to Political Communication*, London: Routledge.
McNair, B. (2017), *An Introduction to Political Communication*, London: Routledge.
McNair, B. (2018), *An Introduction to Political Communication*, London: Routledge.
Mecham, Q. and J. C. Hwang (2014), *Islamist Parties and Political Normalization in the Muslim World*, Philadelphia, PA: Pennsylvania University Press.

Melucci, A. (1988), 'Social Movements and the Democratization of Everyday Life', in J. Keane (ed.), Civil *Society and the State*, London: Verso.

Melucci, A. (1996), *Challenging Codes: Collective Action in the Information Age*, Cambridge: Cambridge University Press.

Meyer, D. S., N. Whitter and B. Robnett, eds (2002), *Social Movements: Identity, Culture, and the State*, Oxford: Oxford University Press.

Michel, T. (2014), *Peace and Dialogue in a Plural Society*, New Jersey: Blue Dome Press.

Mills, C. W. (1959), *The Sociological Imagination*, New York: Oxford University Press.

Mitchell, R. (1969), *The Society of the Muslim Brothers*, Oxford: Oxford University Press.

Moffit, B. (2016), *The Global Rise of Populism: Performance, Political Style, and Representation*, Stanford, CA: California University Press.

Moghadam, V. M. (1993), 'Rhetorics and Rights of Identity in Islamist Movements', *Journal of World History*, 4 (2) (Fall): 243–64.

Moghadam, V. M. (2009), *Globalization and Social Movements: Islamism, Feminism, and the Global Justice Movement*, Lanham, MD: Rowman & Littlefield.

Monshipouri, M. (2009), *Muslims in Global Politics: Identities, Interests, and Human Rights*, Philadelphia, PA: Pennsylvania University Press.

Morse, J. M. (1991), 'Approaches to Qualitative-Quantitative Methodological Triangulation', *Nursing Research*, 40: 120–3.

Moser, C. A. and G. Kalton (1971), *Survey Methods in Social Investigation*, Gaybst: Gower Publishing.

Mudde, C. (2004), 'The Populist Zeitgeist', *Government and Opposition*, 39 (4): 541–63.

Munson, Z. (2001), 'Islamic Mobilization: Social Movement Theory and the Egyptian Muslim Brotherhood', *Sociology Quarterly*, 42 (4) (Autumn): 487–510.

Musallam, A. A. (2005), *From Secularism to Jihad: Sayyid Qutb and the Foundations of Radical Islamism*, Westport, CT: Praeger.

Nasr, V. (2009), *The Rise of Islamic Capitalism: Why the New Muslim Middle Class Is the Key to Defeating Extremism*, New York: Free Press.

Negrine, R. (2008), *The Transformation of Political Communication: Continuities and Changes in Media and Politics*, New York: Palgrave Macmillan.

Negrine, R. and S. Papathanassopoulos (1996), 'The "Americanization" of Political Communication: A Critique', *Harvard International Journal of Press/Politics*, 1 (2): 45–62.

Negrine, R. and S. Papathanassopoulos (2007), 'The Americanization of Political Communication', in R. Negrine and J. Stanyer (eds), *The Political Communication Reader*, Abingdon: Routledge.

Negrine, R. and J. Stanyer (2007), *The Political Communication Reader*, Abingdon: Routledge.

Negrine, R., P. Mancini, C. Holtz-Bacha and S. Papathanassopoulos (2007), *The Professionalisation of Political Communication*, Chicago: Intellect Books.

Nelson, C., P. A. Treichler and L. Grossberg (1992), 'Cultural Studies', in L. Grossberg, C. Nelson and P. A. Treichler (eds), *Cultural Studies*, 1–16, New York: Routledge.

Neuendorf, K. A. (2002), *The Content Analysis Guidebook*, Thousand Oaks, CA: Sage.
Neuman, W. L. (2014), *Social Research Methods: Qualitative and Quantitative Approaches*, Boston: Pearson Education.
Nielsen, J. S., S. Akgönül, A. Alibasic and E. Racius, eds (2014), *Yearbook of Muslims in Europe*, Leiden: Brill.
Orwell, G. (1946), *Politics and the English Language*, London: Penguin.
Oswald, H. (2010), 'Wie heißt qualitativ forschen? Warnungen, Fehlerquellen, Möglichkeiten' (What Is Qualitative Research? Warnings, Sources of error, Possibilities), in B. Friebertshaeuser, A. Langer and A. Prengel (eds), *Handbuch qualitative Forschungsmethoden in der Erziehungswissenschaft* (Handbook of Qualitative Research Methods in Pedagogics), Weinheim: Beltz.
Özbudun, E. (1976), *Social Change and Political Participation in Turkey*, New Jersey: Princeton University Press.
Özdalga, E., ed. (2005), *Late Ottoman Society: The Intellectual Legacy*, Abingdon: Routledge.
Özkan, N. (2019), *Kahramanın Yolculuğu: Yeni nesil siyasetin zaferi* (Hero's Journey: New Generation Politic's Triumph), Istanbul: MediaCat.
Özdenören, R. (2005), 'Necip Fazıl Kısakürek', in B. Tanıl and M. Gültekingil (eds), *Modern Türkiye'de Siyasi Düşünce: İslamcılık* (Political Thinking in Modern Turkey: Islamism), Istanbul: İletişim.
Özüdoğru, Ş. (2016), 'Ottoman Costume in the Context of Modern Turkish Fashion Design', in M. A. Jansen and J. Craik (eds), *Modern Fashion Traditions: Negotiating Tradition and Modernity Through Fashion*, London: Bloomsbury Academic.
Oxford Dictionary of English (2010), 3rd ed., Oxford: Oxford University Press.
Pakulski, J. (1991), *Social Movements: The Politics of Moral Protest*, Melbourne: Longman Cheshire.
Paltridge, B. (2006), *Discourse Analysis: An Introduction*, London: Continuum.
Pappe, I. (2004), *A History of Modern Palestine: One Land, Two Peoples*, Cambridge: Cambridge University Press.
Paul, T. V. (2014), *The Warrior State: Pakistan in the Contemporary World*, Oxford: Oxford University Press.
Perloff, R. M. (2014), *The Dynamics of Political Communication: Media and Politics in a Digital Age*, Abingdon: Routledge.
Phillips, D. L. (2017), *An Uncertain Ally*, Abingdon: Routledge.
Piscatori, J., ed. (1983), *Islam in the Political Process*, Cambridge: Cambridge University Press.
Piscatori, J. (2006), *Reinventing the Ummah? The Trans-Locality of Pan-Islam*, Lecture at the Tenth Anniversary Conference entitled 'Translocality: An Approach to Globalising Phenomena', Zentrum Moderner Orient, Berlin, 26 September.
Plasser, F. and G. Plasser (2002), *Global Political Campaigning: A Worldwide Analysis of Campaign Professionals and Their Practices*, Westport, CT: Praeger.

Polletta, F. and J. M. Jasper (2001), 'Collective Identity and Social Movements', *Annual Review of Sociology*, 27: 283–305.

Porta, D. D. and M. Diana (1999), *Social Movements*, Oxford: Blackwell.

Povey, T. (2015), *Social Movements in Egypt and Iran*, Hampshire: Palgrave Macmillan.

Qualter, T. H. (1962), *Propaganda and Psychological Warfare*, New York: Random House.

Rahat, G. and T. Schaefer (2007), 'The Personalization(s) of Politics: Israel, 1949–2003', *Political Communication*, 24 (1) (29 January): 65–80.

Ramadan, T. (2012), *Islam and the Arab Awakening*, Oxford: Oxford University Press.

Resnik, D. B. (2009), *Playing Politics with Science: Balancing Scientific Independence and Government Oversight*, Oxford: Oxford University Press.

Rida, R. (2007), *İttihad-ı Osmanî'den Arap İsyanına* (From Ittihad-ı İslam to the Arab Revolt), Istanbul: Klasik.

Riffe, D., S. Lacy and F. G. Fico (2008), *Analyzing Media Messages: Using Quantitative Content Analysis in Research*, New York: Routledge.

Ritchie, J. and J. Lewis, eds (2003), *Qualitative Research Practice: A Guide for Social Science Students and Researchers*, London: Sage.

Roy, O. (1994), *The Failure of Political Islam*, Cambridge, MA: Harvard University Press.

Roy, O. (2004), *Globalised Islam: The Search for a New Ummah*, New York: Columbia University Press.

Roy, O. (2013), *Holy Ignorance: When Religion and Culture Part Ways*, Oxford: Oxford University Press.

Rubin, B., ed. (2010), *The Muslim Brotherhood; The Organization and Policies of a Global Islamist Movement*, New York: Palgrave Macmillan.

Rubin, H. J. and I. S. Rubin (1995), *Qualitative Interviewing: The Art of Hearing Data*, Thousand Oaks, CA: Sage.

Ruggiero, V. and N. Montagna, eds (2008), *Social Movements: A Reader*, Abingdon: Routledge.

Sabato, L. J., M. Stencel and S. R. Linchter (2000), *Peepshow – Media and Politics in an Age of Scandal*, Lanham, MD: Rowman & Littlefield.

Said, E. (1978), *Orientalism*, New York: Random House.

Samuel, H. (1914), *The Future of Palestine*, CAB 37/123/43.

Sanjek, R., ed. (1990), *Fieldnotes: The Makings of Anthropology*, Ithaca, NY: Cornell University Press.

Sayyid, S. (2003), *A Fundamental Fear: Eurocentrism and the Emergence of Islamism*, London: Zed Books.

Sayyid, S. (2014), *Recalling the Caliphate: Decolonization and World Order*, London: Hurst.

Scammell, M. (1997), 'The Wisdom of the War Room: U.S. Campaigning and Americanization', Research Paper R-17, The Joan Shorenstein Center, Harvard University John F. Kennedy School of Government, April.

Scammell, M. (2007), 'The Wisdom of the War Room: US Campaigning and Americanization', in R. Negrine and J. Stanyer (eds), *The Political Communication Reader*, Abingdon: Routledge.

Schafferer, C. (2006), *Election Campaigning in East and Southeast Asia: Globalization of Political*, New York: Routledge.

Schatzman, L. and A. L. Strauss (1973), *Field Research: Strategies for a Natural Sociology*, Englewood Cliffs, NJ: Prentice-Hall.

Schensul, S. L. (1999), *Essential Ethnographic Methods: Observations, Interviews, and Questionnaires*, Maryland: AltaMira Press.

Schmitt, C. (1927), *Der Begriff des Politischen* (Concept of the Political), Berlin: Duncker und Humblot.

Schweizer, A. (1984), *The Age of Charisma*, Chicago: Nelson-Hall.

Seligman, B. Z. (1951), *Notes and Queries on Anthropology*, 6th ed., London: Routledge & Kegan Paul.

Sen, M. (2011), 'Transformation of Turkish Islamism and the Rise of the Justice and Development Party', in B. Yesilada and B. Rubin (eds), *Islamization of Turkey under the AKP Rule*, Abingdon: Routledge.

Sevinc, K., R. W. Wood Jr., and T. Coleman (2017), 'Secularism in Turkey', in P. Zuckerman and J. Shook (eds), *The Oxford Handbook of Secularism*, Oxford: University Press.

Sharma, R. K. (2008), *Sociological Methods and Techniques*, New Delhi: Atlantic.

Shively, K. (2016), 'Pragmatism Politics: The Gülen Movement and the AKP', in Ü. Cizre (ed.), *The Turkish Ak Party and Its Leader: Criticism, Opposition and Dissent*, Abingdon: Routledge.

Shlaim, A. (2000), *The Iron Wall: Israel and the Arab World*, London: Penguin.

Silverman, D. (1985), *Qualitative Methodology & Sociology*, Aldershot, UK: Gower Publishing.

Singleton, R., B. Straits, M. Straits and R. McAllister (1988), *Approaches to Social Research*, Oxford: Oxford University Press.

Smith, H. L. (2019), *Erdogan Rising: The Battle for the Soul of Turkey*, London: William Collins.

Spradley, J. P. (1979), *The Ethnographic Interview*, New York: Holt, Rinehart and Winston.

Stacey, M. (1969), *Methods of Social Research*, Oxford: Pergamon Press.

Stein, A. (2014), *Turkey's New Foreign Policy: Davutoglu, the AKP and the Pursuit of Regional Order*, Abingdon: Routledge Journals.

Stokes, J. (2003), *How to Do Media and Cultural Studies*, London: Sage.

Strömbäck, J. (2008), 'Four Phases of Mediatization: An Analysis Of the Mediatization of Politics', *International Journal of Press/Politics*, 13 (3): 228–46.

Strömbäck, J. and S. Kiousis, eds (2011), *Political Public Relations*, New York: Routledge.

Swanson, D. L. and P. Mancini, eds (1996), *Politics, Media, and Modern Democracy: An International Study of Innovations in Electoral Campaigning and Their Consequences*, Westport, CT: Praeger.

Szanto, G. H. (1978), *Theatre and Propaganda*, Austin: University of Texas Press.

Taithe, B. and T. Thornton, eds (1999), *Propaganda: Political Rhetoric and Identity 1300–2000*, Gloucestershire: Sutton Publishing.

Tanıl, B. and M. Gültekingil (2005), *Modern Türkiye'de Siyasi Düşünce: İslamcılık* (Political Thinking in Modern Turkey: Islamism), Istanbul: İletişim.

Tarrow, S. (2008), 'Power in Movement', in V. Ruggiero and N. Montagna (eds) *Social Movements: A Reader*, Abingdon: Routledge.

Tarrow, S. T. (1994), *Power in Movement*, Cambridge: Cambridge University Press.

Thaeker, A. (2004), *The Public Relations Handbook*, Abingdon: Taylor and Francis.

Thomson, O. (1977), *Mass Persuasion in History*, Edinburgh: Paul Harris.

Thussu, D. K. (2006), *International Communication: Continuity and Change*, 2nd ed., London: Arnold.

Thussu, D. K., ed. (2007), *Media on the Move: Global Flow and Contra-flow*, Abingdon: Routledge.

Thussu, D. K. (2009), *News as Entertainment: The Rise of Global Infotainment*, London: Sage.

Tilly, C. (1978), *From Mobilization to Revolution*, Reading, MA: Addison-Wesley.

Toch, H. (1965), *The Social Psychology of Social Movements*, New York: Bobbs-Merrill Company.

Touraine, A. (1981), *The Voice and the Eye: An Analysis of Social Movements*, Cambridge: Cambridge University Press.

Tourine, A. and R. Eyerman (1992), 'Modernity and Social Movements', in H. Haferkamp and N. Smelser (eds), *Social Change and Modernity*, Berkeley: University of California Press.

Turkey: Labor Laws and Regulations Handbook, Vol. 1 (2015), Washington DC: International Business Publications.

Turkey: Research and Development Policy Handbook (2015), Washington DC: International Business Publications.

Uçar, S. (2000), *Savunan Adam* (The Defender), Istanbul: Yasin Yayınevi.

Ünsal, F. B. (2005), 'Mehmet Akif Ersoy', in B. Tanıl and M. Gültekingil (eds), *Modern Türkiye'de Siyasi Düşünce: İslamcılık* (Political Thinking in Modern Turkey: Islamism), Istanbul: İletişim.

Van Dijk, T. A. (2003), 'The Discourse-Knowledge Interface', in G. Weiss and R. Wodak (eds), *Theory, Interdisciplinarity and Critical Discourse Analysis*, 85–109, London: Palgrave.

Van Jisk (2008), *Power and Discourse*, New York: Palgrave Macmillan.

Volpi, F. (2011), *Political Islam: A Critical Reader*, Abingdon: Routledge.

Waisbord, S. (2012), 'Democracy, Journalism, and Latin American Populism', *Journalism*, 14 (5): 504–21.

Waldman, S. A. and E. Caliskan (2016), *The New Turkey and Its Discontents*, London: Hurst.
Webb, B. and S. Webb (1932), *Methods of Social Study*, London: Longmans Green.
Weber, M. (1968), *On Charisma and Institution Building*, Chicago: University of Chicago Press.
Weiss, C. H., ed. (1977), *Uses of Social Research in Public Policy*, Lexington, MA: DC Heath.
Whitaker, U. G. Jr., ed. (1960), *Propaganda and International Relations*, San Francisco: Chandler Publishing.
White, J. B. (2002), *Islamist Mobilization in Turkey*, Seattle, WA: University of Washington Press.
White, J. (2014), *Muslim Nationalism and the New Turks*, New Jersey: Princeton University Press.
Wiarda, H. J. (2013), *Exploring the World: Adventures of a Global Traveller*, Bloomington: iUniverse.
Wickham, C. R. (2002), *Mobilizing Islam: Religion, Activism, and Political Change in Egypt*, New York: Columbia University Press.
Wickham, C. R. (2015), *The Muslim Brotherhood: Evolution of an Islamist Movement*, New Jersey: Princeton University Press.
Wiktorowicz, Q., ed. (2004), *Islamic Activism: A Social Movement Theory Approach*, Bloomington, IN: Indiana University Press.
Wilcox, D. L., P. H. Ault and W. K. Agee (1992), *Public Relations Strategies and Tactics*, London: HarperCollins.
Wilson, J. (1973a), *Introduction to Social Movements*, New York: Basic Books.
Wilson, J. Q. (1973b), *Political Organizations*, New Jersey: Princeton University Press.
Wodak, R. (2001), 'The Discourse-Historical Approach', in R. Wodak and M. Meyer (eds), *Methods of Critical Discourse Analysis*, 63-94, London: Sage.
Wodak, R. and M. Meyer, eds (2009), *Methods of Critical Discourse Analysis*, London: Sage.
Wolcott, H. F. (1999), *Ethnography*, London: Sage.
Wolf, A. (2017), *Political Islam in Tunisia*, London: Hurst.
Wright, R. (1990), *In the Name of God: The Khomeini Decade*, New York: Touchstones Books.
Wring, D., J. Green, R. Mortimore and S. Atkinson, eds (2007), *Political Communications: The General Election Campaign of 2005*, London: Palgrave.
Yanıkdağ, Y. (2013), *Healing the Nation: Prisoners of War, Medicine and Nationalism in Turkey, 1914-1939*, Edinburgh: Edinburgh University Press.
Yasamee, F. A. K. (1996), *Ottoman Diplomacy: Abdulhamid II and the Great Powers 1878-1888*, Istanbul: Isis Press.
Yavuz, M. H. (2003), *Islamic Political Identity in Turkey*, Oxford: Oxford University Press.

Yavuz, M. H. (2006), ed. *The Emergence of a New Turkey: Islam, Democracy, and the Ak Parti*, Utah: University of Utah Press.

Yavuz, M. H. (2009), *Secularism and Muslim Democracy in Turkey*, Cambridge: Cambridge University Press.

Zirakzadeh, C. E. (1997), *Social Movements in Politics*, London: Longmans, Green

Zubaida, S. (1989), *Islam, the People and the State: Political Ideas and Movements in the Middle East*, London: Routledge.

Zubaida, S. (2011), *Beyond Islam: A New Understanding of the Middle East*, London: I.B. Tauris.

Zürcher, E. J. (2010), *The Young Turk Legacy*, London: I.B. Tauris.

Zürcher, E. J. (1993), *Turkey; A Modern History*, London: I.B. Tauris.

Websites

ABC News (2017), 'Erdogan-Style Mustaches Trending in Turkish Ruling Party', http://abcnews.go.com/amp/International/wireStory/erdogan-style-mustaches-trending-turkish-ruling-party-46746917.

Açık Medeniyet (2019), 'Biz dünyanın neresinde bir mazlum varsa elini uzatan bir ülkeyiz' (We Are a Nation that Extends Its Hand Wherever There Is an Oppressed), http://www.acikmedeniyet.com/tr/guncel-yazi/biz-dunyanin-neresinde-bir-mazlum-varsa-elini-uzatan-bir-milletiz.

AK Party (2017), 'Cumhurbaşkanı Erdoğan, İmam Hatip Gençlik Buluşması'nda konuştu' (President Erdoğan Talks at Imam Hatip Youth Meeting), https://www.akparti.org.tr/site/haberler/cumhurbaskani-erdogan-imam-hatip-genclik-bulusmasinda-konustu/90526#1.

AK Party (no date), 'Party Programme', http://www.akparti.org.tr/english/akparti/parti-programme#bolum_.

AKP (2002), '3 Kasım 2002 Parlamento Seçim Sonuçları' (3 October 2002 Parliamentary Election Results), http://www.akparti.org.tr/site/secimler/2002-genel-secim.

AKP (2007), '22 Temmuz 2007 Parlamento Seçim Sonuçları' (22 July 2007 Parliamentary Election Results), http://www.akparti.org.tr/site/secimler/2007-genel-secim.

Akyol, M. (2015), 'Did the West Write Erdogan off for Israel's Sake?', *Al-Monitor*, http://www.al-monitor.com/pulse/originals/2015/01/turkey-west-erdogan-davutoglu-davos.html.

Al Jazeera (2010), 'Erdogan "Is No Gamal Abdel Nasser"', http://www.aljazeera.com/focus/2010/06/201062093027892694.html.

Al Jazeera (2017), 'Turkey's Failed Coup Attempt: All You Need to Know', http://www.aljazeera.com/news/2016/12/turkey-failed-coup-attempt-161217032345594.html.

Al Jazeera (2018), 'Erdogan: Turkey "Tired" of EU Membership Process', http://www.aljazeera.com/news/2018/01/erdogan-turkey-tired-eu-membership-process-180105213814481.html.

Al Jazeera (2019), '"Neutral" Pakistan Pulls out of Malaysia Summit of Muslim Nations', https://www.aljazeera.com/news/2019/12/pakistan-pulls-malaysia-summit-muslim-nations-191218082917256.html.

Al Jazeera Turk (2014), 'Portre: Abdullah Gül' (Portrait: Abdullah Gül), http://www.aljazeera.com.tr/portre/portre-abdullah-gul.

Anadolu Agency (2014), 'Cumhurbaşkanlığı seçimi takvimi belli oldu' (Timetable of the Presidential Election Is Ready), http://aa.com.tr/tr/turkiye/cumhurbaskanligi-secimi-takvimi-belli-oldu/176514.

Anadolu Agency (2017), 'Şehit Erol Olçok'un reklam ajansına Brüksel'den 4 ödül' ('Four Awards from Brussels to Martyr Erol Olçok's Commercial Agency'), http://aa.com.tr/tr/turkiye/sehit-erol-olcokun-reklam-ajansina-brukselden-4-odul/830407.

Anadolu Agency (2018a), 'Bosnian Leader Asks Turks to Help Erdogan', https://www.aa.com.tr/en/europe/bosnian-leader-asks-turks-to-help-erdogan/1152201.

Anadolu Agency (2018b), 'Bosnian Leader: Erdogan Long-Awaited Mentor for Muslims', https://www.aa.com.tr/en/politics/bosnian-leader-erdogan-long-awaited-mentor-for-muslims/1143070.

Anadolu Agency (2019), 'Mohamed Morsi's Son Thanks Erdoğan for Support', https://www.aa.com.tr/en/middle-east/mohamed-morsis-son-thanks-erdogan-for-support/1513885.

Arsu, S. (2020) 'Erdogan's Push for More Social Media Laws Is Another Step Towards Silencing Dissent', *Independent*, https://www.independent.co.uk/voices/president-erdogan-turkey-social-media-twitter-youtube-netflix-internet-a9637446.html.

Atlantic (2016), 'The Thinnest-Skinned President in the World', https://www.theatlantic.com/international/archive/2016/04/turkey-germany-erdogan-bohmermann/479814/.

Atlantic (2017), 'The Strongman in Plaid: Recep Tayyip Erdoğan Has Started a Fashion Trend among Loyalists', https://www.theatlantic.com/magazine/archive/2017/12/recep-tayyip-erdogan-plaid-jackets/544122/.

Avrupa Birliği Bakanlığ, T. C. (2007), 'Dinler Bahçesi Açılış Töreni – Derleme' (Opening Ceremony of Garden of Religions), https://www.ab.gov.tr/31332.html.

BBC (2009), 'Turkish PM Storms off in Gaza Row', http://news.bbc.co.uk/1/hi/business/davos/7859417.stm.

BBC (2016), 'Turkey HDP: Blast after Pro-Kurdish Leaders Demirtas and Yuksekdag Detained', http://www.bbc.co.uk/news/world-europe-37868441.

BBC (2017), 'Why Did Turkey Hold a Referendum?', http://www.bbc.co.uk/news/world-europe-38883556.

BBC Türkçe (2017), 'Cumhurbaşkanı Erdoğan: Bizim Avrupa Birliği üyeliğine ihtiyacımız kalmadı' (President Erdoğan: We Don't Need the European Union Anymore), http://www.bbc.com/turkce/41461446.

Binder, D. (2003), 'Alija Izetbegovic, Muslim Who Led Bosnia, Dies at 78', *New York Times*, http://www.nytimes.com/2003/10/20/world/alija-izetbegovic-muslim-who-led-bosnia-dies-at-78.html.

Bobin, F. (2016), 'Rached Ghannoushi: Il n'y a plus de justification à l'islam politique en Tunisie' (There Is No Justification for Political Islam in Tunisia), *Le Monde*, http://www.lemonde.fr/international/article/2016/05/19/rached-ghannouchi-il-n-y-a-plus-de-justification-a-l-islam-politique-en-tunisie_4921904_3210.html.

Çakırözer, U. (2014), 'Museviler: Panikteyiz' (We Jews Are in Panic), *Cumhuriyet*, http://www.cumhuriyet.com.tr/koseyazisi/103091/Museviler__Panikteyiz.html#.

CNN (2019), 'This Is the World's Happiest Country in 2019', https://edition.cnn.com/travel/article/worlds-happiest-countries-united-nations-2019/index.html.

CNN Türk (2013a), 'Başbakan Erdoğan Kazlıçeşme'de konuştu' (PM Erdoğan Talked in Kazlıçeşme), https://www.cnnturk.com/2013/turkiye/06/16/basbakan.erdogan.kazlicesmede.konustu/711858.0/index.html.

CNN Türk (2013b), 'Erdoğan'dan 'kürtaj ve sezaryen' yorumu' (Erdoğan Comments on 'Abortion and Caeserean'), https://www.cnnturk.com/2013/guncel/06/19/erdogandan.kurtaj.ve.sezaryen.yorumu/712176.0/index.html.

CNN Türk (2014), 'İşte Erdoğan'ın yeni uçağı' (Erdoğan's New Plane), https://www.cnnturk.com/fotogaleri/turkiye/iste-erdoganin-yeni-ucagi?page=1.

CPJ (2017), 'Record Number of Journalists Jailed as Turkey, China, Egypt Pay Scant Price for Repression', https://cpj.org/reports/2017/12/journalists-prison-jail-record-number-turkey-china-egypt.php.

Daily Sabah (2016), 'Erdogan Criticizes Gaza Flotilla Organizer Group IHH for Undermining Deal with Israel', https://www.dailysabah.com/diplomacy/2016/06/29/erdogan-criticizes-gaza-flotilla-organizer-group-ihh-for-undermining-deal-with-israel.

Daily Sabah (2017), 'Erdoğan Invites OIC Countries to Convene over Jerusalem Issue', https://www.dailysabah.com/diplomacy/2017/12/06/erdogan-invites-oic-countries-to-convene-over-jerusalem-issue.

Daragahi, B. (2019), 'Mohammed Morsi Death: Ousted Egyptian President Dies during trial', *Independent*, https://www.independent.co.uk/news/world/middle-east/mohamed-morsi-dead-egypt-president-coup-court-died-muslim-brotherhood-al-sisi-a8962471.html.

Demir, N. and M. D. Erdem (2006), 'Türk Kültüründe Destan ve Battal Gazi Destanı' (Epic in Turkish Culture and Epic of Battal Gazi), *Turkish Studies, International Periodical for the Language Literature and History of Turkish or Turkic*, 1 (1) (Summer), http://www.turkishstudies.net/Makaleler/1895091786_7necatidemirmderdem.pdf.

Dinc, G. (2008), 'A Close Look at AKP's Election Success', Friedrich Ebert Stiftung, http://library.fes.de/pdf-files/bueros/tuerkei/05726.pdf.

Diyanet (2020), 'Cuma Hutbesi – 24 Nisan 2020' (Friday Sermon – 24 April 2020), https://www.diyanethaber.com.tr/hutbeler/cuma-hutbesi-24-nisan-2020-h10239.html/.

Dogan, T. (2019) 'Why Couldn't Erdogan's Populist Politics Win Istanbul?', *Middle East Eye*, https://www.middleeasteye.net/opinion/why-couldnt-erdogans-populist-politics-win-istanbul.

Duvar English (2020), 'Erdoğan Could Not Islamize Minds, So He Is Islamizing Stones Instead', https://www.duvarenglish.com/columns/2020/07/21/erdogan-could-not-islamize-minds-so-he-is-islamizing-stones-instead/.

DW (2019), 'Türkiye'de akademide 1071 gerilimi' (1071 Tension in Turkish Academia), https://www.dw.com/tr/türkiyede-akademide-1071-gerilimi/a-49813176.

DW (2020), 'Recep Tayyip Erdogan Targets Social Media in Turkey', https://www.dw.com/en/recep-tayyip-erdogan-targets-social-media-in-turkey/a-53792631.

Economist (2019), 'Turkey Leads the World in Jailed Journalists', https://www.economist.com/graphic-detail/2019/01/16/turkey-leads-the-world-in-jailed-journalists.

Ensonhaber (2011), 'Erdoğan'dan fakir aileye gece ziyareti' (Erdoğan's Nightly Visit of a Poor Family), http://www.ensonhaber.com/erdogandan-fakir-aileye-gece-ziyareti-2011-10-18.html.

Erdogan, S. and F. Ünal (2013), 'Problems of the Turkish Political Parties and Turgut Özal's Motherland Party (ANAP)', *Journal of US-China Public Administration*, 10 (6) (June 2013): 601–7, http://www.davidpublishing.com/davidpublishing/Upfile/9/10/2013/2013091000072325.pdf.

Ete, H. (2014), 'Gülen ve Takipçilerini Tanımlama Zor(unlu)luğu' (The Difficulty of Characterizing Gülen and His Follower), *SETA Analysis*, http://setav.org/tr/gulen-ve-takipcilerini-tanimlama-zorunlulugu/yorum/14431.

Ete, H., Y. Akbaba, G. Dalay, S. O. Ersay, K. B. Kanat and K. Üstün (2014), 'Turkey's 2014 Local Elections', *SETA Analysis*, March, http://file.setav.org/Files/Pdf/20140322163202_turkeys-2014-local-elections.pdf.

European Commission (2005), 'Turkey 2005 Progress Report', https://www.ab.gov.tr/files/AB_Iliskileri/Tur_En_Realitons/Progress/Turkey_Progress_Report_2005.pdf.

Evrensel Daily (2019), 'Constitutional Court of Turkey Decrees Peace Academics' Rights Violated', https://www.evrensel.net/daily/383786/constitutional-court-of-turkey-decrees-peace-academics-rights-violated.

Filiu, J. P. and M. Khalaji (2011), 'The Muslim Brotherhood Today: Between Ideology and Democracy', The Washington Institute, http://www.washingtoninstitute.org/policy-analysis/view/the-muslim-brotherhood-today-between-ideology-and-democracy.

Financial Times (2016), 'Davutoglu's Departure Thrusts Erdogan Son-in-law into Limelight', https://www.ft.com/content/2cdd0178-1395-11e6-839f-2922947098f0.

Foreign Policy (2015), 'How President Erdogan Mastered the Media', http://foreignpolicy.com/2015/08/12/how-president-erdogan-mastered-the-media/.

France 24 (2019), 'Ekrem Imamoglu: From Opposition Underdog to Istanbul Mayor', https://www.france24.com/en/20190404-turkey-imamoglu-opposition-underdog-istanbul-mayor.

Freedom House (2016), 'Freedom of the Press 2016', https://freedomhouse.org/report/freedom-press/2016/turkey.

Freedom House (2017), 'Country Profile: Turkey', https://freedomhouse.org/report/freedom-net/2017/turkey.

Freedom House (2019), 'Turkey', https://freedomhouse.org/report/freedom-world/2019/turkey.

Freedom House (2020), 'Turkey', https://freedomhouse.org/country/turkey/freedom-world/2020.

Gerçek Gündem (2015), 'Erdoğan'dan Fethullah Gülen'e sert sözler' (Strong Words from Erdoğan to Gülen), https://www.gercekgundem.com/erdogandan-fethullah-gulene-sert-sozler-163914h.htm.

GlobeScan (2017), 'Sharp Drop in World Views of US, UK: Global Poll', https://globescan.com/sharp-drop-in-world-views-of-us-uk-global-poll/.

González López, J. L. and P. R. Hernández (2011), 'Quantitative versus Qualitative Research: Methodological or Ideological Dichotomy', Index de Enfermería, http://www.index-f.com/index-enfermeria/v20n3/0189e.php.

Guardian (2013), 'Erdogan's Chief Adviser Knows What's Behind Turkey's Protests – Telekinesis', https://www.theguardian.com/commentisfree/2013/jul/13/erdogan-turkey-protests-telekinesis-conspiracy-theories.

Guardian (2014), 'Turkey's New Presidential Palace Unveiled – in Pictures', https://www.theguardian.com/world/gallery/2014/oct/29/turkeys-new-presidential-palace-unveiled-in-pictures.

Guardian (2016), 'Erdogan: Turkey "Tired" of EU Membership Process', https://www.theguardian.com/world/2016/may/24/turkey--eu-migration-deal-visa-free-travel-recep-tayyip-erdogan.

Guardian (2016), 'Turkey Coup Attempt: Erdogan Demands US Arrest Exiled Cleric Gulen Amid Crackdown on Army – as It Happened', https://www.theguardian.com/world/live/2016/jul/15/turkey-coup-attempt-military-gunfire-ankara.

Guardian (2017), 'Defiant Donald Trump Confirms US Will Recognise Jerusalem as Capital of Israel', https://www.theguardian.com/us-news/2017/dec/06/donald-trump-us-jerusalem-israel-capital.

Guardian (2017), 'I Will Return Saudi Arabia to Moderate Islam, Says Crown Prince', https://www.theguardian.com/world/2017/oct/24/i-will-return-saudi-arabia-moderate-islam-crown-prince.

Haberler (2013), 'Başbakan Erdoğan'ın Renkli Kravatlarının Sırrı' (Secret of PM Erdoğan's Colourful Ties), https://www.haberler.com/basbakan-erdogan-in-renkli-kravatlarinin-sirri-5143049-haberi/.

Habertürk (1991), 'Genel Seçim 1991' (General Election 1991), http://www.haberturk.com/secim1991/Konya.

Habertürk (1995), 'Genel Seçim 1995' (General Election 1995), http://www.haberturk.com/secim1995/Konya.

Habertürk (2002), 'Genel Seçim 2002' (General Election 2002), http://www.haberturk.com/secim2002/Konya.

Habertürk (2015), 'Cumhurbaşkanı Erdoğan'dan Netanyahu'ya sert tepki' (Strong Reaction to Netanyahu from President Erdoğan), http://www.haberturk.com/gundem/haber/1029712-hangi-yuzle-oraya-gitti.

Habertürk (2017), 'İşte "Türklerin AB'ye bakışı" araştırmasının sonuçları' (the Results of the 'Turks View on the EU' Research), http://www.haberturk.tv/gundem/haber/1736940-turkiye-ab-ye-uye-olacak-mi.

Habertürk (2018), 'Faruk Acar: MHP desteği olmazsa Ak Parti büyükşehirlerin bazılarını kaybetme potansiyeli taşıyabilir' (Faruk Acar: Without MHP's Support There Is a Risk for the AK Party to Lose Some Metropolises), https://www.haberturk.com/faruk-acar-mhp-destegi-olmazsa-ak-parti-buyuksehirlerin-bazilarini-kaybetme-potansiyeli-tasiyabilir-2197336.

Hamid, S. (2017), 'How Much Can One Strongman Change a Country', *The Atlantic*, https://www.theatlantic.com/international/archive/2017/06/erdogan-turkey-islamist/531609/.

Hoffman, B. (May 2006), 'The Use of the Internet by Islamic Extremists', RAND Corporation, http://www.rand.org/pubs/testimonies/CT262-1.html.

Hürriyet (2006), 'Adnan Menderes'i suçlamaktan vazgeçin! Arapça ezanı DP ile CHP beraber serbest bırakmışlardı' (Stop Accusing Adnan Menderes. Arabic Call to Prayer Were Allowed with the Efforts of DP and CHP), http://www.hurriyet.com.tr/adnan-menderes-i-suclamaktan-vazgecin-arapca-ezani-dp-ile-chp-beraber-serbest-birakmislardi-4560385.

Hürriyet (2011), '2011 Yılı Genel Seçim Sonuçları' (2011 General Election Results), http://www.hurriyet.com.tr/secim2011/default.html.

Hurriyet (2011), 'Başbakan'ın zafer turu ve laiklik mesajinin adresi' (PM Erdoğan's Victory Tour and Laïcité Message), http://www.hurriyet.com.tr/basbakan-in-zafer-turu-ve-laiklik-mesajinin-adresi-18742520.

Hürriyet (2011), 'Genel Seçim' (General Elections), http://secim2011.hurriyet.com.tr/ildetay.aspx?cid=42.

Hürriyet (2014), 'Adaylar Oy Dağılımı' (Candidates Vote Share), http://www.hurriyet.com.tr/cumhurbaskanligisecimi/.

Hürriyet (2014), 'Cumhurbaşkanı Recep Tayyip Erdoğan Necip Fazıl ile olan anısını anlattı' (President Recep Tayyip Erdoğan Memory with Necip Fazıl), http://www.hurriyet.com.tr/cumhurbaskani-recep-tayyip-erdogan-necip-fazil-ile-olan-anisini-anlatti-27506507.

Hürriyet (2015), '2015 Türkiye Genel Secimi' (2015 Turkish General Election), http://www.hurriyet.com.tr/secim-2015/aydin-secim-sonuclari-9-0.

Hürriyet (2017), 'Ben ayakta gömülüyüm, sadece başım dışarıda' (I've Been Buried Standing Up, Only My Head Is Looking Out), http://www.hurriyet.com.tr/yazarlar/ayse-arman/ben-ayakta-gomuluyum-sadece-basim-disarida-40449722.

Hürriyet (2017), 'Erdoğan neden yelek giydiğini açıkladı' (Erdoğan Explained Why He Is Wearing a Vest), http://www.hurriyet.com.tr/erdogan-neden-yelek-giydigini-acikladi-40419694.

Hürriyet (2017), 'Erdoğan'ın eliyle Rabia tarifi' (Rabia Explanation by Erdoğan), http://www.hurriyet.com.tr/erdoganin-eliyle-rabia-tarifi-40594955.

Hürriyet (2018): TBMM Başkanı Kahraman: 'Çamlıca Camii'nin ismi Recep Tayyip Erdoğan olsun' (Speaker of the Turkish Grand National Assembly Kahraman: Çamlıca Mosque's Name Should Be Recep Tayyip Erdoğan), https://www.hurriyet.com.tr/gundem/tbmm-baskani-kahraman-camlica-camiine-ismi-recep-tayyip-erdogan-olsun-40737604.

Hürriyet Daily News (1999), 'Erdoğan Goes to Prison', http://www.hurriyetdailynews.com/erdogan-goes-to-prison.aspx?pageID=438&n=erdogan-goes-to-prison-1999-03-27.

Hürriyet Daily News (2010), 'Turkey's First Five Referendums: A Look Back', http://www.hurriyetdailynews.com/turkeys-first-five-referendums-a-look-back.aspx?pageID=438&n=the-five-referendums-in-the-history-of-turkey-2010-07-28.

Hürriyet Daily News (2014), 'Turkey's New Presidential Palace Has 1,150 Rooms, Not 1,000, Erdoğan Reveals', http://www.hurriyetdailynews.com/turkeys-new-presidential-palace-has-1150-rooms-not-1000-erdogan-reveals-75281.

Hürriyet Daily News (2016), 'Turkey's Erdogan Slams Gaza Flotilla Organizers over Objection to Israel Deal', http://www.hurriyetdailynews.com/turkeys-erdogan-slams-gaza-flotilla-organizers-over-objection-to-israel-deal-101085.

Hürriyet Daily News (2017a), 'Erdoğan Criticizes Saudi Crown Prince's "Moderate Islam" Pledge', http://www.hurriyetdailynews.com/erdogan-criticizes-saudi-crown-princes-moderate-islam-pledge-122262.

Hürriyet Daily News (2017b), 'Europe Is Only Pretending to Fight Against Terrorism: Erdoğan', http://www.hurriyetdailynews.com/europe-is-only-pretending-to-fight-against-terrorism-erdogan-122194.

Hürriyet Daily News (2017c), 'Turkish TV Series Draw Great Interest in Israel', http://www.hurriyetdailynews.com/turkish-tv-series-draw-great-interest-in-israel-142291.

Hürriyet Daily News (2018), 'MHP to Support Erdogan in 2019 Presidential Election, Calls on AKP for Alliance', http://www.hurriyetdailynews.com/mhp-will-not-present-presidential-candidate-for-2019-election-bahceli-125379.

Hürriyet Daily News (2019a), 'IMF Chapter Will Not Be Reopened, Says Erdoğan', http://www.hurriyetdailynews.com/imf-chapter-will-not-be-reopened-says-erdogan-141029.

Hürriyet Daily News (2019b), 'Morsi Was Murdered: President Erdoğan', http://www.hurriyetdailynews.com/erdogan-condemns-inaction-before-morsis-death-144303.

IDP (2016), 'İslamcı Dergiler Projesi' (Islamist Journal Project), http://idp.org.tr/zaman-cizelgesi.
IHA (1994), 'Seçim Sonuçları' (Election Results), http://secim.iha.com.tr/Bolgeler.aspx?il=34&ilce=0&belde=0&parti=0&skod=1051&stip=6&s=27%20Mart%201994%20B%C3%BCy%C3%BCk%C5%9Fehir%20Belediye%20Se%C3%A7imi.
IHH Official Website, https://www.ihh.org.tr/en/history.
Ikhwanweb (2006a), 'El-Shater: We Do Not Promote an Anti Western Agenda', http://ikhwanweb.com/article.php?id=930.
Ikhwanweb (2006b), 'Muslim Brotherhood Rejects Al Zawahiri Statements and Stresses on Peaceful Reform', http://ikhwanweb.com/article.php?id=4993.
Ince, Ö. (2012), 'Necip Fazıl Kısakürek', *Aydınlık*, http://www.aydinlikgazete.com/yazarlar/183-oezdemir-nce/12557-ozdemir-ince-necip-fazil-kisakurek-1904-1983.html.
Independent (1993), 'Obituary: Turgut Ozal', http://www.independent.co.uk/news/people/obituary-turgut-ozal-1456191.html.
Independent (2012), 'Abortions Are Like Airstrikes on Civilians: Turkish PM Recep Tayyip Erdogan's Rant Sparks Women's Rage', http://www.independent.co.uk/life-style/health-and-families/health-news/abortions-are-like-air-strikes-on-civilians-turkish-pm-recep-tayyip-erdogans-rant-sparks-womens-rage-7800939.html.
Independent (2017), 'MHP to Support Erdogan in 2019 Presidential Election, Calls on AKP for Alliance', http://www.independent.co.uk/news/world/europe/recep-tayyip-erdogan-turkey-president-stir-up-the-world-germany-speech-ban-threat-a7613606.html.
Independent (2017), 'Recep Tayyip Erdogan: US Recognising Jerusalem as Israel's Capital Makes It a Partner in Bloodshed', http://www.independent.co.uk/news/world/middle-east/recep-tayyip-erdogan-us-jerusalem-israel-capital-partner-bloodshed-donald-trump-turkey-president-a8103096.html.
Independent (2017), 'Turkey Constitutional Changes: What Are They, How Did They Come About and How Are They Different?', http://www.independent.co.uk/news/world/europe/turkey-president-recep-tayyip-erdogan-referendum-constitutional-reform-a7539286.html.
Independent Turkey (2019), Davutoğlu Ak Parti'den istifa etti (Davutoğlu Resigns from the Ak Party), https://www.independentturkish.com/node/70341/siyaset/Davutoglu-ak-parti'den-istifa-etti.
Internet Society (2015), 'The Internet and Sustainable Development', http://www.internetsociety.org/doc/internet-and-sustainable-development.
Internethaber (2014), 'Davutoğlu ve Erdoğan'a koruma Ordusu! Sayi Inanilmaz' (An Army of Bodyguards for Davutoğlu and Erdoğan! The Number Is Unbelievable), http://www.internethaber.com/davutoglu-ve-erdogana-koruma-ordusu-sayi-inanilmaz-713112h.htm.
Jerusalem Post (2013), 'Turkish PM Erdogan Hosts Increasingly Isolated Hamas Leader Mashaal in Ankara', http://www.jpost.com/Diplomacy-and-Politics/

Turkish-PM-Erdogan-hosts-increasingly-isolated-Hamas-leader-Mashaal-in-Ankara-328176.

Kara, I. (2013), Interview by Ruşen Çakır for *Vatan*, 23 May, http://www.gazetevatan.com/rusen-cakir-541144-yazar-yazisi--erbakan-hicbir-zaman-sistem-karsiti-olmadi-/.

Kara, I. (2017), 'Islam and Islamism in Turkey: A Conversation with Ismail Kara', 24 October, https://themaydan.com/2017/10/islam-islamism-turkey-conversation-ismail-kara/.

Karar (2017), 'Gül ve Davutoğlu' (Gül and Davutoğlu), http://www.karar.com/yazarlar/hakan-albayrak/gul-ve-davutoglu-3826#.

Kadir Has Üniversitesi (2019), 'Türk Dış Politikası Kamuoyu Algıları Araştırması 2019 Sonuçları Açıklandı' (Turkish Foreign Policy Public Perceptions Survey 2019 Results Has Been Announced), https://www.khas.edu.tr/tr/haberler/turk-dis-politikasi-kamuoyu-algilari-arastirmasi-2019-sonuclari-aciklandi.

Khaleej Times (2020), 'UAE Envoy Reacts to Trump's Palestine-Israel Peace Plan', https://www.khaleejtimes.com/news/government/uae-ambassador-reacts-to-trumps-palestine-israel-peace-plan-.

Kırmızı, A. (2016), 'Erdoğan Abdülhamid'e değil, Mustafa Kemal'e benziyor' (Erdoğan's Is Rather Similar to Mustafa Kemal Than Abdülhamid), *Al Jazeera Turk*, http://www.aljazeera.com.tr/gorus/erdogan-abdulhamide-degil-mustafa-kemale-benziyor.

KONDA (2020), 'What has changed in 10 years?', https://interaktif.konda.com.tr/en/HayatTarzlari2018/#firstPage.

Lauria, J. (2010), 'Reclusive Turkish Imam Criticizes Gaza Flotilla', *Wall Street Journal*, https://www.wsj.com/articles/SB10001424052748704025304575284721280274694.

Lewins, A., C. Taylor and G. Gibbs (2005), 'What Is Qualitative Data Analysis?' School of Human & Health Sciences, University of Huddersfield. United Kingdom, http://onlineqda.hud.ac.uk/Intro_QDA/what_is_qda.php.

Lyrictranslate (2012), 'We Walked Together by Muazzez Abacı', http://lyricstranslate.com/de/beraber-yürüdük-we-walked-together.html.

Marks, M. (2016), 'How Big Were the Changes Tunisia's Ennahda Party Just Made at Its National Congress?', *The Washington Post*, https://www.washingtonpost.com/news/monkey-cage/wp/2016/05/25/how-big-were-the-changes-made-at-tunisias-ennahda-just-made-at-its-national-congress/?utm_term=.e93449652677.

Marks, M. L. (2014), Brookings Doha Centre, 'Convince, Coerce, or Compromise?: Ennahda's Approach to Tunisia's Constitution', https://www.brookings.edu/wp-content/uploads/2016/06/Ennahda-Approach-Tunisia-Constitution-English.pdf.

Middle East Eye (2019a), 'Facing Expulsion, Former Erdogan Ally Davutoglu Resigns from AKP', https://www.middleeasteye.net/news/facing-expulsion-former-erdogan-ally-davutoglu-resigns-akp.

Middle East Eye (2019b), 'Turkey's "Anti-imperialist" FOX TV Is No Friend of Trump – or Erdogan', https://www.middleeasteye.net/news/turkeys-anti-imperialist-fox-tv-no-friend-trump-or-erdogan.

Middle East Eye (2019c), 'UAE and Saudi Arabia Back Trump's "Deal of the Century" Economic Conference', https://www.middleeasteye.net/news/uae-backs-trump-administrations-deal-century-economic-conference.

Migdalovitz, C. (2007), 'CRS Report for Congress, Turkey's 2007 Elections: Crisis of Identity and Power', http://www.fas.org/sgp/crs/mideast/RL34039.pdf.

Milli Gazete (2016), 'Karar'cı Elif Çakır'dan Erdoğan'ın Mavi Marmara sözlerine tepki: Acı gülüyorum' (Karar Affiliated Elif Çakır Criticises Erdoğan's Approach on Mavi Marmara: I Laugh Bitterly), http://www.milligazete.com.tr/haber/891082/kararci-elif-cakirdan-erdoganin-mavi-marmara-sozlerine-tepki-aci-aci-guluyorum#.

Milliyet (1994), Erdoğan: Elhamdulillah Şeriat istiyoruz' (Erdoğan: Thank God We Are for the Sharia), http://gazetearsivi.milliyet.com.tr/Arsiv/1994/11/21.

Milliyet (2003), 'Gömlek kavgası' (Ideology Fight), thttp://www.milliyet.com.tr/2003/05/22/siyaset/asiy.html.

Milliyet (2013), 'Dünya 'beş'ten büyüktür' (The World Is Bigger Than 'Five'), http://www.milliyet.com.tr/dunya-bes-ten-buyuktur/siyaset/detay/1767594/default.htm.

Milliyet (2013), 'Erdoğan alkol yasakları hakkında konuştu' (Erdoğan Spoke About Alcohol Ban), http://www.milliyet.com.tr/erdogan-alkol-yasaklari-hakkinda/siyaset/detay/1713431/default.htm.

Milliyet (2014), 'Özal ve Hamido'nun Ölüm Yıldönümü' (Özal and Hamido's Death Anniversary), http://www.milliyet.com.tr/ozal-ve-hamido-nun-olum-yildonumu-malatya-yerelhaber-150745/.

Milliyet (2015), 'Ak Parti Olağan Büyük Kongresi'ne Katılan Yabancı Konuklar' (Foreign Guests Participating in the Ak Party Ordinary Great Congress), http://www.milliyet.com.tr/ak-parti-olagan-buyuk-kongresi-ne-katilan-ankara-yerelhaber-967809/.

Milliyet (2015), 'Seçim sonuçları kesinlik kazandı' (Election Results Became Final), http://www.milliyet.com.tr/secim-sonuclari-2015-istanbul--gundem-2141026/.

Milliyet (2015), 'Türkiye'de Üniversite Sayisi 193'e ulaştı' (The Number of Universities Increased to 193 in Turkey), http://blog.milliyet.com.tr/turkiye-deki-universite-sayisi-193-e-ulasti/Blog/?BlogNo=498323.

Milliyet (2016), '15 Temmuz'un hedefi Cumhurbaşkanı Erdoğan'ı şehit etmekti' (The Aim of 15 July Was to Martyr President Erdoğan), http://www.milliyet.com.tr/-15-temmuz-un-hedefi-cumhurbaskani-gundem-2309559/.

Milliyet (2016), 'MGK Kararları açıklandı (National Security Council Decisions Announced), http://www.milliyet.com.tr/mgk-kararlari-aciklandi-gundem-2281286/.

Mis, N., A. Aslan, M. E. Ayvaz and H. Duran (2015), 'Dünyada Başkanlık Sistemi Uygumaları' (Implementation of Presidential System across the World), file:///C:/Users/abfc123/Downloads/20150526181848_51_baskanlik_raporu_web.pdf.

Nation (2014), 'Turkey in Turmoil', https://www.thenation.com/article/turkey-turmoil/.

Negrine, R. and S. Papathanassopoulus (1995), 'The "Americanization" of Political Communication', *Academia*, https://www.academia.edu/1944470/The_Americanization_of_Political_Communication_A_Critique.

Nerantzaki, E. (2012), 'Turkey-Hamas-Hezbollah: A New Trinity?', Centre for Mediterranean, Middle East and Islamic Studies (CEMMIS), http://www.cemmis.edu.gr/index.php?option=com_content&view=article&id=349%3Aturkey-hamas-hezbollah-a-new-trinity&catid=68%3Apolicy-papers&Itemid=65&lang=en.

New York Times (2003), 'The Erdogan Experiment', http://www.nytimes.com/2003/05/11/magazine/the-erdogan-experiment.html.

New York Times (2010), 'Sponsor of Flotilla Tied to Elite of Turkey', http://www.nytimes.com/2010/07/16/world/middleeast/16turkey.html.

New York Times (2016), 'The Arc of a Coup Attempt in Turkey', https://www.nytimes.com/interactive/2016/07/16/world/europe/turkey-coup-photos.html.

New York Times (2016), 'Turkey Was an Unlikely Victim of an Equally Unlikely Coup', https://www.nytimes.com/2016/07/17/world/europe/turkey-was-an-unlikely-victim-of-an-equally-unlikely-coup.html.

New York Times (2017), 'Inside Turkey's Purge', https://www.nytimes.com/2017/04/13/magazine/inside-turkeys-purge.html.

New York Times (2019), 'Intercepts Solidify C.I.A. Assessment That Saudi Prince Ordered Khashoggi Killing', https://www.nytimes.com/2018/12/02/us/politics/crown-prince-mohammed-qahtani-intercepts.html.

NPR (2014), 'Turkey's President and His 1,100-Room "White Palace"', https://www.npr.org/sections/parallels/2014/12/24/370931835/turkeys-president-and-his-1-100-room-white-palace.

NTV (2012), 'Erdoğan şampiyondan 3 çocuk istedi' (Erdoğan urged the Champion to have at least three Children), https://www.ntv.com.tr/turkiye/erdogan-sampiyondan-3-cocuk-istedi,T9xkYTXyHkOvSrf3a0qhvA.

NTV (2017), 'Cumhurbaşkanı Erdoğan'dan idam açıklaması' (Statement on Execution from President Erdoğan), https://www.ntv.com.tr/turkiye/cumhurbaskani-erdogandan-idam-aciklamasi,D1bEy45Fb0qdC1A_jBieaA.

NZZ Standpunkte (2015), 'Heinrich August Winkler: Der Westen, mächtig und angreifbar' (Heinrich August Winkler: The West, Powerful and Vulnerable), https://www.youtube.com/watch?v=Q2x6bdDSRQM.

Ogur, Y. (2020), 'Hagia Sophia: Ataturk and the Rich Americans Who Changed Icon's Fate', https://www.middleeasteye.net/opinion/hagia-sophia-mosque-museum-why-ataturk-converted.

Oxford Dictionary (2017), Definition of Hadith, https://en.oxforddictionaries.com/definition/hadith.

Peraino, K. (2006), 'Winning Hearts and Minds', *Newsweek*, 2 October, http://www.newsweek.com/winning-hearts-and-minds-111623.

Peterson, S. (2016), 'As Post-Coup Purge Intensifies, a Vision of Erdogan's Turkey', *Christian Science Monitor*, https://www.csmonitor.com/World/

Middle-East/2016/0719/As-post-coup-purge-intensifies-a-vision-of-Erdogans-Turkey.

Pew Research (2017), 'Key Middle East Publics See Russia, Turkey and U.S. All Playing Larger Roles in Region', http://www.pewglobal.org/2017/12/11/key-middle-east-publics-see-russia-turkey-and-u-s-all-playing-larger-roles-in-region/.

Pew Research Center (2006), 'Islam and the West: A Conversation with Bernard Lewis', http://www.pewforum.org/2006/04/27/islam-and-the-west-a-conversation-with-bernard-lewis/.

Quran (2016), 'Surah Fatihah', https://quran.com/1.

Radikal (2010), 'Hamido'nun eşi 32 yıl sonra konuştu: Fail Ergenekon' (Hamido's Wife Spoke after 32 years: Perpetrator Is Ergenekon), http://www.radikal.com.tr/turkiye/hamidonun-esi-32-yil-sonra-konustu-fail-ergenekon-992565/.

Radikal (2014), 'Mehmet Şimşek: Erdoğan logosu'nda Arapça ile "Muhammed" ismi kullanıldı' (Mehmet Şimşek: The Name 'Muhammad' in Arabic calligraphy was applied in Erdoğan's Logo), http://www.radikal.com.tr/politika/mehmet-simsek-erdogan-logosunda-arapca-ile-muhammed-ismi-kullanildi-1200474/.

Radikal (2014), 'Türkiye'de siyaset tarihine yön vermiş 10 el işareti' (Ten Hand Signs That Has a Meaning in Political History of Turkey), http://www.radikal.com.tr/radikalist/turkiyede-siyaset-tarihine-yon-vermis-10-el-isareti-1225867/.

Recep Tayyip Erdoğan (2020), 'Gençlerle Video Konferans Buluşması' (Video Conference Meeting with Youth), https://www.youtube.com/watch?v=nhXz8783eOU.

Republic of Turkey Ministry of Foreign Affairs (no date), 'The Alliance of Civilizations Initiative', http://www.mfa.gov.tr/the-alliance-of-civilizations-initiative.en.mfa.

Reuters (2016), 'At Height of Turkish Coup Bid, Rebel Jets Had Erdoğan's Plane in Their Sights', https://www.reuters.com/article/us-turkey-security-plot-insight/at-height-of-turkish-coup-bid-rebel-jets-had-erdogans-plane-in-their-sights-idUSKCN0ZX0Q9.

Sabah (2014a), '17 Aralık dibacesi 7 Şubat' (7 February Was the Foreword for 17th December), http://www.sabah.com.tr/Perspektif/Yazarlar/ozhan/2014/02/08/17-aralik-dibacesi-7-subat.

Sabah (2014b), 'İşte Erdoğan'ın balkon konuşması' (Erdoğan's Balcony Speech), https://www.sabah.com.tr/gundem/2014/08/10/iste-erdoganin-balkon-konusmasi.

Sabah (2017a), 'Erol benim yol arkadaşımdı' (Erol Was My Companion), https://www.sabah.com.tr/onbes-temmuz-ihaneti/2017/07/15/erol-benim-yol-arkadasimdi.

Sabah (2017b), 'Sabah Abone Bayilerimiz' (Sabah Subscriber Dealers), http://www.aboneturkuvaz.com/index.php?p=Bayi.

Sezgin, Y. (2014), 'Turkish Local Elections: One Victor, Many Losers', *Al Jazeera*, http://www.aljazeera.com/indepth/opinion/2014/04/turkish-local-elections-one-vict-20144211532875833.html.

Sharma, S. (2017), 'Analysis: Erdogan, Champion of Palestine and Player to Arab Street', *Middle East Eye*, http://www.middleeasteye.net/news/erdogan-turkey-islam-and-arab-street-894402812.

Shlaim, A. (2005), 'A Debate: Is Zionism Today the Real Enemy of the Jews?', *New York Times*, http://www.nytimes.com/2005/02/04/opinion/a-debate-is-zionism-today-the-real-enemy-of-the-jews-2005020493240380407.html.

Smith, H. L. (2019), 'Fahrettin Altun: The Rise and Rise of Turkey's Second Most Powerful Man', *Times*, https://www.thetimes.co.uk/article/fahrettin-altun-the-rise-and-rise-of-turkeys-second-most-powerful-man-pzntf29kp.

Sontag, D. (2003), 'The Erdogan Experiment', *New York Times*, http://www.nytimes.com/2003/05/11/magazine/the-erdogan-experiment.html.

Spiegel Online (2003), 'Erdogan verspricht mehr Demokratie' (Erdogan Promises More Democracy), http://www.spiegel.de/politik/ausland/tuerkei-und-eu-erdogan-verspricht-mehr-demokratie-a-264159.html.

Spiegel Online (2009), 'Gaza-Eklat in Davos – Erdogan stürmt vom Podium' (Gaza-Éclat in Davos – Erdogan Storms off Podium), http://www.spiegel.de/wirtschaft/debatte-mit-peres-gaza-eklat-in-davos-erdogan-stuermt-vom-podium-a-604429.html.

Star (2014), 'Necip Fazıl ödülleri verildi' (Necip Fazıl Awards Were Handed Out), https://www.star.com.tr/kultur-sanat/necip-fazil-odulleri-verildi-haber-960444/.

Steinworth, D. (2009), 'Erdogan Rides Wave of Popularity in Muslim World', Spiegel, http://www.spiegel.de/international/world/a-new-direction-for-turkey-erdogan-rides-wave-of-popularity-in-muslim-world-a-606900.html.

T24 (2014), 'Erdoğan'dan Gül'e gönderme: Sisi'ye giden tebrik kabul edilemez' (Erdogan to Gül: Congratulating Sisi Is Unacceptable), http://t24.com.tr/haber/erdogandan-gule-gonderme-sisiye-giden-tebrik-kabul-edilemez,262286.

T24 (2016), '"Barış İçin Akademisyenler" in 1128 imzayla açıkladığı bildirinin tam metni' (Detailed Text of the 'Petition for Peace Academics' with 1128 Signatures), https://t24.com.tr/haber/baris-icin-akademisyenlerin-1128-imzayla-acikladigi-bildirinin-tam-metni,324471.

T24 (2020), 'AKP'de 'dijital dönüşüm' stratejisi: Hedef Z kuşağından 7 milyon yeni seçmen' (AKP's Digital Transformation Strategy: The Goal Is to Reach 7 Million Generation Z), https://t24.com.tr/haber/akp-de-dijital-donusum-stratejisi-hedef-z-kusagindan-7-milyon-yeni-secmen,884769.

TCCB (2014), 'Bizim Mücadelemiz Hak, Hukuk, Adalet ve 200 Yıldır Esirgenen Hakların Teslimi Mücadelesidir' (Our Struggle Is for Right, Law, Justice and the Challenge of 200 Years of Spared Rights), https://www.tccb.gov.tr/haberler/410/1548/bizim-mucadelemiz-hak-hukuk-adalet-ve-200-yildir-esirgenen-haklarin-teslimi-mucadelesidir.html.

TCCB (2017a), 'All OIC Member States Are Determined to Defend Al-Quds' Sanctity and Historical Status', https://www.tccb.gov.tr/en/news/542/87722/kudusun-sahipsiz-olmadigini-tum-dunyaya-gosterdik.html.

TCCB (2017b), 'We Strive To Build a Country Which Is a Source of Confidence for the Oppressed and the Victims', https://www.tccb.gov.tr/en/news/542/87743/turk-milleti-olarak-dunyaya-son-sozumuzu-henuz-soylemedik.html.

TCCB (2018), 'Our Motto "The World Is Bigger Than Five" Is the Biggest-Ever Rise against Global Injustice', https://www.tccb.gov.tr/en/news/542/89052/our-motto-the-world-is-bigger-than-five-is-the-biggest-ever-rise-against-global-injustice.

TCCB (2019a), 'We Will Tightly Embrace Our Eternal Brotherhood and Work for the Peace of Our Citizens', https://www.tccb.gov.tr/en/news/542/103767/-we-will-tightly-embrace-our-eternal-brotherhood-and-work-for-the-peace-of-our-citizens-.

TCCB (2019b), 'Önder Imam Hatipliler Buluşmasında Yaptıkları Konuşma' (Speech at Önder İmam Hatip Meeting), https://www.tccb.gov.tr/konusmalar/353/109575/onder-imam-hatipliler-bulusmasinda-yaptiklari-konusma#.

TCCB (2020a), 'We Have Mobilized All Our Means to Eliminate the Virus Threat', https://www.tccb.gov.tr/en/news/542/117038/-we-have-mobilized-all-our-means-to-eliminate-the-virus-threat/.

TCCB (2020b), 'İnsanlığın ortak mirası olan Ayasofya, yeni statüsüyle herkesi kucaklamaya çok daha samimi, çok daha özgün şekilde devam edecektir' (With Its New Status, Hagia Sophia, the Shared Heritage of Humanity, Will Continue to Embrace All), https://www.tccb.gov.tr/haberler/410/120583/-insanligin-ortak-mirasi-olan-ayasofya-yeni-statusuyle-herkesi-kucaklamaya-cok-daha-samimi-cok-daha-ozgun-sekilde-devam-edecektir-.

Telegraph (2014), 'Turkey's President Moves into World's Biggest Palace Costing £384 million', http://www.telegraph.co.uk/news/worldnews/europe/turkey/11210083/Turkeys-president-moves-into-worlds-biggest-palace-costing-384-million.html.

Telegraph (2015), 'Turkey's Most Powerful President since Ataturk: A Profile of Recep Tayyip Erdogan', http://www.telegraph.co.uk/news/worldnews/europe/turkey/11548369/Turkeys-most-powerful-president-since-Ataturk-A-profile-of-Recep-Tayyip-Erdogan.html.

TEPAV (2020), 'Support for EU Membership Rises to 66 Percent among Young People between the Ages of 18-24', https://www.tepav.org.tr/en/haberler/s/10077.

Terkan, B. (2010), 'Siyasi Partilerin Kadına İlişkin Söylem ve Politikaları: AKP ve CHP örneğ' (Discourse and Politics of Political Parties with Regard to Women: AKP and CHP as a Case Study), https://www.google.co.uk/url?sa=t&rct=j&q=&esrc=s&source=web&cd=6&ved=0ahUKEwjgqu6g4L_SAhViBcAKHavjA6IQFghFMAU&url=http%3A%2F%2Fjosc.selcuk.edu.tr%2Farticle%2Fdownload%2F1075000114%2F1075000109&usg=AFQjCNGJz5n9_57dI15xRHstw7BqNtSXSA&cad=rja.

TGRT Haber TV (2020), 'Cumhurbaşkanı Erdoğan: Sosyal Medya Düzene Sokulmalı' (President Erdoğan: Social Media Needs to Be Regulated), https://www.youtube.com/watch?v=GV0ZPSt5C7Q.

Türkiye (2014), 'İşte Erdoğan'ın yaptığı Rabia'nın anlamı' (The Meaning of Erdoğan's Rabaa Gesture), http://www.turkiyegazetesi.com.tr/gundem/142657.aspx.

TV5 Haber (2014), 'Erbakan ve Gülen'in İslam Birliği ve Dinlerarası Diyalog hakkında düşünceleri' (Erbakan and Gülen's Views on the Organisation of Islamic Cooperation and Interfaith Dialog), http://www.tv5haber.

com/25212_Erbakan-ve-Gulen-in-Islam-Birligi-ve-Dinlerarasi-Diyalog-hakkinda-dusunceleri.html.

Wall Street Journal (2010), 'Turkey's Radical Drift', http://www.wsj.com/articles/SB10001424052748703561604575282423181610814.

Wall Street Journal (2014), 'From His Refuge in the Poconos: Reclusive Imam Fetullah Gulen Roils', http://online.wsj.com/news/articles/SB10001424052702304027204579332670740491570.

Weise, Z. (2018), *How Did Things Get So Bad for Turkey's Journalists?*, The Atlantic, https://www.theatlantic.com/international/archive/2018/08/destroying-free-press-erdogan-turkey/568402/.

Welt (2008), 'Das sagte Ministerpräsident Erdogan in Köln' (This Is What Prime Minister Erdogan Said in Cologne), https://www.welt.de/debatte/article1660510/Das-sagte-Ministerpraesident-Erdogan-in-Koeln.html

White House (2020), 'Remarks by President Trump Announcing the Normalization of Relations between Israel and the United Arab Emirates', https://www.whitehouse.gov/briefings-statements/remarks-president-trump-announcing-normalization-relations-israel-united-arab-emirates/.

Yeni Şafak (2007), '2007 Anayasa Referandumu Sonuçları' (2007 Constitution Referendum Results), http://www.yenisafak.com/secim-referandum-2007/konya-secim-sonuclari-referandum.

Yeni Şafak (2015), 'Halkımızla arama hiç kimse giremez' (No One Should Intervene Between Me and My People), https://www.yenisafak.com/gundem/halkimizla-arama-hic-kimse-giremez-2148930?p=1.

Yeni Şafak (2017), 'Erdoğan'ın 2002 Genel Seçimleri sonrası yaptığı konuşma' (Erdoğan's Speech after the 2002 General Elections), https://www.yenisafak.com/video-galeri/secim/erdoganin-2002-genel-secimleri-sonrasi-yaptigi-konusma-2133848.

Yeni Şafak (2019), 'Bıyık meselesi nasıl başladı?' (How Did the Mustache Issue Begin?), https://www.yenisafak.com/yazarlar/kemalozturk/biyik-meselesi-nasil-basladi-2038597.

Yerlikaya, Hamza (2020), Tweet on 11 May, https://twitter.com/hamzayerlikaya/status/1259907353463476226?s=20.

Yılmaz, M., B. Özipek and V. Coşkun (2014), 'Cumhurbaşkanı Adaylarının Seçim Stratejilerinin Analizi' (Analysis of Election Strategies of Presidential Candidates), http://www.sde.org.tr/userfiles/file/Cumhurba%C5%9Fkanl%C4%B1%C4%9F%C4%B1%20analiz.pdf.

YSK (2015), '1987–2007 Yillari Arasi Milletvekili Genel Secimleri' (General Elections between 1987 and 2007), http://www.ysk.gov.tr/ysk/faces/HaberDetay?training_id=YSKPWCN1_4444010920&_afrLoop=101938963603313&_afrWindowMode=0&_afrWindowId=t0fftl8iw_10#%40%3F_afrWindowId%3Dt0fftl8iw_10%26_afrLoop%3D101938963603313%26training_id%3DYSKPWCN1_4444010920%26_afrWindowMode%3D0%26_adf.ctrl-state%3Dt0fftl8iw_22.

Videos

Aktif Haberci (2013), 'Eğitim seviyesi arttıkça AKP oyları azalıyor' (As the Level of Education Increases, the Support for the AKP Decreases), https://www.youtube.com/watch?v=0UadGDmDljM.
Clinton Global Initiative (2012), 'President Muhammad Morsi and President Bill Clinton', https://www.youtube.com/watch?v=kVS5BEcmA-k.
Euronews (2014), 'Erdoğan AK Parti'de 'hoş bir seda' bıraktı' (Erdoğan Left an Imprint at the AKP), https://www.youtube.com/watch?v=CxzEGR25_ws.
Herkul (2013), 'Yolsuzluk' (Corruption), http://www.herkul.org/bamteli/yolsuzluk/.
Medyascope (2020), 'Günümüz Türkiye'sinde dini tartışmalar ve İslamcılık: Prof. İsmail Kara ile söyleşi' (Islamism and Religious Discussion in Today's Turkey: Interview with Prof. Ismail Kara), https://www.youtube.com/watch?v=e8g0izXlUic.
Milli Haber (2013), 'Necmettin Erbakan anlatıyor Tayyip Erdoğan ve Siyonizm hakkında' (Necmettin Erbakan about Erdoğan and Zionism), https://www.youtube.com/watch?v=k7yiYGNZKsA.
Saadet Partisi Karatay Gençlik Kolları (Saadet Party Karatay Youth Branches) (2014), 'Erbakan Hoca Tayyip Erdoğan'ı anlatıyor' (Erbakan Speaks about Tayyip Erdoğan), https://www.youtube.com/watch?v=8YGC_ud_tME.
Sosyal Pencere (2013), 'Fethullah Gülen'den 'Yolsuzluk' gündemi hakkında yorum' (Fethullah Gülen's Comments on 'Corruption' Agenda), https://www.youtube.com/watch?v=M99L4t_RfTY.
Subasi94 (2017), 'Cumhurbaşkanı Erdoğan Imam Hatip Gençlik Buluşması' (President Erdoğan Imam Hatip Youth Gathering), https://www.youtube.com/watch?v=qiGxb7VleGU.
TRT Kurdi (2016), 'Fethullah Gülen Beddua' (Fethullah Gülen Curse), https://www.youtube.com/watch?v=zyAdAaWzsmI.
Turkish Journal (2008), 'Başbakan Erdoğan Columbia Üniversitesi' (PM Erdoğan Columbia University Speech), https://www.youtube.com/watch?v=57Yup-6ALZ4.
Ulke Uplink (2014),'Cumhurbaşkanı Adayı Recep Tayyip Erdoğan'ın Konya Mitingi' (Presidential Candidate Recep Tayyip Erdoğan's Konya Rally) https://www.youtube.com/watch?v=WZH1-9G6Gvs&t=6s.
UN (2019), 'Turkey – President Addresses General Debate', 74th Session https://www.youtube.com/watch?v=Bve1yt0SEb4.
Yeneroglu, Mustafa (2020), ' "Türkiyenin Adalet Karnesi" üzerine TBMM Genel Kurul Konuşması' (Speech on 'Turkey's Justice Report' at the Grand National Assembly of Turkey), 15 April https://www.youtube.com/watch?v=AfUvmEGRflY.
140 Journos (2020) *Sakın kader deme* ('Do Not Dare Call It Destiny') https://www.youtube.com/watch?v=kD5vEQmIgZI.

Index

Afghanistan 78, 99, 109
Akşener, Meral 115
  see also Good Party (IYI Party)
Al-Assad, Bashar 52
  see also Syria
Albayrak, Berat 63, 150
Albayrak, Serhat 150
Alevis 2, 11, 89, 110
Al-Sisi, Abdel Fattah 60, 125
  see also Egypt
Al-Thani, Tamim bin Hamad 60, 162–3
  see also Qatar
Altun, Fahrettin 79, 96, 150–1, 163
  see also Communications Directory
Arab street 3, 74, 94
Arab uprisings 1, 45, 53, 164–5
Armenia 2
  Armenian crisis 32
  Armenians 51, 89
Atatürk, Mustafa Kemal 4, 8, 22, 34, 70, 79, 89–90, 109–10, 113, 129–32, 134–9, 141, 159, 168–70, 172, 176
authoritarianism 5, 61, 71, 77, 90, 92–3, 126–8, 146, 148, 150, 158, 164

Babacan, Ali 5, 89, 120, 155, 161
Balkans 1, 45, 157, 161
Battle of Manzikert 6, 62
Ben Ali, Zine El Abidine 52
Blue homeland 3, 175
Byzantine Empire 6, 37, 88

Çamlıca Mosque 11, 89, 133, 156
China 3, 4, 127, 165
Chora Museum 1, 175
Communications Directory 16–17, 76, 78–9, 82, 118, 150–2, 154, 163
conservative democracy/democrats 2, 44, 49, 50, 53, 55, 63, 158–9
COVID-19 6, 21, 101

Davos debate 2, 45–7, 56–9, 61, 145, 161
Davutoğlu, Ahmet 5, 45, 47, 51–2, 58, 72, 100, 120–1, 128, 169
dawah 97–8, 116, 118, 167
Demirtaş, Selahattin 76, 115–16
  see also Peoples' Democratic Party (HDP)
democratization 4, 15, 43–5, 49, 91, 158
DEVA Party 5, 72
  see also Babacan, Ali
Diyanet 21, 160, 172

Eastern Mediterranean 3, 6, 175
  Blue homeland 3, 175
Egypt 21, 26, 30, 37, 44, 46, 52, 54, 58–60, 83, 84, 87, 90–1, 94–6, 113, 124–5, 143, 157, 162, 165
Ennahda 25–6, 53–4, 83, 165
Erbakan, Necmettin 1, 4, 10, 23, 27, 36–43, 50–1, 53–7, 65–5, 69, 74–5, 88, 95, 98, 113, 125, 127, 137, 139, 141–3, 158, 161, 166–7, 174
  see also Milli Görüş
Erdoğan, Emine 83–4, 100, 121–2, 156
Erdoğan, Necmettin Bilal 37, 62
Ersoy, Mehmet Akif 33, 86–7, 110
European Union (EU) 4, 135, 67, 91–2, 124, 135–8, 140–1, 146, 174
  membership 2, 35–7, 43–5, 85, 133
  membership, Brussels 3, 124

France 15, 28, 33, 132, 149, 165
freedom of expression (in Turkey) 2–3, 8, 42–4, 49, 61, 63, 68, 71–2, 109, 110, 112, 114, 117, 137–7, 140–1, 146, 163–4, 166, 171, 174–5
Future Party (GP) 5

Gaza 46–7, 57, 99, 108, 113, 123
  see also Palestine/Palestinian

Generation Z 3, 32, 62, 64, 72–3, 79, 96–7, 115, 154, 173
  digital natives 5
Germany 15, 36, 72, 86, 102, 146, 151
  Merkel, Angela 102
Gezi Park protests 3, 5, 7–8, 11, 46, 52, 58–9, 68, 71, 81, 89, 91, 93, 109, 120, 127–9, 145, 151, 157–8, 164–5, 172
Ghannouchi, Rashed 25, 53–4
  see also Ennahda
Good Party (IYI Party) 108, 115, 169
Greater Middle East Initiative 45
Gül, Abdullah 5, 10, 23, 40–1, 43, 59–60, 71–2, 87, 120–1, 128, 139, 164
Gülenists 5, 13, 58–9, 65, 73, 107–9, 131, 135–7, 143–5, 165, 172, 175
  Gülen, Fethullah 13, 58–9, 108–9, 144–5, 165

Hagia Sophia 1, 3, 37, 79, 88–90, 109, 133, 157, 170, 175
Hamas 162
  see also Palestine/Palestinian
Hezbollah 103
  see also Nasrallah, Hasan
Humanitarian Relief Foundation (IHH) 57–8

Ihsanoğlu, Ekmeleddin 67, 76
Imam Hatip schools 1, 32, 62–4, 82, 91, 119, 133, 140–1, 160
Imamoğlu, Ekrem 5, 68–9, 168–70
Independent Industrialists and Businessmen's Association (MÜSIAD) 40, 63
institutionalization 11, 22, 28, 33, 36, 68, 70–1, 73–4, 77, 87–8, 92–3, 110, 138, 143, 148, 174–5
International Monetary Fund (IMF) 37, 62, 161
Iran 27, 127, 129, 139
Iraq 78, 87, 99, 113, 125
Islamism 7, 25–7, 29–31, 44–5, 50, 53–7, 59, 66, 84, 104, 166
  pan-Islamism 30, 57, 174
  political Islam 36, 40, 53–6, 84, 89
  populist Islamism 3–5, 8, 24, 27, 42, 56, 66, 84, 89–90, 124, 145, 147–8, 166, 168, 171–2, 174
  post-Islamism 4, 26–7, 166

Islamic State of Iraq and Syria (ISIS) 87, 131
Islamophobia 1, 127, 134, 175
Israel 1–4, 36–8, 44–7, 57–8, 78, 92, 99, 103, 108–9, 134–7, 143, 146, 158, 160–4, 167
Istanbul Convention 156
Istanbul elections *see* 2019 local elections
Izetbegovic, Alija 111
Izetbegovic, Bakir 111–12

Jihad 31, 88, 139
July 15 coup attempt 3, 7, 8, 21, 59, 65, 68, 74, 89, 108, 114, 124, 128, 130, 133, 145, 148, 157, 159, 165–6, 171
Justice and Development Party in Morocco (PJD) 21, 26, 83, 104–6, 154

Kalın, Ibrahim 43–4, 50, 60, 141, 151–2
Karakoç, Sezai 33–6, 38, 69, 82, 170
  Büyük Doğu 34–5
Kemalism 22, 27, 34, 38, 41, 64–6, 84, 118–19, 130, 138, 140, 166, 168, 174
Khashoggi, Jamal 162
Khomeini, Ayatollah 139
Kısakürek, Necip Fazıl 33–5, 38, 69, 82, 125, 134, 155
  see also poem
Kotku, Mehmet Zahit 38, 98
Kurdish Democratic Union Party (PYD) 6, 159
Kurdish Peace Process 61
Kurdistan Workers' Party (PKK) 8, 61, 107, 131, 135, 145, 148, 159, 169
Kurds 2, 61, 89, 153

laïcité/laicism/laicization 1, 27, 83–4, 92, 159, 174
LGBTQ+ 3, 21, 89, 133
liberalism 4, 6, 8, 174
Libya 79, 113

Mavi Marmara (Gaza flotilla) 2, 45, 47, 56–8, 65, 92, 98, 109, 143–5, 160–1
Middle East and North Africa (MENA) 2, 6, 15, 33, 36, 39, 42, 45, 56–7, 94, 98, 126, 143–4, 148, 157–8, 161–5
Milli Görüş 1–2, 10, 18, 20–1, 25–7, 36–40, 43, 50, 53–5, 57, 60, 64, 69, 86, 88, 98, 130, 139, 143, 167

Adil düzen (Just order) 4, 37, 40, 167
D-8 4, 127, 167
Felicity Party (SP) 23, 40–1
National Order Party (MNP) 38–9
National Salvation Party (MSP) 38–9
Welfare Party (RP) 23, 27, 39–40, 43, 50–1, 55, 112–13
see also Erbakan, Necmettin
Mohammad bin Salman (MBS) 163
see also Saudi Arabia
Mohammad bin Zayed (MBZ) 163
see also UAE
Morsi, Muhammad 46, 59–60, 124–5, 165
see also Egypt
Mubarak, Husni 44, 52
Muslim Brotherhood (MB) 21, 26, 44, 46, 59–60, 83, 90, 95–6, 108, 124–5, 162–3, 165
Muslim world 1, 3, 8, 30, 45, 57, 67, 74, 90, 99, 111–13, 119, 123–5, 127, 146, 156, 162, 164–5, 167, 171, 173, 175
Arab world 30, 161, 167

Nasrallah, Hasan 103
National Intelligence Organization (MIT) 59, 144
Nationalist Movement Party (MHP) 73, 107–8, 115, 159, 169
nationalist/nationalism 8, 22, 34, 49–50, 54, 61, 79, 92, 108, 115, 120, 124–5, 147, 157–9, 165–6, 168, 175
National Turkish Student Union (MTTB) 41–2, 69, 143
Netflix 3, 63, 133
see also Social media law
New Turkey 8, 51, 61, 89, 122, 161, 171, 176

Obama, Barack 16, 77, 80, 83, 102, 104–5
Olçok, Erol 16, 74–8, 80, 82–3, 118, 123, 149, 150
Ottoman Empire 7, 21, 26–8, 30–1, 33, 36, 40, 51, 66, 86–7, 106, 119, 127, 131, 135, 137, 139, 146, 149, 157, 173
Committee of Union and Progress (CUP) 32–3, 66
Ittihad-ı Islam 30–1, 57
Ottoman Sultan(s) 3, 32, 87, 109, 146, 156–7, 171
Tanzimat 28–9, 173

Young Turks 33, 66

Palestine 46, 90, 99, 125, 134, 163
Palestine, Palestinian 1, 44, 47, 58, 74, 99, 103, 108, 134, 158, 160–4, 167, 175
People's Republican Party (CHP) 5, 22, 68, 70, 73, 99, 108, 116, 169–0
Peoples' Democratic Party (HDP) 8, 61, 73, 115–16, 147, 169
pluralism/pluralist 1–2, 4, 24, 44, 66, 77, 89, 128, 133, 158, 174
political communication 1, 3–9, 12–20, 22–3, 26, 39, 42, 49, 56, 71, 73, 75–9, 80–3, 92–4, 96, 98, 100, 102, 104, 126, 147–50, 152–4, 157, 160–1, 165, 171, 173–5
Americanization 6–7, 14–18, 71, 74, 77–8, 80–3, 93–4, 100, 104, 132, 147–9, 152, 154, 173–4
candidate-centred electioneering 7, 17, 81, 94, 97, 100, 123
charisma 2–3, 5, 7, 18–19, 21, 42, 68–70, 73–5, 78, 81–2, 94, 102, 116, 119, 132, 147, 157–8, 161, 170, 175
one-to-one communication (face-to-face communication) 7, 94, 102
personalization 7, 15, 17–18, 70–1, 81, 100–2, 112, 152, 155, 173
political public relations 4, 7, 9–11, 13–14, 16, 74, 77–8, 88, 122, 145, 153
professionalization 18, 80, 149, 152–3
Rabaa hand gesture 108, 124–5, 157, 165
balcony speech 114, 117–19, 121–4, 129
logo 18, 100, 104–7, 121–2, 151, 157
poem and Islamic metaphor 23, 34, 41, 67, 69, 82, 87, 103, 125, 140, 155, 166
US Presidential elections 102, 123, 155
postmodern coup (in 1997) 1, 40, 43, 50, 53–4, 64–5, 84, 119, 140, 158, 170–1
Presidential Palace/Complex 130–2, 151, 157
Publicity and Media Department, AKP 94, 100–1, 114–19, 132, 150–1
Putin, Vladimir 4
see also Russia

Qatar 60, 127, 162–3
Quran 31, 34, 79, 86, 89–90, 101, 108, 114, 119, 155, 170

rhetoric 3, 8, 27, 39, 59, 61, 66, 85–6, 99, 106, 109, 116, 124, 158–9, 162, 167, 175
Rohingya 127, 167
Russia 3–4, 35, 78, 151, 165
  see also Putin, Vladimir

Sabah, Daily Sabah 126, 150
  see also Turkuaz media
Saudi Arabia 87, 162–3
  see also Muhammad bin Salman
secularism/secularization/secularist 4, 15, 22–3, 29, 31, 33, 43–4, 85, 89–90, 109, 134–5, 137–41, 159, 168, 173, 175
Selim III 27–9, 86
SETA 52, 150
17/25 December corruption scandal 46, 71, 74, 127, 144–5, 165
social media law 3
social movement 5, 19–24, 37, 46, 53–5, 60, 77, 88, 95, 103, 111, 125, 145, 155
  collective identity 5, 15, 22–3, 46, 53, 55, 59–60, 77, 88, 95, 98, 110, 112, 128, 131, 159, 164, 172–5
Somalia 1, 113, 157, 162
Strategy Team 50, 75, 77–8, 82, 94, 104, 106, 118, 150, 152
Sultan Abdulhamid II 7, 27, 29–32, 57, 65–6, 87, 112, 126–7, 156, 167, 172, 174
Sultan Mahmud II 28, 86
Sultan Mehmet II (also known as Sultan Fatih) 37, 79, 87–8, 170
Sultan Selim III 27–8, 86
Syria 2, 6, 37, 45, 52, 78–9, 87, 95, 99, 113, 135, 146, 159, 165, 167, 175

Taksim Square 11, 52, 89, 109, 164
  see also Gezi Park protests
1994 local elections 2, 18–9, 23, 39, 69, 75, 112, 128
Topçu, Nurettin 34, 41, 69
True Path Party (DYP) 40
Trump, Donald 4, 16, 78, 80, 102, 151, 162–3, 167
  see also United States (US)
Turkish Cooperation and Coordination Agency (TIKA) 157
Turkish Radio and Television Corporation (TRT) 61, 76
Turkish soap opera 161–2
Turkuaz media 150
  see also Sabah, Daily Sabah
Twitter 7, 16, 62–3, 78–80, 96, 103–4, 123
2018 presidential elections 64, 73, 76, 104, 108, 115, 150
2011 parliamentary elections 58, 112, 153
2015 parliamentary elections 54, 73, 75, 100, 116
2014 presidential elections 17, 46, 60, 67, 73, 75–6, 93–9, 102–4, 107, 114–23, 130, 133, 141, 145, 153, 159
2019 local elections 5, 8, 58, 62, 69, 72, 77, 82, 97, 99, 103–4, 108, 133, 154–5
2007 parliamentary elections 76, 85, 98, 102, 123, 148, 152, 175
2002 parliamentary elections 43–4, 140, 148

ummah 30, 35, 127, 156
Ünal, Aydın 50–1, 55, 58–60, 73, 86–8, 91, 144, 152–3, 157
United Arab Emirates (UAE) 162–3
United Kingdom (UK) 15, 53, 72, 101, 151, 165
United States (US) 14–16, 45, 64, 77–8, 83, 94, 132, 144, 149–51, 154–5, 163, 165, 167

Virtue Party (FP) 23, 40–1
  see also Milli Görüş
Vision 2023 (Vision 2053, Vision 2071) 6, 128

World Economic Forum (WEF) 2, 46, 56
  see also Davos debate

Xi Jinping 4, 127
  see also China

Yavaş, Mansur 5, 68–9, 169
Yıldırım, Binali 5, 77, 120–1, 169

zero-problem 2, 45
  see also Davutoğlu, Ahmet
Zionism 37, 142–3, 160

www.ingramcontent.com/pod-product-compliance
Lightning Source LLC
Chambersburg PA
CBHW072146290426
44111CB00012B/1992